CHILD CARE:
Concerns and Conflicts

A Reader

D0239146

edited by

Sonia Morgan and Peter Righton

Department of Health and Social Welfare, the Open University, Milton
Keynes

Hodder & Stoughton

A MEMBER OF THE HODDER HEADLINE GROUP

in association with the Open University

British Library Cataloguing in Publication Data
Child care: concerns and conflicts: a reader.
  1. Great Britain, Children, Care
  I. Righton, Peter II. Morgan, Sonia
  362.7'0941

ISBN 0 340 51330 6

First published 1989
Impression number 10 9 8 7 6 5 4 3 2
Year 1999 1998 1997 1996 1995 1994

Typeset by Input Typesetting Ltd, London.
Printed in Great Britain for Hodder & Stoughton Educational, a division of Hodder
Headline Plc, 338 Euston Road, London NW1 3BH by Athenæum Press Ltd,
Newcastle upon Tyne.

Contents

Acknowledgements

The publishers would like to thank the following for permission to reproduce material in this volume:

Academic Press for 'Two value positions in recent child care law and practice' by Lorraine M. Fox Harding from *British Journal of Social Work* 12, 1982; Aldine de Gruyter for 'Observing and recording children's behaviour' by J. K. Whittaker from *The Other Twenty Three Hours: Child Care Work with Emotionally Disturbed Children in a Therapeutic Milieu* by A. E. Trieschman, J. K. Whittaker and L. K. Brendtro (1969); The Association of Workers for Maladjusted Children for 'In defence of residential care' by Lorraine Waterhouse from *Maladjustment and Therapeutic Education* Vol. 5, 1987 and for 'Senses and sensibility' by Leonard F. Davis from *New Growth* Vol. 1, Spring, 1981; Ann Brechin and John Swain for their article 'Professional/client relationships: creating a "working alliance" with people with learning difficulties' from *Disability, Handicap and Society* Vol. 3, No. 3, 1988; British Agencies for Adoption and Fostering for 'What kind of permanence?' by June Thoburn from *Adoption and Fostering* Vol. 9 (4), 1985 and for 'Fostering in the eighties and beyond'; by Jane Rowe, abridged and updated version of *Fostering in the Eighties* (1983); Batsford and British Agencies for Adoption and Fostering for 'Rethinking child care policy' by M. Fisher, P. Marsh and D. Phillips with E. Sainsbury from *In and Out of Care* (1986), 'Transracial placements: conflicts and contradictions' by John Small from S. Ahmed, J. Cheetham and J. Small (eds) *Work with Black Children and their Families* (1986) and 'Assessing children's needs' by M. Adcock with R. Lake and A. Small from J. Adgate and J. Simmons (eds) *Direct Work with Children* (1988); CCETSW for 'Daily experience in residential care for children and their caregivers' by Juliet Berry from *Good Enough Parenting*, Study No. 1, Report of a Group on Work with Children and Young People and the Implications for Social Work Education (1978); *Child Care Quarterly Review* for 'Communicating with children' (abridged) by Clare Winnicott, Vol. 18, 1964; Gower Publishing Company Ltd, for 'Are links important?' (abridged) from *Lost In Care* by S. Millham, R. Bullock, K. Hosie and M. Haak (1986); The National Children's Bureau for 'Services for under fives: current provision in context and a glossary of terms' (abridged) by Gillian Pugh from *Services For Under Fives: Developing a Co-ordinated Approach* (1988); The Open University for 'Effective co-operation in child protection work' by W. Stainton Rogers, 'Residential child care: matching services with needs' by Lorraine Waterhouse, 'The case for residential special education' by T. Cole and 'Access between children in care and their families' by J. Tunnard; The Open University and Harper and Row for 'Children in care: the racial dimension in social work assessment' by Shama Ahmed from J. Cheetham (ed.) *Social and Community Work in a Multi-Racial Society* (1981); *Spare Rib* for 'Working with girls' by Val

Carpenter, No. 94, 1980; Whiting and Birch for 'Family Centres' (abridged) by Bob Holman from *Children and Society* No. 2, 1987

Preface

This collection of readings and a second volume entirely of original material entitled *Child Care Research, Policy and Practice* (edited by Barbara Kahan, and also published by Hodder and Stoughton) are integrated components of the Open University's multi-media course *Working with children and young people (K254)*.

The decision to produce the course resulted from concern about the level of training available to those working in the child care field. A major grant from the Department of Health and Social Security enabled the Department of Health and Social Welfare at the Open University, The Gatsby Project (formerly the Child Care Open Learning Project) and four Certificate in Social Service Schemes – Cleveland and North Yorkshire, Greater Manchester, South and West Wales, and West of Scotland – to come together to develop the course. The Central Council for Education and Training in Social Work has approved the course as a contribution to qualifying training in social work.

The core of the course consists of a series of workbooks which consider key issues in 'ordinary' human development and major problem areas affecting children and young people which their care workers are called on to deal with. In addition, the course includes three hours of video and six hours of audio material designed to stimulate thinking about practice issues, as well as a workbook containing practical guidance on those areas of the law which carers need to know and understand. The approach adopted throughout the course is anti-racist and anti-sexist, and challenges social class bias.

The course materials may also be purchased in pack form, and more information about the course and the packs is available from: The Department of Health and Social Welfare, The Open University, Walton Hall, Milton Keynes, MK7 6AA.

We would like to express our thanks to members of the course team and colleagues in the Department of Health and Social Welfare at the Open University – in particular, Jan Walmsley and Fiona Williams – for their help and advice in selecting and commenting on the writings contained in this Reader. Thanks are also due to Julie Fletcher and Giles Clark of the Open University Publishing Division for their editorial advice, and to the course secretaries, Pat Kirkpatrick, Betty Morris and Rae Smyth, for their ever cheerful and efficient secretarial support.

Introduction

Peter Righton

The articles and chapters from books assembled in this Reader bring together a variety of perspectives on key issues in child care policy, provision and practice. Unlike its companion volume, *Child Care Research, Policy and Practice*, it is not a review of research in the child care field (although many of our authors allude to relevant research), nor does it examine how research might be more effectively used in our planning and delivery of services to children and young people or in our ways of working with them. Instead, it seeks to complement the research book by engaging us in a critical analysis of some current child care policies; an exploration of the range of provisions available as supplements to, or substitutes for, the day-to-day care parents give their children; and opportunities to consider and reconsider how certain aspects of our practice with children and young people might be improved.

It is important for readers to bear three points in mind as they study the writings collected here. First, there are inevitably many more issues for debate than space has allowed us to include. Like all editors of similar material we have had to be selective, and our selection is based on three criteria: what appears to us to be particularly controversial; what seems likely to be of continuing concern during the next decade; and what is most significant, in our view, for the well-being and future of children in care or at risk of reception into care. Secondly, some contributors examine their chosen topic through several pairs of theoretical spectacles, others through one pair only. Some leave the readers to draw their own conclusions, others argue forcefully in favour of a particular viewpoint. Four contributions were specially commissioned for this volume; while most of the remainder were written relatively recently, two made their first appearance more than twenty years ago. In all cases we made our selection because of our belief that the authors have something to tell us that is both valuable and of contemporary relevance. Thirdly, the whole child care field is subject to continual, and sometimes rapid, change. Even as this Reader goes to press a new child care bill is before Parliament; innovative thinking and organisational restructuring in social service agencies are altering the range and balance of provisions for children and young people; and debate continues about the implications for practice of the recent Wagner report on residential services and the Griffiths report on community care. Within a year or two at most, the issues discussed here will need to be re-evaluated in the light of developments such as these. We believe nonetheless that the greater part of what our authors have to say will remain both topical and crucial for some time to come. They do not, of course, all agree cosily with each other. The word 'conflicts' in the title of this publication refers as much to differences of opinion among the contributors as to controversies in the child care field generally.

Readers will search in vain for tidy solutions to knotty problems; what they will find, we hope, is stimulus and challenge. The critical and questioning approach they bring to the book's contents will be every bit as important as anything the authors themselves have written.

Any contribution (such as this Reader) to the continuing debate on child care issues needs to be viewed against the social background of its time. While the major constituents of this background are as old as human history, they are continually changing their shape. In Britain, as we enter the 1990s, three constituents in particular exhibit features that are associated with potential stress and turmoil for certain children – especially for those whose individual circumstances render them more liable than most to intervention by statutory or voluntary agencies of the personal social services. We have something to say now about each of these in turn – and have allowed ourselves a certain licence in the conclusions we draw from the second of them.

The family

While the family continues to be the most highly valued institution in our society for the care and upbringing of children, the last decades have seen major changes in characteristic family structures. There has been a sharp increase in the rate of divorce and remarriage, so that a substantially higher proportion of children than hitherto are now living in single-parent families (most commonly with their mother) or in step-families. The shock and distress experienced by children whose families of origin break up have been extensively documented in recent years – including the impact on them of increasing marital discord, of the departure from home of one or other much-loved parent, of the harrowing uncertainties of divorce proceedings and arrangements for custody, of the emotional and financial strains on the parent who stays with them, and of the difficult (and by no means always successful) adjustment to that parent's new partner. Cumulatively, the effect of these events is scarcely less traumatic for a child than the experience of reception into or committal to care; yet we know also that the majority of children who have undergone them are as anxious to keep in touch with the absent parent as children in care are to maintain links with their families – brothers and sisters as well as parents. Whatever the divorce court decides about custody and access, it remains the case that the majority of divorced parents share the care of their children between them – however unevenly.

Such considerations seem to us to have two important policy implications for the provison of supplementary or substitute care for children who cannot – for whatever reason, and for however short or long a period – live with their own families. First, it would be helpful if the present processes of reception into or committal to care, with their sharp separation between 'being with one's family' (normal and natural) and 'being in care' (abnormal and stigmatised) were to be replaced as far as possible by the practice of 'shared care'. Within this concept, children would remain legally in the care of their parents while living temporarily or intermittently with other caregivers under the auspices of a statutory or voluntary agency. Such an arrangement would make it easier for a *partnership* to develop between parents and agencies rather than the uneasy (and sometimes resentful) rivalry that occurs all too frequently at present. Moreover, there is no good reason why, in other than specified circumstances (such as serious abuse of a child), shared care, rather than reception into or committal to care, should not be employed even when a child is being prepared for permanent placement in another family. Secondly, the increasing evidence of the extent to which many children find the break-up of their family a highly disturbing experience should help to make agencies more alert than they sometimes are to the likelihood of serious difficulties – even of failure – when they take the decision to place a child in care with a foster-family. To say this is not to devalue the practice of fostering. It is rather to urge agencies to recognise that there are occasions when a child needs a temporary moratorium from family life before he or she is ready to cope with and benefit from the intensity and intimacy of relationships that are inseparable from family living, but which have become associated for him or her with deep levels of pain or anxiety. Despite our increasing knowledge about the damage that families are capable of inflicting on children, we are still too apt to draw glib contrasts between the virtues of the family and the vices of 'institutional' life. This is to ignore the uncomfortable truth that families too are institutions, and may be pathological as well as benign. Group living of high quality, whether in its day-care or residential care guise, has an important function to perform in helping children to overcome family-generated traumata, as well as in maintaining children's contacts with their families: it is disquieting, in our view, that in several places group care has become a dwindling and undervalued resource.

Child abuse

Like the family, child abuse and neglect is an age-old phenomenon. But it is only in the past twenty-five years that research in Britain and the United States has shown us how unexpectedly widespread is the incidence and prevalence within families of abusive behaviour by parents (including step-parents) towards their children. From the first coinage of the term baby-battering in the 1960s, we have been compelled with bewildering speed to recognise the existence of an immense variety of abuse and neglect, both physical and emotional, and that children of all ages (not only the very young) may be victims of it. In Britain there has been a succession of official reports on abused children from the case of Maria Colwell onwards; the blame for allowing abuse to continue has been placed primarily on social workers; a large number of recommendations has been put forward, some of which have been enacted in legislation, and some woven into the complex child abuse procedures drawn up by local authority social services or social work departments. The most recent – and still very much current – concern has centred on child sexual abuse. Both before and after the events in Cleveland, professional and lay opinions have been agonisingly divided not only on the extent to which sexual abuse is taking place, but also on the most appropriate ways of intervening with abusers and with the children they have abused. Those who are convinced that the estimated levels of sexual abuse represent only the tip of the iceberg are equally matched by those who believe that large numbers of parents are falsely suspected of such abuse. Within the medical profession there are acrimonious differences of opinion as to whether (for example) anal dilatation should invariably be taken as indicating that abuse has occurred. On one side there are social workers and administrators who hold that the first priority should be to remove a child from the family as soon as there are serious grounds for supposing that abuse has taken place; on the other are those who fear that such precipitate removal, together with the investigative procedures that precede or accompany it, may inflict greater damage than the abuse itself. If we feel sure that a child is the victim of abuse, but he or she is reluctant to tell us so (either through fear of the abuser or through fear of losing him), how far are we justified in putting pressure on the child to disclose it? Once the disclosure has been made, should child and abuser invariably be separated? What is the best way of helping the child work through his or her experience, or of working with the abuser?

In all of these controversial matters, while many relevant research studies have been undertaken, and some helpful guidelines for action have been produced, none of them is as yet conclusive. We are in the realm of conjectures rather than certainties. This last statement, it may be convincingly argued, is applicable to many aspects of child care other than sexual abuse. Very true; and we are uttering here what may seem to many to be no more than an obvious cliché only because sexual abuse emphasises for us more poignantly, perhaps, than any other childhood misfortune the awesome responsibilities – and dilemmas – with which workers are burdened as they strive to make 'good enough' decisions in their child care practice. Imagine, if you can, the feelings of a boy or girl who time and again, in the face of relentless persistence on the part of the worker, has denied that he or she has been subject to molestation by a parent, yet knows that denial is not believed. Imagine, conversely, the agony experienced by a child who *has* been abused by a parent whom he or she none the less loves, yet knows that disclosure will entail either removal from home or the disappearance of the parent (if not both consequences), when all the child wants is for the abuse to stop. Imagine, further, the feelings of the worker, who having acted in good faith on the basis of the best available evidence and the prevailing codes of practice, comes to realise that his or her actions were misguided. The situations we have just sketched are distressing by any standards: no one would willingly subject either a child or a worker to any of them. Yet they are no different in principle from the situation of a child placed involuntarily in a foster family when he or she would rather have gone to a children's home; or that of a child received into care because his or her circumstances do not fit the criteria for admission to the local day nursery. If they seem different it is because we can scarcely conceive that anything done to a child can be more damaging than subjecting him or her to sexual abuse, so that the consequences of bad decisions in such a case must be worse for that child than those made in response to any other contingency. But this is to miss the point: that *all* decisions in child care are problematic (which is not the same as saying they are always, or even often, wrong); that fresh evidence from research and practice is constantly accumulating, sometimes, but by no means always, contradicting what preceded it; and that it is the continuing professional responsibility of the worker to keep abreast of new developments and to use them selectively, bearing in mind that every situation encountered is in some respects similar to others of its type, in other respects unique. Above all, it is vital for the worker to listen to what the child has to say (with an inner as well as an outer ear) and to give what is heard the same respect and attention as would be granted to a parent or to an adult colleague.

Children's rights

The final sentence of the previous paragraph brings us to the third and last of the social background constituents we have chosen to discuss – that of children's rights. For practical purposes (and to steer clear of the well-intentioned but often empty rhetoric in which many 'human rights' issues are couched) we see rights as comprising two elements: the *entitlement* of a person to do something he wants to do, have something he considers he needs, or be protected from what he perceives to be harmful; and the *claim* such entitlements make on others to create the opportunities needed for their enjoyment and to apply sanctions to those who infringe them. The first element carries two obvious implications. Since my choices and preferences may conflict with yours (you want to use that field as a playground for your children, while I want to graze my cattle on it), rights are *limited*, for at least one party to the conflict, and *negotiable*, at least in principle. From the second element come two further implications. If my rights are to be upheld in the face of opposition or infringement, the society I live in must devise effective and enforceable *rules* for doing so (in practice these rules are almost always embodied in common or statute law, which is either supported or challenged by social custom and convention). If there are to be opportunities for me to enjoy my rights, rules that define and enforce them are not of themselves sufficient: I will also need the appropriate *resources* (a judgment in your favour that you may use the hypothetical field as a children's playground will be of no use whatever if, in the meantime, someone has built a supermarket on it).

The last illustration reminds us of the harsh reality that underlies all four of the implications carried by the concept of rights – namely *power*: who holds it, how it is exercised, and whether it is concentrated or diffused. If rights are limited, who sets the limits and in whose interests? If rights are negotiable, how are the terms of the negotiation decided? Are the legal enactments concerned with rights equitable across all groups in society, or do they favour some at the expense of others? To what extent are resources equally or unequally distributed? One has only to ask such questions to be very forcibly reminded of the power inequalities that persist in Britain: those between rich and poor, men and women, and white and black, to name only the most obvious examples. Yet it is between the relative power of adults and children that we find the widest gulf. While adults who are poor, female or black are to a greater or lesser extent disadvantaged in their struggle to secure equal rights with their rich, male or white counterparts, it is at least acknowledged that, as adults, they are capable of considering what is in their own best interests, and are qualified to strive for it. By contrast, while there is in our society a very genuine concern to create conditions that are in the best interests of children and young people, there is also a widespread (and rarely questioned) assumption that it is for adults to determine what those interests are. Children themselves are seldom consulted about them and tend to be heard with patronising condescension on the infrequent occasions when consultation does take place. Very few effective changes in legislation or child care practice were made, for example, in response to the strikingly clear and coherent complaints voiced by the young people who took part in the National Children's Bureau initiative (1977) to ascertain their views about their experiences in care. Since that time, the National Association of Young People in Care (NAYPIC) has been set up, has campaigned vigorously for improved conditions for children in care, and has drawn up a charter of children's rights. Despite the publicity and the support from some professional adults that the movement has received, its impact on child care policy has as yet been minimal, and at the time of writing the funding and future of the organisation is by no means assured.

Now the virtual monopoly that adults enjoy in respect of deciding what is in the best interests of a child is on the whole exercised from the most honourable of motives – and it is precisely those honourable motives that make the monopoly so impervious to attack. Very young children are undoubtedly more vulnerable and dependent than adults; their very eagerness to learn, to explore their world and to master basic skills exposes them to risks from which they must rightly be protected; their capacity to balance their own wishes and needs against those of others is initially markedly limited and egocentric. It is, therefore, entirely appropriate that adults should act as trustees for children's interests and rights during their early years – though it should be more widely recognised than it is that, in these circumstances, children's 'rights' are the rights that adults choose for them, not necessarily those they would choose for themselves. (For many if not most children, for example, the 'right' to education is at some stage in their school career perceived by them not as a right but as an obligation – and an oppressive one at that.) The point is, however, that the majority of children develop very rapidly the ability to contribute sensible views about what is in their best interests, and by the age of early adolescence can match most adults in their capacity to make responsible decisions. In other words their need for adult trusteeship in the matter of interests and rights tapers off close to vanishing point long before most parents – or other adults with authority over them – are prepared to relinquish it. As John Holt (1975) points out, there is remarkably little progression in the acknowledged rights of children to make independent choices for themselves between the day of their birth and the day on which they reach the legal age of majority – when they acquire almost instantly not only the full rights but also the full responsibilities of adulthood. During the intervening period, it is adults exclusively who set limits to, and control the negotiations for, what children are entitled to receive, and who make the rules and supply (or withhold) the resources that underwrite their claims to those entitlements. To illustrate the point we are making: in comparison with a five-year-old child, a young person of fifteen will often express intelligent preferences as to the subjects he or she wants to study at school, the circumstances in which they can be learnt most effectively, and even the wisdom of leaving school rather than remaining there. But the young person has very little more power than the younger child to make those preferences prevail; teachers and parents will continue to decide what he or she studies; teachers will still be in charge of classroom ethos and procedures; he or she cannot afford to pay a private tutor, and in any case law and social custom will impose virtually irresistible pressures to stay on at school.

The rights of a child or a young person can appear even more threadbare when the inequalities of power between adults and children are reinforced by one or more of the social inequalities we referred to earlier. It is, perhaps, the powerlessness resulting from poverty that provides the most striking example. If there is any right that human beings – adults and children – should unquestionably be able to enjoy, few people are likely to disagree that this ought to be the right to adequate shelter and a minimal standard of living. Yet a young person of sixteen or seventeen who is both unemployed and homeless (because, say, life with the family has become intolerable) is now no longer entitled to income support unless he or she can produce evidence of estrangement from the family. Without a job it will be virtually impossible to persuade a landlord to provide accommodation; without accommodation it will be difficult to get a job. If driven to join the ranks of young people (now numbered in their thousands) who sleep in cardboard boxes on town pavements, he or she may well muse with some cynicism on the theoretical 'right' to shelter that well-wishers claim. In practice the entitlement does not exist: social security legislation has set income support limits that are negotiable only if the young person can prove estrangement (which may be a long and tedious process even if it is eventually successful); there are no alternative regulations permitting the young person to make a claim; and there are few, if any, other resources on which he or she can call.

It has been well established in research studies that the children of poor parents are at substantially greater risk of being received into or committed to care than those of the comparatively well-to-do; also that a relatively higher proportion of black children than white children are in the care of local authorities. The 'welfare principle' underlying child care legislation lays it down that:

> in reaching any decision relating to a child in their care, a local authority shall give first consideration to the need to safeguard and promote the welfare of the child throughout his childhood; and shall so far as practicable ascertain the wishes and feelings of the child regarding the decision and give due consideration to them, having regard to his age and understanding. (Child Care Act 1980, Section 18)

It is not, therefore, that the rights of children in care are ignored in legislation: the reverse is true. What happens in practice, however, is that 'due consideration' of the child's wishes and feelings is far more commonly demonstrated through decisions taken by adult carers, however bene-volently, on the child's or young person's behalf than through joint adult–child consultations in which the child can feel an equally respected participant. It is social workers and carers, in general, who decide unilater-ally where the child is to be placed, the extent and duration of access to parents, and the arrangements made to prepare the young person for independent living. There is as yet no unqualified right for a child to see his or her own files; and while it is now common for children in care to be directly involved in their periodic case reviews, the observations of many young people who have submitted evidence to NAYPIC show us how often this involvement has appeared to them to be no more than an empty formality. Children from black ethnic communities all too often find, if they are placed in children's homes, that little opportunity is provided for them to practise customs, consume food or celebrate festive occasions specific to their culture or religion. Those who are placed with white foster-parents may incur a serious risk of loss or diminution of their ethnic identity.

Finally, whether a child comes from a wealthy or a poor family, is a boy or a girl, is white or black, a possible reason for care proceedings is that he or she has been physically or sexually abused. It is a wry comment on the status of children's rights at this point in time that the action taken to prevent further abuse – so often the removal of the child from the family where the abuser lives – is perceived by the child as a harsh punishment rather than as a welcome sign that his or her rights are being protected.

It seems to us that we have no reason to be complacent about the rights of children and younger people. In their work with them social workers and care staff can do something, through the development of partnerships, to establish and confirm their right to share in decision making, whatever the current state of legislation or the prevailing policy of their employing agency. But this, by itself, is not enough. We concur with the view of M. D. A. Freeman (1988) that we will make little headway in this important sphere of human relationships in the absence of two highly desirable developments: first, the requirement that all future legislation be accompanied by *child impact statements*, clarifying the implications that such legislation has for children's interests and rights; and secondly, the establishment of the office of Children's Ombudsman, equipped with adequate resources and powers, and making itself freely accessible to all children and their representatives.

References

FREEMAN, M. D. A. (1988) 'Taking children's rights seriously', *Children and Society*, Vol. 4 (1987–8), pp. 299–319.

HOLT, J. (1975) *Escape from Childhood*, Harmondsworth, Penguin.

NATIONAL CHILDREN'S BUREAU (1977) '*Who Cares? Young People in Care Speak Out*', London, NCB.

Section I   Policy issues

1 Rethinking child care policy

Mike Fisher, Peter Marsh and David Phillips with Eric Sainsbury

The raising of children is an intensely private family matter which is nevertheless the subject of equally intensive public debate and concern. We have all been children, some of us are parents, and we all in various ways take responsibility for children. We are all curious to know what really goes on in other families and all equally determined to preserve the privacy of our own family life. Despite this interest in the way families raise their children, there nevertheless remains a fundamental belief that parents have an inviolable right to determine their children's upbringing independently of outside interference. The families and the professionals have been concerned with the care of children and with negotiating the criteria that govern state intervention in that care.

Changing families and changing policy

The public system of child care in the UK has been dominated by the twin themes of rescue and compensation. The law has long recognised the right of society to remove children from parents who are believed to be damaging them and, in recent times, has become alert to more subtle kinds of damage. This judicial readiness to sanction rescue was revised in post-war years in the light of Bowlby's work on maternal deprivation. However, the effect of Bowlby's studies has been contradictory. In one sense, he re-emphasised the sanctity of the maternal relationship and its centrality to psychological health. This served to raise the rescue threshold by warning of the possible damage to the child of removal from the family. In another sense, however, the research could be interpreted as pointing to the necessity to ensure that, once crossed, the threshold of removal should lead to a particular, compensatory form of care in recognition of the child's maternal loss. These themes are alive and well in British child care policy at both a national and a local level.

These psychological principles which once guided thinking about the planning of child care services are, of course, founded on particular notions about the composition of 'normal' families and about the nature of family relationships. The child's alleged psychological need for unbroken maternal presence fits neatly with dominant conceptions of 'proper' family life, in which the mother's role in upbringing far outweighs that of the father. Such a view of family life coincided in the UK with an intense concentration during the 1950s on the mother as the primary guarantor of children's health and welfare (Oakley, 1981; Wilson, 1977) and aligns comfortably with the period's economic boom and reconstructionist philosophy.

These are, however, highly questionable principles in the moral and practical minefield of child care policy. The decision about whether and when to intervene in unhappy families cannot be resolved simply by reference to psychological theories, nor can it be based on folk precepts about not interfering. When to intervene, who should be given powers to do so, and with what long-term aims, are questions which challenge our fundamental social organisation and values.

Moreover, these traditional wisdoms of family life do not survive modern scrutiny. In the first place, the very composition of families is changing. The pattern of permanent two-parent, two-children families has shifted, and the boundaries of family membership are now more fluid (see Rapoport *et al.*, 1982). It is becoming more common for families to consist of a series of parent figures in various relationships to a series of children. As is so often the case, the evolving terminology used to describe families epitomises these changes. When the family norm was permanence, the term 'broken family', with its aura of irretrievable loss and disgrace, was used. A current term, 'reconstituted families' (Burgoyne and Clark, 1982), describing families where a new parent figure is incorporated, neatly encapsulates the concept of an evolving family unit whose nature is changed, rather than destroyed, by the arrivals and departures of various members.

Related changes have also occurred in the nature of parenting itself. The concept of the father's and the mother's discrete and unconnected contributions to the psychological and physical well-being of the child is less tenacious in modern child psychology. The 'discovery' of the role of the father in child development, in particular his ability to achieve significant interaction with the child despite the apparent handicap of significantly less time to do so (see, for example, Lamb, 1981), has led to a revision of the basic tenets of parenting. So too has the rise of feminist versions of the nature of parenting, in which, for example, the daily physical care of children has been demystified to lay bare the sheer labour involved, and hence the need to share this burden equally rather than regard it as an unequivocal privilege (see, for example, Oakley, 1974).

Increasingly parents regard their contributions as interchangeable and allocate parental roles on the basis of competence, availability and equality and not simply gender. These changes have considerable implications for the criteria for social work intervention in the lives of families and for the nature of public child care provision.

Political dimensions of child care policy

If these changes in family structure and parental roles are of recent origin, current political dimensions of child care policy, which have rarely been more prominent than today, surely have a longer history.

The tension between the rights of parents, of their children, and of the state, which attracted increasing legislative attention in the UK during the nineteenth century, continues to be demonstrated in the concerns of pressure groups in recent years. The increasing emphasis on the rights of children in the campaigns of Equality For Children and of Justice for Children are mirrored in increasing legislative concern for the child's wishes. Equally vociferous are the parent-oriented Campaign For One-Parent Families and the Family Rights Group, whose arguments for the rights of parents in the face of state intervention have contributed to the pressure which produced the recent DHSS Code of Practice relating to access to children in care. Thus the pendulum of public pressure swings back and forth, reflecting the unresolved tensions within public policy.

In political terms, the relationship between the family and the state has always included at its core both the right of the family to raise children as it sees fit, and the corresponding right of the state to intervene if the family's care or control falls short of what the state requires. Law and custom thus defend the family as the prime agent of socialisation only in so far as it fulfils the task currently prescribed. The construction of the task is a dynamic process which varies from age to age and society to society.

A constant theme in this process has been the family's duty to take responsibility for its members, to inculcate socially acceptable behaviour, and to safeguard virtues in danger of erosion through either time or opposition. Thus hard work, education and moral tutelage are some of the guiding principles behind parent–child relationships, and much parental ingenuity and anxiety is expended in finding opportunities to introduce or reinforce these messages. However, in legitimating these tasks, the legal framework established by the state has inevitably suffered from some confusion over whether it is primarily directed at helping families to achieve social control of their children or at ratifying state intervention.

The evolution of British law governing the moral and physical welfare of children exemplifies this confusion. Legal authority over children was vested in kin until the demand, engendered by the industrial revolution, for cheap factory labour from children (Alcock and Harris, 1982; Morris *et al.*, 1980; Dingwall *et al.*, 1983) caused children to work outside the parent's sphere of authority, rendering children's behaviour and working circumstances a target for state as well as family control.

Thus the generation of the framework of British child welfare legislation never derived simply from the interests of the child; instead the dominant force was the need for social regulation. As Dingwall and his colleagues (1983) comment, 'Attention was first focused on protection from children and only latterly on protection of children.' There is, in fact, a tension between legal concepts designed to facilitate state control over family life, and those designed to protect the family from undue state intervention and to boost family autonomy.

Nowhere is this tension better demonstrated than in the provision of the British system of social services. The particular relationship between the state and the family embodied in the system of public welfare gives rise to considerable concern over the extent to which such provisions boost or erode family autonomy. Family responsibility to care for its members has become shared with health and education authorities, social security and social services to a greater extent than ever before, and there has always been a concern that the welfare state may undermine family ties and produce welfare dependency. One political response to this has been to attempt to reinforce the role of the family as the primary carer, and to identify why some families appear throughout generations to be unable to solve their problems without recourse to public assistance.

The identification of family authority over children with the interests of the state is strongly aligned with the political view that the family should be encouraged to accept total responsibility for its members. Such a strong family unit has both emotional appeal, as underpinning moral virtues under current threat, and considerable economic appeal, as reducing the demand for costly public care of dependency groups. This philosophy finds expression in some recent social thought and has been most notably promulgated in the area of social services, producing on the far right a philosophy of welfare in which the care of family members is increasingly seen as a private problem, to be undertaken using family resources only, and to be underpinned only in extreme circumstances by a residual network of statutory services.

In the UK (and the USA) this has been the recent drift of government programmes. In Britain, the Social Services Minister, Sir Keith Joseph, made the now famous speculations on the inadequacy of working-class parenting and the need for better 'preparation for parenthood'. The funds given by the DHSS under Sir Keith for research into the 'cycle of deprivation' were the practical expression of this policy. At the inception of this UK research programme designed to examine the intergenerational transmission of poverty, Harriet Wilson (1974) investigated the relevance of Sir Keith's ideas on 'preparation for parenthood' to resolving the problems of poor families in inner cities. She concluded that the research indicated the need not for social training, but for:

> large-scale fiscal measures to speed up slum clearance and housing schemes, to improve local amenities, to boost family incomes by generous family allowances, to improve the job market in the inner city, and to implement the proposed extension of nursery provision.

Not surprisingly, the research commissioned by the DHSS failed to identify any attitudinal mechanism by which poverty was somehow 'transmitted' from parent to child. Instead, the studies pointed to a complex exchange between traditional attitudes and stark economic deprivation of the kind described by Wilson (see Blaxter and Paterson, 1982; Coffield *et al.*, 1982). Despite this, primary preventive measures of the sort recommended by Wilson have not emerged in public policy.

Furthermore, the fear that the welfare state is undermining family responsibility is unfounded (Longfield, 1984). Policy changes are being pressed on the basis of myths. British studies of family life and family preferences for care for dependants indicate that family members have essentially retained their primary caring role, and prefer care in *partnership* with public agencies rather than wishing to hand it over (see Moroney, 1976; West, 1984).

The child care legacy

In relation to child care policy, this fear of undermining responsibility results from a fundamental misunderstanding of the role of parents, and reinforces the antipathy between public and private care of children. As other commentators have noted (Millham *et al.*, 1984), the history of social policy in this field has bequeathed a legacy of disregard for the potential of the family as a continuing source of security for children identified in some way as being at risk.

This disregard of the family's potential for constructive future contact where the question of the adequacy of a child's parenting has arisen, has led to a polarisation of public care and private family life. Public care is seen as inevitably damaging the psychological health of the child and as a verdict on the parents' abilities to offer appropriate care. By contrast, the family remains the haven of proper child development. The evidence presented earlier indicating that there are many different patterns of family composition, and that caring is frequently shared with others than the direct family, changes radically our conceptions of what help is relevant when parents find child care difficulties beyond their solution.

Clearly the very notion that responsibility for child development is best shared among a range of people, with stimuli for education and play, attention for health matters and so on deliberately shared between parents and professionals, has immediate implications for the public response when families encounter difficulties in child care. Add to this the notion that in very many families, as a matter of daily routine, the simple care of children (other than for educational or health purposes) is entrusted to minders, friends and wider family, and it is clear that there is no such thing as the exclusive care of children by their parents. All parenting is shared between the family and the wider kinship and friendship network, and between this system and state provision.

The consequence of this is that public services designed to develop the potential of children and to safeguard their health and welfare must aim for an approach which incorporates the concept of *partnership* at its core, and that the legal framework relating to intervention in families should recognise and encourage this sense of partnership. In some services, this recognition already exists, at least in a rudimentary form. Few dispute that the health of children is primarily the responsibility of the parents, and much intervention is designed to educate parents in the physical care of their children. Nursing and medical intervention is therefore dependent on parental notification, and subsequent care, particularly in relation to young children, can often be exercised only through the parents. However, imperfectly practised, this approach at least recognises that health care intervention must supplement that of the parents rather than substitute for it. It is this emphasis on *supplementary* rather than *substitute* care (Davis, 1981), growing out of a recognition of the fundamentally shared nature of parenting, which should be the driving force behind a new direction for child care policy.

Collaboration or compulsion?

It is, of course, nothing new to propose that the legal framework of child welfare and professional intervention should reflect the need to work with, rather than against, families. As the government circular explaining the 1948 Children Act (Circular 48/160) put it:

> To keep the family together must be the first aim, and the separation of the child from its parents can only be justified when there is no possibility of securing adequate care for that child in his own home.

Much of the legislation governing public intervention in family life is in fact concerned with laying a duty on public authorities to 'diminish the need to receive children into or keep them in care' (Child Care Act 1980, S.1), while the terminology of the law emphasises the *reception* of children into care, rather than the popular phrase 'taking them into care'. This is not mere semantics. Public authorities have extensive discretion in their operation of the law relating to child welfare (Alcock and Harris, 1982), and are legally empowered to offer a preventive service aimed at support-ing families in their caring for children. The popular image of the 'welfare' removing children, however well it may reflect the service given by social services in the eyes of its recipients and of ratepayers, is only a pale reflection of the legal obligations on public authorities. As with every area of social welfare, practical intervention and the legal authority for it may be worlds apart in their nature and effects.

The potential emphasis in the legislative framework on permissive inter-vention, implying the co-operation of families in ensuring the adequate care of their children, relates primarily to services designed to prevent the need for admission to care. In its practical implementation by public authorities, the legislative framework may well give some scope for recog-nising the potential of family care *prior* to care. When admission has taken place, however, the legacy of public and professional attitudes towards parents whose children have entered public care often appears an insur-mountable obstacle to any further constructive contact between parents and their children.

The aura of compulsion in the public child care services has been extensively analysed in recent years. Parton (1979, 1981) and Packman

(1981) both highlight an apparently increasing tendency for intervention in family life to be based on compulsion rather than informal permission, and attribute this either to defensive practice in the context of possible exposure (Packman), or to the fact that social work practice is merely reflecting a change in the moral climate of society towards greater social control of deviance (Parton). As this is being written (in 1985), the publicity given to the case of Jasmine Beckford, who died after she was returned from public care to her parents' care, will ensure that social workers will once again be reminded of the need to respond to the apparently contradictory demands of society both to intervene effectively and to respect family autonomy.

These theories regarding the increasing use of compulsion have been criticised by Dingwall and his colleagues (1983) as lacking in authoritative statistical basis, and lacking any overview of the *relative*, as opposed to *absolute*, use of compulsory intervention. According to these critics, the use of compulsory powers to protect children is, in fact, declining in relation to the number of children who may require such protection.

Although the question whether there is any way of determining those in need of protection is at the heart of this debate, this is unlikely to be the prime determinant of professional practice. It seems clear that, no matter how those at risk may be identified and quantified, social workers will, in practice, increasingly want to ensure that their actions are directed by legislative requirements, both as protection for themselves and as a means of pointing to at least some external criteria for the validity of the protective actions taken in respect of children. Thus there seems a prima-facie risk that social work intervention will increasingly be characterised by recourse to legal justification, and that, regardless of the debate about whether compulsion is on the increase, the public care of children will be further identified with compulsory removal and thus as antipathetic to family care. The findings from this study point to an alternative way forward.

The clients' contribution

This danger calls increasing attention to a second issue, namely how such intervention is experienced by families. The analysis of the effects of social policy by interpreting official statistics remains the favourite method of social commentators, despite now extensive evidence that such an approach relies on social indicators which are at best artificially constructed and at worst downright misleading. In the area of child care policy, juvenile crime is the prime example where figures based on actual offences overlook both the discretion applied by law enforcement agencies and the effects of detection efficiency. There is now evidence both that the police charge some children and not others (Cigourel, 1967; Parker *et al.*, 1981), and that the actual rate of offending is much higher than that revealed by official figures (Hindelang, 1976; West and Farrington, 1973). Clearly, an accurate account of the effects of social policy in the area of juvenile crime could not be undertaken by reference solely to official statistics.

The same is true of the effects of social services' intervention in the lives of families. For many years, until Mayer and Timms published *The Client Speaks* in 1970, it was accepted practice that the effects of social work intervention were assessed by asking social workers to describe their practice and (sometimes) by objective assessment of clients. The concept that social intervention could have effects unintended by the practitioners, and which could be revealed only by asking the clients for their *subjective* impressions, took a long time to achieve currency, and had to do battle with the time-honoured attitude in professional practice that the client could not be expected to know what he, or more usually she, wanted. The even more extraordinary notion, that clients' opinions could be used to reshape social work practice into a more effective intervention, and that social policy itself could be responsive to the views of its recipients, has taken even longer to achieve respectability amongst social commentators.

Launched by Mayer and Timms and continued by, among others, Sainsbury and his colleagues at the University of Sheffield, this new approach to the evaluation of social work has revealed previously uncharted areas of knowledge, and has been extensively reviewed in recent years (Sainsbury, 1980; Craig, 1981; Rees and Wallace, 1982; Fisher, 1983). One overriding finding from these reviews is that social work has many effects on its clients of which its practitioners are unaware and which they cannot intend. The potential for misinterpretation and imperfect communication in the interactions between workers and clients is enormous, and no analysis of the effects of social work intervention can be complete without some attention to the views of those on the receiving end.

This dimension to social policy is especially relevant to the question of how public intervention in the lives of families where child care difficulties have arisen can be most effective. As we have seen, for example, the raw fact that an admission to care takes place as a result of a care order made by the court, and thus appears in official statistics as further evidence of compulsion, may tell us little about how this action is experienced either by the child or by his or her family. Our research revealed that a significant number of such admissions were, in fact, perceived by the parents as a direct result of their requesting help, and that in such cases the parents actually welcomed the care order as an attempt to meet the needs of their children. This is not to say that all care orders were welcomed by the families; and there is clearly the possibility that, while this intervention was favoured by the parents, it was resented by the children.

Nevertheless, such findings illustrate the dangers of using apparently incontrovertible facts to develop an argument about the changing nature of public intervention in child care. Our evidence points to the need both to be sensitive to the many different recipients of public policy and their potentially different views on its effects, and to the need to understand the meaning, to those on the receiving end, of actions taken in the name of public policy.

A new approach

Our argument is therefore that evidence about the changing nature of family life, about the characteristics of present-day parenting, and about the views of clients, points to a clear need to review both the legal/moral framework governing state intervention in the lives of families and the professional practice of those working in child care.

We accept the view advanced by Parton (1981) that all debate over the proper role of the state in guaranteeing acceptable family life for children centres on judgments of what is acceptable parenting and child behaviour, and that such judgments are essentially influenced by the ideological context. In the end, as Dingwall and his colleagues (1983) point out, child care policy amounts to a statement on what constitutes 'the good society'.

We are convinced that the philosophy which was originally intended to predominate in the post-war UK child care legislation – namely that the work of public agencies was to provide supportive services to families, part of which could include admission to care as a means ultimately of preserving family relationships in the long run – has been lost from current practice. This loss is both accidental, in the sense of resulting from neglect and omission, and deliberate, in the sense that current social policy is founded on myths and misinformation about family life which tend to polarise the public and private care of children. In our view, this philosophy of *partnership* with clients, in which the primary caring role of the family is reasserted but effectively *supplemented* by public services, must be reintroduced into national policy and practice. The 'good society' must, in our view, treat those in need of child care services as fellow citizens rather than as 'inadequate' parents or children.

References

ALCOCK, A. and HARRIS, P. (1982) *Welfare Law and Order*, London, Macmillan.

BLAXTER, M. and PATTERSON, E. (1982) *Mothers and Daughters*, Oxford, Heinemann Educational.

BURGOYNE, J. and CLARK, D. (1982) 'Reconstituted families' in Rapoport *et al.* (1982).

CIGOUREL, A. (1967) *The Social Organisation of Juvenile Justice*, Chichester, John Wiley.

COFFIELD, F., ROBINSON, J. and SARSBY, J. (1982) *A Cycle of Deprivation? A Case Study of Four Families*, Oxford, Heinemann Educational.

CRAIG, G. (1981) *Review of Studies of the Public and Users' Attitudes, Opinions and Expressed Needs with Respect to Social Work and Social Workers*, National Institute for Social Work.

DAVIS, A. (1981) *The Residential Solution*, London, Tavistock.

DINGWALL, R., EEKELAAR, J. and MURRAY, T. (1983) *The Protection of Children: State Intervention in Family Life*, Oxford, Blackwell.

FISHER, M. (ed.) (1983) *Speaking of Clients*, Joint Unit for Social Services Research, University of Sheffield.

HINDELANG, M. J. (1976) 'With a little help from their friends: group participation in reported delinquent behaviour', *British Journal of Criminology*, No. 16, pp. 109–125.

LAMB, M. (ed.) (1981) *The Role of the Father in Child Development*, Chichester, John Wiley.

LONGFIELD, J. (1984) *Ask the Family*, London, Bedford Square Press.

MAYER, J. E. and TIMMS, N. (1970) *The Client Speaks*, London, Routledge and Kegan Paul.

MILLHAM, S., BULLOCK, R., HOSIE, K. and HAAK, M. (1984) 'The problem of maintaining links between children in care and their families: a study of the child care process', in *Report to DHSS*.

MORONEY, R. (1976) *The Family and the State*, Harlow, Longman.

MORRIS, A., GILLER, H., SZWED, E. and GEACH, H. (1980) *Justice for Children*, London, Macmillan.

OAKLEY, A. (1974) *The Sociology of Housework*, Oxford, Martin Robertson.

OAKLEY, A. (1981) *Subject Women*, Oxford, Martin Robertson.

PACKMAN, J. (1981) *The Child's Generation*, 2nd edn, Oxford, Blackwell.

PARKER, H., CASBURN, M. and TURNBULL, D. (1981) *Receiving Juvenile Justice*, Oxford, Blackwell.

PARTON, N. (1979) 'The natural history of child abuse: a study in social problem definition', *British Journal of Social Work*, Vol. 9, No. 4, pp. 431–451.

PARTON, N. (1981) 'Child abuse, social anxiety and welfare', *British Journal of Social Work*, Vol. 11, No. 4, pp. 391–414.

RAPOPORT, R., FOGARTY, M. and RAPOPORT, R. N. (eds) (1982) *Families in Britain*, London, Routledge and Kegan Paul.

REES, S. and WALLACE, A. (1982) *Verdicts on Social Work*, London, Edward Arnold.

SAINSBURY, E. (1980) 'Research into client opinion', *Social Work Today*, Vol. 11, No. 37.

WEST, D. and FARRINGTON, D. (1973) *Who Becomes Delinquent?* London, Heinemann Educational [for the Cambridge Institute of Criminology].

WEST, P. (1984) 'Public preferences for the care of dependency groups', *Social Science and Medicine*, Vol. 18, No. 4, pp. 287–295.

WILSON, E. (1977) *Women and the Welfare State*, London, Tavistock.

WILSON, H. (1974) 'Parenting in poverty', *British Journal of Social Work*, Vol. 4, No. 3, pp. 241–254.

2 Two value positions in recent child care law and practice

Lorraine M. Fox Harding

Interest in this area arose originally from a consideration of the concept of 'parental rights', of how this concept is defined in law and social services practice relating to child care and adoption, and to what extent it might be reasonable to speak of there being any extant meaningful 'parental rights' in the contemporary scene. While a broad historical trend was noted towards the limitation of the once near-absolute rights of parents over children by state agencies, with the declared objective of protecting the child's interests and welfare, it seemed that in recent policies a number of different themes could be identified, involving potentially conflicting values and assumptions about children, parents, the state and the rights and roles of different parties in the child care situation. A study of the literature relating to recent child care legislation, policy and practice, together with a number of interviews carried out with individuals prominent in this field (academics, practitioners and representatives of pressure groups) focusing on policy shifts during the 1970s,[1] suggested that at least two broad value positions, differing from each other on child care policy in important ways, might usefully be defined. These two schools of thought are termed here the 'kinship defenders' and the 'society as parent protagonists'.

It is suggested that views diverge on the central question of the rights of parents to custody and control of their children in relation to the right of the state (acting through courts and social work agencies) to intervene in the parent–child relationship, to remove children from their parents, to allocate their care and control to other parties, and to determine their subsequent upbringing. To some extent these differing viewpoints may be regarded as ideological positions advanced in the defence of the interests of particular groups, notably the natural parents and the 'substitute carers' (foster- and adoptive parents). The differing viewpoints are here polarised into the two major value positions set out below, though it is recognised that these positions represent relatively extreme points on a *dimension* of views, rather than two all-embracing categories. Other viewpoints may be defined which occupy an intermediate location between these two, and there are also schools of thought which are not readily assimilable to the dimension suggested, for example those which put emphasis on a radical definition of 'children's rights'. A 'practitioner' view was also identified which was pragmatic, accepting elements of both the major value positions outlined here but being more aware of the need for different approaches in different individual cases, and more concerned about matters of detailed practice than of principle (though this may mean simply that values and principles were not made explicit).

The 'kinship defenders'

The position of the 'kinship defenders' may be briefly outlined as follows.
In this view the natural – that is, biological – family is perceived as being
of unique value to the child and as being, for the vast majority of children,
the optimum context for their growth, upbringing and development. State
intervention should therefore be directed to preserving, supporting and
strengthening the family unit; only in unusual and extreme situations
should it be disrupted. Where obviously inadequate parenting occurs, the
response of the statutory services in most cases should be to support
parents and help improve their parenting, whilst keeping the child within
the family. Commentators in this school tend to emphasise class and
economic variables as factors producing poor standards of child care, and
to de-emphasise parental culpability and personal inadequacy. Thus, in
this view parents as well as children tend to appear as victims and, in
particular, working-class parents are seen as vulnerable and powerless *vis-
à-vis* statutory agencies. It is thought that the separation of children from
poor parents, the keeping of children apart from parents and the removal
of parental rights are undertaken too readily by these agencies. Ideally,
steps should not be taken to remove children from parental care unless
there is clearly no other way to prevent harm to them and unless other
options, such as day-care, financial and housing help, have been investigated first. When children *have* been removed, positive efforts should be
made to rehabilitate them with their parents as soon as possible.

Of the 'kinship defenders', the most notable is probably Holman, whose
position is outlined in his pamphlet *Inequality in Child Care*[2] and elsewhere. He argues that a good deal of the apparent need for substitute
child care is produced by social deprivation and its attendant pressures,
rather than by parental inadequacy or culpability *per se*. The ties between
parents and child are strong; parents may be forced into, rather than
willingly accepting of, separation from their children; when separated,
they may not want to make the final break via adoption. The response of
the social services to poor standards of parenting should be the provision
of more supportive services to enable natural families to cope better,
rather than facilitating the removal of children to substitute care and the
ultimate separation of adoption. Holman speaks emotively of parents
'losing' their children, which suggests that he identifies the wishes and
feelings of parents as being of not insignificant importance alongside the
needs of children. Indeed, in writing about unmarried mothers and child
separation, he specifically states that the wishes of the mothers should be
taken into consideration more strongly in the legislation concerning the
future of their children.[3]

Holman is critical of the 1975 Children Act for taking no cognisance of
the link between child separation and poverty. The major child care need
is to provide the necessary environmental facilities to prevent families
from breaking up, or to bring separated families together again. In Hol-

man's view – and in contrast to beliefs held in some quarters – social work practice tends *not* to encourage contact between parents and children in care, or the reunification of separated families. In support of this contention he quotes research done by Thorpe,[4] who found in a study of long-term foster-children that only 27 per cent had contact with their parents every six months or more frequently and that over 60 per cent of natural parents did not know where their children were living, with only 21 per cent feeling encouraged by their social worker to maintain contact. In only 5 per cent of cases was rehabilitation considered by the social worker to be a possibility and in no case at all was there any definite plan towards rehabilitation. Holman stresses that lack of contact did not necessarily reflect parental wishes (in fact nearly half of the parents wanted their children back), but parents felt they were being tacitly excluded by the agency.

In a recent article Holman reiterates his arguments.[5] In his view, in the 1970s the drop in children available for adoption led adoption pressure groups to advocate a kind of fostering closer to adoption, with the natural parents having fewer rights to intervene in the foster placement. At the same time, influential psychodynamic doctrine[6] held that children can only relate to one set of parent figures and that psychological ties are more important than biological ones. The 1975 Act contained various provisions to limit parental rights, the effects of which were to increase the likelihood of parents losing touch with their children and to encourage quasi-adoptive fostering exclusive of natural parents, while no extra community resources were provided to prevent children having to leave their parents at all. Since 1975 community services such as day care, which have a role in preventing reception into care, have contracted under government spending cuts. In the light of these cuts, much might be achieved by stimulating localities to care for their own children – that is, by the greater use of informal sources of substitute child care. And Thoburn's research[7] has shown that persistent social work can in fact bring about the return of children to natural parents who previously could not cope.

Other writers in the field have made similar points. Tunstill[8] attacks practice guides for social workers issued by the Association of British Adoption and Fostering Agencies, for emphasising the removal of parental rights and placement of children for adoption and long-term fostering. Tunstill is critical of these guides for leaning heavily to the side of the substitute carers and for stressing the advantages of removal from inadequate natural parents and placement with long-term substitute families if the child is in care from an early age and if the relationship with the natural parent is not consistent and affectionate. She suggests that this is a hard-line criterion against natural parents which does not take account of social workers' failure to encourage regular contact between natural parents and children in care. It is also worth mentioning some of the work of Wilson,[9] who, though mainly concerned with factors influencing delinquency, comments that material shortages in the home and poor environmental conditions adversely affect child rearing. Life in the slum forces parents to adopt child-rearing methods of which they do not approve, and Wilson concludes that 'in the world of poverty the material preconditions necessary for child-centred parenting do not exist'. This underlines the argument that it is poor children whose rearing is most likely to appear to agencies to be unsatisfactory.[. . .]

A number of pressure groups should also be referred to as being among the 'kinship defenders'. The British Association of Social Workers attacked the care provisions of the 1975 Act as an attempt to undermine working-class parents in particular. In their response to the Houghton Report which preceded the Act in 1972,[10] BASW argued that the law should not allow parental responsibilities to be removed (under Section 2 of the 1948 Act) unless there were good reason to suppose that the local authority's judgment of the child's interests was better than the parents'. They also stressed the difference between adoption and fostering, not seen as simply one of length of placement: often the aim of fostering was restoration of the child to the natural family, or at least the maintenance of contact with it. And BASW were generally unhappy about the introduction of arbitrary time limits into the legislation. The Child Poverty Action Group, in their comments on the 1975 Act when it was still in bill form,[11] stressed the link between poverty and children being received into or committed to care, and the fact that the latter often occurred because of a lack of housing or day-care facilities. The Group believed that the Children Bill further eroded the already inadequate rights of poor families by allowing for the progressive transfer of parental rights to foster-parents and by widening the powers to dispense with parental consent to adoption. The National Council for One-Parent Families is, understandably, concerned about the number of one-parent family children who go into substitute care, arguing that they are more vulnerable to separation because the help they need is often withheld. Many social workers fail to visit on a regular preventive basis and requests for assistance or cries for help are often ignored. It is argued that lone parents have children taken away from them as a punishment for their failure to cope with society's shortcomings and its failure to offer adequate support.[12]

Some quotations from individuals interviewed[13] on child care policy illustrate further the main concerns of the 'kinship defenders'. Points raised frequently by these respondents concerned the nature and problems of adoption, the difficulties of the 'time limits' provisions in the 1975 Act and the value of the natural family for the child.[. . .]

One respondent in this school of thought commented on the strength of the bond between even inadequate parents and children, saying: 'The astounding thing, in my experience as a social worker, is that for the most part kids are crazy about their parents, even when they're being badly treated.' Questioned as to whether she thought there really was a blood tie, this respondent replied:

> Well, I think the children don't like being taken into care, for the most part. It isn't what most of them want. And parents have to be appallingly bad before they do. I'm not talking about the Maria Colwell . . . I'm talking about

the whole grey area, where Social Services Departments define parents as inadequate or not good enough or just generally at risk. My experience is that kids really like their parents best, unless the very worst is going on.

This respondent was also concerned about the failure of social workers to work for rehabilitation, stating, 'There are lots of social workers who think it quite appropriate to take a child away from dodgy natural parents and work avidly towards replacing it with adoptive ones.'

Another respondent commented on the child's relationship to the foster family and the natural family as follows:

I see fostering, except under exceptional circumstances, as the 'in trust for the natural family' thing, and I think some of the efforts made to safeguard the child are in fact safeguarding the foster-parents . . . I think there's always a danger of being a bit simplistic about children who I think have a right to their own family, and that doesn't just mean parents, it means grandparents, people who can talk to them about their past, the past of the family.

And a third reiterated that it is the poor who come into contact with Social Services Departments, while:

middle-class people, rich people, go elsewhere; they go and see their GP, they have a wider network of people that they could perhaps draw on; and if they don't they have the nine-to-five freedom from their children, the release from the pressures of having kids around; they have boarding schools which are a legitimate way of getting rid of our children if you have the money to do it.

The central concerns of the kinship school hardly need restating. There is a focus upon natural families, and in particular poor natural families, whose ties are threatened by the powers of courts and social workers to remove children and keep them away from their parents, perhaps permanently. The alternative and desired emphasis of policy would be to provide more resources to parents caring for their children at home so that they could do their job better, and to reunite with their parents, wherever possible, those children who have been removed. The 1975 Children Act, however, constitutes a step in the opposite direction.

The 'society-as-parent protagonists'

In contrast to the 'kinship defenders' the 'society-as-parent protagonists' seem to place greater faith in the possibility of beneficent state intervention to protect children's well-being. Indeed, the responsibility and necessity for such action to defend children against parental mistreatment is strongly emphasised. When parental care is inadequate, children should be placed with those who are best able to care for them. Because of the emphasis on good care rather than biological bonds, this school of thought tends to hold a fairly favourable view of good substitute carers and to wish to strengthen their position *vis-à-vis* the natural parents. A high value tends to be placed on certainty and permanence, so that when a child is removed from his natural parents and rapid rehabilitation seems unlikely, he should not be confused by multiple parent figures or uncertain plans for his future. It may then be better for his welfare to sever contact with the family of origin completely and enable the substitute carers to assume the full parental role. The emphasis is on the child as a unit distinct from his [or her] family, and on the responsibility of society to care for [the child] in the best way possible – if necessary by giving care of him or her, permanently and legally, to adults other than the parents. This view is critical of the concept of 'parental rights' which is seen as being still too influential in popular thinking about parents and children. Proponents of this view tend to see the idea of parental possession as one that is still protected and upheld by the law and by social agencies; and they believe this state of affairs to be damaging to children, given that parents' and children's interests sometimes conflict.

Kellmer Pringle[14] is among the most outspoken proponents of the society-as-parent type of view. She is critical of attitudes stressing the paramountcy of biological parenthood as being ambivalent and contradictory. In her view society overvalues children's ties with their parents and is too slow to cut them permanently. Society suffers from a misplaced faith in the 'blood tie' and an over-romanticised picture of parenthood. The idea that children belong to their parents like other possessions over which [the parents] may experience exclusive rights has no factual foundation and should be rejected; children are only on temporary loan to their parents. Kellmer Pringle argues that we need a concept of responsible and informed parenthood and a recognition that the ability and willingness to undertake the responsibilities of parenthood are not dependent on, or necessarily a consequence of, biological parenthood. The stress is on *psychological* parenthood. Kellmer Pringle believes that we go too far in asserting that the way parents bring up their children is solely their own concern. In law and practice, we often act as though the overvalued blood ties ensured satisfactory parenting, with the result that the child's well-being is sacrificed to that of the adult.

Tizard[15] puts a similar, though less emphatic, case in *Adoption: A Second Chance*, which reports a study that compared children in institutional care in early life who were subsequently adopted, with similar children who were restored to their natural parent. Tizard's findings led her to conclude that the adopted children were the most fortunate – as a group they had fewer problems than the restored children. With reference to the natural mothers whose children had been restored to them, she says, 'The blood tie by no means implied a love tie', and comments that the adoptive mothers were warmer on the whole than the natural mothers. In Tizard's view, fostering does not offer children the security of adoption: the uncertainty disturbed the children and contacts with the natural parents aroused anxiety in them. Her study suggested that social work decisions were influenced by a number of underlying and often implicit assumptions, which included the primacy of the blood tie and the primacy of natural parental possession. The parents' right to dispose of their child overrode considerations of the child's own rights: it was accepted that children should be put in care while the parents made up their minds whether to relinquish them or not. Parental contact, though irregular, prevented the child from forming an alternative parent–child relationship.

Tizard argues that her study, together with others, suggests that attempts to restore a child to his [or her] natural family may not be in the best interests of the child. Children need someone unconditionally and permanently committed to them, and it is difficult to see why a parent who takes no responsibility for a child's care has a right to prevent someone else from doing so. However, Tizard does acknowledge that the issue is complicated by social inequality – children who come into care tend to come from the most powerless sector of society. In some cases, parents would have been able to keep the child if minimal material assistance had been available. There is therefore a need for better family support services.

Another study which brings forward similar, though not identical, conclusions is that carried out by Rowe and Lambert, *Children Who Wait*.[16] This was an influential study which broadly supported the view that permanent substitute parents should be found for children in long-term care. The study investigated children in care whose social workers wanted to find homes with substitute families for them, taking as two basic assumptions that every child has a right to a family of his [or her] own, and that adoption and fostering are not completely separate categories but have a considerable area of overlap. It was found that 22 per cent of the whole group of children were thought to need a substitute family; and permanent substitute families were being sought for nearly three-quarters of these. Forty per cent of the children needing placement were considered to need permanent foster homes, 6 per cent direct adoption and 26 per cent a foster home with a view to adoption. It was found that decisions about placements were often long delayed while efforts were made to solve the family's problems. Yet rehabilitation was only expected for a minority – about 25 per cent – of all the children in the study. There was little parental contact – and here the findings of Rowe and Lambert echo those of Thorpe, though different conclusions are drawn from them. Only 5 per cent of the children saw their parents as often as once a month; 41 per cent had no parental contact. The longer the children stayed in care the less parental contact they had.

In discussing the implications of their study, Rowe and Lambert say 'rehabilitation for children in long-term care is still for the most part a slogan rather than a reality'. They emphasise that most of the children judged by their social workers to need placement needed permanent rather than temporary substitute families. They see a need to identify those children requiring new parents, and believe that social workers should be more committed to placing children with new parents in permanent homes; and they note a greater commitment to this policy in the United States. In Rowe and Lambert's view, then, a child should either be speedily returned to his [or her] own family or, if this is not possible [. . .] be securely established in a permanent substitute family.[. . .]

The most important pressure group which may be associated with the 'society-as-parent' school is the British Agencies for Adoption and Fostering (BAAF), formerly the Association of British Adoption and Fostering Agencies (ABAFA). Particularly relevant here is their publication *Terminating Parental Contact*,[17] which considered whether, and in which circumstances, a parent may be prevented from personal contact with a child in care. This paper stressed the need to make plans for children based on a realistic assessment of whether or not rehabilitation with the natural family is possible and to consider the *purpose* of parental contact and its effects on the child. The starting point in assessing the value of contact should be: is it of benefit to the child and, if so, how? The authors say that this is a somewhat uncommon approach to the problem, as access to children in care is more often discussed in terms of the benefit to the parents. But if there is some doubt about the child returning home, then it is necessary to ask if the benefits of contact outweigh the drawbacks. Visits may strengthen bonds with a parent who is unlikely to resume care, and then constitute an obstacle to finding an appropriate placement. As an alternative to actual contact, knowledge about the family of origin can be supplied through discussion, photographs, letters and family albums. Again, there is a concern about certainty in the placement situation. Uncertainty about the future and lack of continuity of decisions make it hard for the substitute parents to make a strong commitment to the child *and* include the natural parent. The paper goes on to say that since 'there is an assumption in our society that the blood tie or relationship with the parent is the ideal, then any alternative is seen as a failure rather than as something in the child's best interest'. This tendency to see alternatives as second best, it is argued, inhibits decisions.

It is useful to refer again to the practice guides which the then ABAFA produced to the 1975 Children Act (1976[18] and 1977[19]) (and which were criticised by Tunstill).[20] These guides, dealing with the Act in general and with the assumption of parental rights, aimed to help social workers understand the new legislation, making use of case histories and similar exercises. The emphasis was on the termination of parental rights in favour of long-term fostering and adoption; Tunstill comments that, in three out of the four case histories in the guide to the assumption of parental rights, the only possibility of a 'happy ending' was by means of such steps. Similar points were made in the guides as in *Terminating Parental Contact*. Children are seen as needing long-term substitute families if their own parents cannot meet all their needs; if for example, there is no consistent or affectionate relationship with the parent, or if contact is only sporadic.

The 'society-as-parent' school is further illustrated by quoting from respondents interviewed by the author, though fewer of these took this position than were committed to a 'defence of kinship' view and their views tended to be less strongly and less explicitly stated. Like the first group of respondents, they had comments to make on the 'time limits' provision in the 1975 Act, on the conflict between the child's rights and interests and those of the parents, and on adoption. One respondent argued in support of time limits as follows:

> It is always my hope and belief that by alerting social workers to the danger for children and parents of the passage of time and requiring them to point these out to the natural parents, that one would be avoiding that sort of drift, and collusion with parents of 'Oh don't worry, you get yourself together and then we'll think about him coming home.' I mean, there's an awful lot that goes on! As though it doesn't matter that time is going on.

She saw the 1975 Act's emphasis on adoption as positive. It would:

> make people think more in terms of adoption for some children, but the problem is authorities don't do anything, they just drift with them . . . I would rather see a few children unnecessarily separated from their parents than thousands of them just remain without any parents at all! [. . .]

In general, then, supporters of the 'society-as-parent' view tend to favour changes in the 1975 Children Act which facilitate the removal and transfer of parental rights. Rowe,[21] for example, believes the Act will be recorded in history as 'another milestone in the long progress towards recognising children as persons and not the possessions of adults'. Proponents of this approach tend to feel that the changes made so far do not go far enough, however, and that excessive consideration for the biological parent–child relationship is still being allowed to put the child's future at risk. An example might be the provisions which state that the child's welfare is to be the first consideration in decisions relating to adoption and children in care (Sections 3 and 59). To some commentators this appears to leave too much scope for giving continued weight to parental wishes, and they would like to see the sections worded 'first and paramount consideration'.[22]

Areas of convergence between the two positions

Before summarising what appear to the writer to be the major points of difference between the two value positions, it might be advisable first to outline their apparent areas of agreement. It should be noted that both points of view would claim to be centrally concerned with the well-being of children.

The problem arises over the *interpretation* of the concept of welfare, or the child's best interests, and of other concepts much used in child care practice, such as 'neglect', 'ill-treatment' or being 'in moral danger'. Walton has commented usefully on this,[23] arguing that the use of the phrase 'the best interests of the child' has often confused rather than helped child care debates, creating the illusion that these interests constitute an objective fact. Walton argues that views of 'best interests' are rather always contingent, depending on the particular position and assumptions of the person expressing them as well as on objective circumstances. Phrases like this are often used like the jargon of politics, as deceptively simple slogans. The term 'best interests' is used to justify action which is taken with respect to children, but it is open to abuse, creates confusion and draws a veil of ignorance over important issues. In Walton's view, there is a need to consider factors to be taken into account if the phrase is to be infused with greater meaning, and to clarify whether what is meant is the best interests of *all* children in a particular community, or of deprived, maladjusted or delinquent children, or of one particular child. Otherwise there is a danger that the phrase will be used merely symbolically, to create the illusion of change, to deflect criticism, or to discredit opposition (because no one would want to be seen to oppose 'the child's best interests'). Walton stresses that there is no simple concept or criterion of the child's best interests which can be applied in a crude rule-of-thumb way, and no group or individual which has sole authority to assume that generally it has the best conception of the child's interests.

Both schools of thought defined here, then, would claim to have as their central focus the child's welfare, although it appears that the 'society-as-parent' school more often uses this phrase or phrases like it, while the other group tends to talk about the family. Another area of apparent convergence is that both schools of thought would acknowledge that in some situations parental care is so bad that children should be removed and kept away from their parents. That is, this viewpoint is not the monopoly of the 'society-as-parent protagonists'. The difference is one of emphasis, of how and under what circumstances children should be removed and when parental contact should be maintained and restoration to the parent attempted. [. . .]

Thirdly, it seems that both groups of critics would want to see greater support given to natural families, in general, to help them to care for their children more effectively and to prevent the need for substitute care arising. Again, the difference is one of emphasis. The 'kinship defenders' are more concerned to press for policy changes, such as more day-care provision to help one-parent families, as urgently necessary; the other group perhaps sees such changes as more long term, as not immediately related to the needs of the children who are currently the subject of placement decisions. But they are not entirely unsympathetic to natural parents. Tizard,[24] for example, mentions the need to support the natural parents to enable them to care adequately; Kellmer Pringle[25] has advocated payment for mothers who stay at home to care; and a further interviewee who may be identified with the 'society-as-parent' view had this to say in answer to the argument that the 1975 Act put already powerless parents in an even more powerless position:

> I think I would respond by saying that I wouldn't in any sense dispute the need to try to prevent things getting to that point. But I can't accept the argument that because you make provision to deal by law as well as by practice with the situations where things have got to that point in order to

safeguard children, that you are thereby saying that you are going to take more children from their parents! I mean, I think that one should put as much service as one possibly can into the preventive end – I can't see it as an either/or!

Major differences between the two positions

The differences between the two value positions outlined are somewhat blurred by the apparent consensus on certain general points – the primacy of the child's welfare as a guiding principle, the need for child removal in some cases, and the need for broad preventive, parent-support policies. However, it is suggested that these points of convergence should not be allowed to disguise important differences in values and assumptions between the two positions. An attempt is now made to summarise the major areas of disagreement or difference of emphasis, under the following nine headings:

1 Differences on the importance of the blood tie and the natural family.
2 Differences on the effects of uncertainty and multiple parent figures.
3 Different views on the emphasis currently given to prevention and rehabilitation in practice.
4 Different views on the success of adoption.
5 Different views on the nature of fostering.
6 Differences on the adequacy of professional and court decision making and the effectiveness of state intervention generally in child care matters.
7 Different views on the existing balance of power between natural parents, statutory agencies and substitute parents.
8 Differential awareness of the class transaction element in child care.
9 Different concepts of the causes of, and remedies for, unsatisfactory parenting.

1 The importance of the blood tie and the natural family

On the whole the 'kinship defenders' defend the *biological* parents and their value to the child, and the 'society-as-parent' school supports the *psychological* parents – those who have given most care and attention to the child and stand in a close, loving relationship to him [or her]. It is not clear to what degree the kinship defenders would want to preserve the link with biological parents who are in no way the psychological parents as well – that is, how much they value the blood tie as such. Perhaps in attacking child removal the kinship defenders have mostly in mind cases where the biological parent is also the psychological parent, albeit an inadequate one. However, one 'kinship defender' interviewed did speak of children 'having intense feelings for their own parents even if they've never seen them'.

2   The effects on the child of uncertainty and multiple parent figures

The 'society-as-parent' supporters seem preoccupied with the necessity for certainty, permanence, security and a stable bond with a single set of parent figures in a relationship where both sides feel safe enough to make a long-term commitment. Those who defend the kinship bond find more acceptable a situation where, say, a child may maintain an active relationship with his [or her] natural parents while living with foster-parents, or may even remain in contact with them after adoption. It should be noted, however, that a concern for certainty and a single set of parent figures might also imply support for a position of minimal state intervention.

3   The emphasis currently given to prevention and rehabilitation with natural parents in practice

While both groups of thinkers tend to admit the lack of preventive policies and the need for more resources here, the kinship school is more acutely conscious of this and perhaps more optimistic about what preventive services might achieve in terms of better parenting. It would therefore like to see a shift in priorities to prevention rather than substitute care. ['Kinship defenders'] also feel that insufficient work is carried out by social workers on the rehabilitation of separated families, while at least some of the 'society-as-parent' school seem more aware of situations where rehabilitation is attempted inappropriately, and perhaps foisted on an unwilling parent, and feel that social workers should be discouraged from holding out unrealistic hopes of restoring the child. One interviewee commented:

> This business of planning rehabilitation and planning adoption – fostering with a potential view to adoption simultaneously, which is what seems to happen now – seems to me absolutely dotty! With one hand people are placing children while on the other hand they are still encouraging the natural parents to think there's some chance of having them back! Well this is unfair to everybody.

4   The success of adoption

On the whole, the 'society-as-parent' school tends to look more favourably on adoption. Tizard's study,[26] for example, gives a positive picture in terms of the effects of adoption on the child's development and the creation of an affectionate family unit, as compared with long-term fostering or restoration of a separated child to the natural mother. The kinship school, however, tends to have two kinds of reservation about studies which seem to demonstrate the success of adoption. One type of reservation relates to the class nature of adoption: it is thought that the observed beneficial effects of adoption stem mostly from the tendency of adoption to move children to a somewhat higher social class than that of the family of origin. Holman,[27] for example, in an article analysing the class nature of adoption, notes the gross underrepresentation found in studies of adoption of Classes IV and V among adoptive parents.

The other reservation concerns the long-term effects of adoption, which it is thought may damage personality and identity. It is hypothesised that most existing studies of adoption are not sufficiently long term to demonstrate these effects. An interviewee of the Holman group observed, 'My experience as a child care officer was that some of the worst adoption breakdowns and problems were for kids in their adolescence.' There is some evidence that adopted children make greater use of the psychiatric services than the general population, though this could be due to class factors.[28] In general, it is more difficult to trace adoption breakdown than foster home breakdown, as the families concerned will not necessarily return to the agencies involved in the original placement. So it can be argued that adoption is in fact a less successful aspect of child care policy than it appears.

5   The nature of fostering

The 'kinship defenders' tend to see adoption and fostering as qualitatively different types of care, the distinction being not merely dependent on the length of the placement. Holman has distinguished between 'inclusive' and 'exclusive' fostering,[29] with a preference expressed for 'inclusive' fostering in which the natural parents are actively involved in the placement. 'Exclusive' fostering, where the foster-parents tend to treat the child rather as though he [or she] were their own or they had adopted him [or her], is thought to be damaging to the child's identity, as well as hindering restoration to the natural parents. By contrast, those who support the 'society-as-parent' position see adoption and fostering not necessarily as mutually exclusive, but as both being forms of substitute care whose boundaries may be blurred. Long-term foster placements may turn into *de facto* or, eventually, legal adoptions. One of the basic assumptions of Rowe and Lambert's study[30] was that adoption and fostering are not completely separate categories but overlap. In the 'society-as-parent' view, long-term, exclusive fostering would not necessarily be deplored, although there may be a wish to see it achieve the more secure legal status of custodianship[31] or adoption.

6   The adequacy of professional and court decision making, and the effectiveness of state intervention generally, in child care matters

The 'kinship defenders' are generally far more sceptical than the other group about the adequacy of both courts and social services agencies in making decisions about child placement and protecting the child's interests and well-being. While natural parents may be inadequate, even neglectful and cruel, this has to be balanced against the unsuitability of state agencies to fulfil the parental role, particularly in the long term. Removing a child to public care is no magic answer to ill-treatment in the natural home, but may result in, for example, placement in a series of unsuitable foster homes, resulting in a cumulative experience of rejection and failure. Indeed, substitute child care might be *worse* than the situation from which the child has been removed. (There have been cases, for example, of child deaths in supposedly supervised foster homes.)[32]

The 'society-as-parent' protagonists seem to place rather more confidence in society's ability, acting through its official agencies, to make wise decisions on the care of children. The state and its machinery is generally viewed as beneficent in this context.

7   The balance of power between natural parents, statutory agencies and substitute parents

The 'kinship defenders' see the natural parents who come into contact with statutory agencies as being in a relatively weak position, with their rights severely eroded by various legal provisions, most recently the 1975 Act which strengthened the powers of both local authorities and foster-parents to an unacceptable degree. Draper says, 'the dice are loaded against the parents';[33] Holman that the 1975 Act 'concentrates exclusively on facilitating the removal of children from their families and on reducing the rights of natural parents'.[34]

The 'society-as-parent' protagonists, on the other hand, tend to see parental rights as a force still to be reckoned with in law, agency practice and social attitudes. Kellmer Pringle,[35] for example, attacks the idea (presumed still commonly held) that children are comparable with other possessions over whom parents may exercise exclusive rights; Tizard[36] objects to the way in which parents were able to prevent others from providing permanent care for their children, although they did not do so themselves. This school would like to see the balance of power shifted further towards statutory decision makers and those who provide substitute care.

8   The class transaction element in child care

Undoubtedly, the Holman kinship school is more aware of the class nature of child care services and policy (as indicated above, under 4). The people who lose their children to public care are, disproportionately, socially deprived, lower-class parents who are prey to such disadvantages as low income, inadequate housing, homelessness, living in deprived inner-city neighbourhoods, unemployment or erratic employment, and frequent changes of home. Social workers, judges, adoptive parents (and, more recently, professional foster-parents) are largely middle class and apply middle-class values and norms to child care situations, resulting in what is in effect discrimination against the poor. While there are inadequate middle-class parents, they suffer less visibility than poor parents, and have a wider range of child care options available to them.

A crude summary of this political position would be that child care policies remove the children of the poor and attempt to absorb them into the middle class. Schorr, for example, has described adoption agencies as 'a system for distributing children from the poor to the middle class'.[37] The 'society-as-parent' thinkers, on the other hand, tend to perceive child care matters in personal rather than political terms and are more inclined to the views expressed or implied in the following comments by respondents from this group: 'you could never have done anything with this poor[38] mother', and:

> I think those are perhaps the hardest cases, where the parents are not able to cope because they just cannot cope, they are subnormal, and you can't in any way say that they are to blame, they're just totally inadequate people.

This relates to the final major point of difference between the two positions.

9 Concepts of the causes of, and remedies for, unsatisfactory parenting

In the view of Holman and others who take a similar approach, bad parenting is firmly linked with social deprivation and its concomitant pressures on families. Holman stresses that poor parents may well share the child care values and objectives of the wider society, but are prevented from achieving them by depriving environments. He comments:

> It is a sobering thought that probably many of the parents whose children are in public care were born with capacities similar to readers of this paper. Given similar external circumstances, we might well have reacted as they have done, and we would have lost our children.[39]

The remedies for bad parenting thus focus on reducing social deprivation through provisions such as day care, financial support and community action by groups of parents. The 'society-as-parent' thinkers, as indicated above, are more likely to construe unsatisfactory parenting in terms of personal inadequacy. (Holman would characterise this as 'blaming the poor'.) The remedies, looking at it in this light, would be, in the main, individualised help or the removal of the children to a 'fresh start' with more adequate parent figures.

The two value positions in context

It may legitimately be asked whether and how the two positions defined may be connected with, or reflect, wider intellectual traditions or ideological stances. For example, may the two schools of thought be most usefully seen as integral to broad political perspectives which propose contrasting views of the state, social work as a part of state intervention, social institutions, and the relations between socioeconomic groups? Or may the most helpful interpretation be to align the two child care positions with opposing camps in the field of psychological explanation?

Only a lightly sketched attempt is made here to place the 'kinship defenders' and the 'society-as-parent protagonists' in the context of broader viewpoints and sets of values; a thorough analysis could be a very lengthy exercise. It is suggested that a useful starting point might be to classify the nine major points of difference which are outlined as distinguishing the two value positions. The following categories of difference seem to emerge. Firstly, differences one and two, concerning questions of (1) the blood tie and the natural family and (2) the effects of uncertainty and multiple parent figures, seem to be essentially differences relating to conflicting ideas about *child psychology*.

Secondly, the following four differences, concerning (3) the emphasis in child care practice on prevention and rehabilitation, (4) the success of adoption, (5) the nature of fostering, and (6) the adequacy of state intervention in child care, reflect different views on *child care policy*.

Thirdly, the three last differences, relating to (7) the balance of power between different parties, (8) the class element in child care, and (9) the causes of, and remedies for, poor parenting, represent broader ideas about *society* – about power, social relations and social influences.

It is argued that the first and third categories of difference, the psychological and the social or political, constitute the most useful bases from which to consider the link with broader intellectual positions.

The psychological assumptions underlying the 'society-as-parent' position may be seen as broadly deriving from psychoanalytic theory. It is not so clear what the theoretical foundations (within psychology) of the kinship school might be. The notion of identity and of healthy identity stemming from knowledge of and contact with one's family of origin seems to be a crucial concept. And it may be noted that Holman[40] draws on psychological research to emphasise the adverse effects on children of separation from their parents, of the failure to develop relationships at all, and of disruptive family relationships. He also argues that poverty causes lowered self-respect and self-image, and cites data showing two contrasting behavioural reactions to this: withdrawal and aggression.

The political assumptions are perhaps easier to identify. The 'kinship' school may reasonably be associated with a radical analysis of society which stresses the importance of class and power. Child care policies are seen as part of a structure of political and economic relations in which dominant groups control subordinate and, in particular, deviant groups by a range of sanctions. Dominant values are upheld and dominant interests protected in the name of universal interests – in the child care case, in the cause of child welfare, which is assumed to be some kind of objectively assessable 'good thing'. In reality, according to this view, only certain groups of children and parents are interfered with by state agencies, with the objectives of upholding dominant values about child rearing, maintaining particular sorts of socialisation, and, to some degree, redistributing deprived children to members of more powerful social groups who, for various reasons, desire to care for them. Finally, the 'kinship defenders' are in harmony with a radical view of society in putting some emphasis on working-class self-help and self-determination, rather than on state paternalism, in finding solutions to social and personal problems (for example, Holman's suggestions about informal child care resources).

If the 'kinship' school may be located within the broader framework of a power or class analysis of society, the 'society-as-parent' supporters might be defined as belonging more to what might be termed a 'personal responsibility analysis' which broadly takes the existing political and economic structure of society for granted, or which does not relate it very strongly to individual families' difficulties. The 'society-as-parent' school perhaps falls into a tradition of paternalistic state intervention in the cause of social welfare, which has its roots in the nineteenth century; a tradition in which the values of the dominant class have been imposed on the poor for their own good, and in which the children of the poor have been removed to make a 'fresh start' in what were adjudged more favourable circumstances than those of their origins. The possibility that this approach might appear to poor parents as a punishment for their poverty was not considered to be a significant part of the equation. Welfare, in the broader view of which this approach to child care might be deemed a part, is construed in individual terms: individuals are deemed responsible for their conduct, and little weight is given to structural, environmental and material determinants of behaviour.

Conclusion

Two value positions in child care have been defined, which differ on questions of child psychology, child care policy and the broader social framework in which child care policy is located. In general, one viewpoint leans towards a class or power analysis of child care, while the other tends to take the existing social structure as given and to construe child care issues in more individualistic terms. Material has been brought forward from the literature and from interviews to illustrate and refine the differences between the two schools of thought. Apparent areas of convergence, such as an ostensible focusing on the 'welfare of the child', should not be allowed to disguise what are regarded as real differences stemming from different psychological and political assumptions underlying the two positions.

Author's note

Lorraine M. Fox Harding is currently writing a book which elaborates the original model of two perspectives by examining four: laissez-faire; paternalism; the defence of kinship; and children's liberation. The book will probably be titled *Perspectives in Child Care Policy* and will be published by Longman in 1990.

Notes

1   Twelve interviews were carried out with thirteen people thought to be influential and well informed in the child care field. They included four senior staff in Social Services Departments, four people connected with 'pressure groups' with an interest in the field, three academics and two other researchers. However, these distinctions were somewhat blurred by the fact, for example, that four of the respondents had been members of the Houghton Committee 1969–72, whose recommendations formed the basis of the Children Act 1975, and that other respondents had presented evidence to the Committee, while one respondent termed 'academic' was also strongly associated with a relevant pressure group, and another classed as associated with a pressure group was also undertaking relevant research and was well known as a researcher in this field. Most respondents, therefore, had a number of bases for their interest, involvement and knowledge.

Interviews were semi-structured and were tape recorded. Discussion focused on the Houghton Committee and its report, reactions to its recommendations, the two Children bills of 1974–5, pressure group involvement and debate at that time, and comments on specific parts of the 1975 Children Act, particularly the welfare clauses and the various 'time limits' provisions. This led to a discussion of general views on the emphases in child care policy, on adoption, fostering, the natural family, and social services practice. Most respondents also provided documentary evidence and suggested further contacts.

The respondents' own positions on child care issues were sometimes clearly defined in terms similar to those used in this paper. Sometimes their position was less clearly put but was deduced from the content of the interview, published material, and the nature of the organisation with which they were associated. Having regard to various relevant sources, it was concluded that four respondents fell definitely into the 'kinship defender' group defined here, while two were fairly clearly 'society-as-parent protagonists' and two other respondents leaned towards this view. The others – four practitioners and one researcher – did not seem to occupy any clear-cut position, and the practitioners seemed to be very aware of the various conflicting arguments and to have rather different preoccupations, such as the clarity of the legislation and matters of practice.

2   Holman, R. (1976 and 1980) *Inequality in Child Care*, London, Child Poverty Action Group (CPAG).

3   Holman, R. (1975) 'Unmarried mothers, social deprivation and child separation', *Policy and Politics*, Vol. 3, pp. 25–41.

4   Thorpe, R. (1974) 'Mum and Mrs So and So', *Social Work Today*, Vol. 4, No. 22, pp. 691–5.

5   Holman, R. (1980) 'A real child care policy for the future', *Community Care*, No. 340, pp. 16–17.

6   Goldstein, J., Freud, A. and Solnit, A. (1973) *Beyond the Best Interests of the Child*, London, Collier-Macmillan and New York, Free Press.

7   Thoburn, J. (1980) *Captive Clients*, London, Routledge and Kegan Paul.

8   Tunstill, J. (1977) 'In defence of parents', *New Society*, Vol. 42, No. 785, pp. 121–2.

9   Wilson, H. (1974) 'Parenting in poverty', *British Journal of Social Work*, Vol. 4, No. 3, pp. 241–54.

10   Comments on the Houghton Report (unpublished) (1973) British Association of Social Workers.

11   CPAG (1975) *The Children Bill, Rescue or Prevention?*, London, CPAG.

12   Fletcher, H. (1979) National Council for One-Parent Families, quoted in *Community Care*, No. 247, p. 5.

13   See note 1.

14   Kellmer Pringle, M. (1974) *The Needs of Children*, London, Hutchinson.
15   Tizard, B. (1977) *Adoption: A Second Chance*, London, Open Books.
16   Rowe, J. and Lambert L. (1973) *Children Who Wait*, London, ABAFA.
17   ABAFA (1979) *Terminating Parental Contact*.
18   ABAFA (1976) *Practice Guide to the Children Act 1975*.
19   ABAFA (1977) *Assumption of Parental Rights and Duties: Practice Guide*.
20   Tunstill, op. cit.
21   Rowe, J. (1975) 'A children's charter for happiness?' *Community Care*, No. 84, pp. 14–15.
22   See Bevan, H. and Parry, M. (1978) *The Children Act 1975*, London, Butterworths.
23   Walton, R. (1976) 'The best interests of the child', *British Journal of Social Work*, Vol. 6, No. 3, pp. 307–13.
24   Tizard, op. cit.
25   In a number of statements.
26   Tizard, op. cit.
27   Holman, R. (1978) 'A class analysis of adoption reveals a disturbing picture', *Community Care*, No. 210, p. 13.
28   Kellmer Pringle, M. (1967) *Adoption, Facts and Fallacies*, London, Longman.
29   Holman, R. (1975) 'The place of fostering in social work', *British Journal of Social Work*, Vol. 5, No. 1, pp. 3–27.
30   Rowe and Lambert, op. cit.
31   Sections 33–55 of the 1975 Children Act. Not yet implemented.
32   For example, the case of Dennis O'Neill (1945).
33   Draper, J. (1978) 'When social services abused a family', *Community Care*, No. 242, pp. 4–5.
34   Holman, R. *Inequality in Child Care*, op. cit.
35   Kellmer Pringle, op. cit.
36   Tizard, op. cit.
37   Schorr, A. (1978) quoted by R. Holman in 'A class analysis of adoption', op. cit., p. 13.
38   It seems clear that 'poor' was not meant in the economic sense.
39   Holman, R. *Inequality in Child Care*, op. cit.
40   Ibid.

3   What kind of permanence?

June Thoburn

There is no doubt in my mind that issues surrounding permanent family placement with a child's own family are very similar to those which surround permanent family placement in substitute families. Because of my research experience working with two aspects of permanence, related in my book *Captive Clients* (1980) and the evaluation of The Child Wants a Home project (*Adoption and Fostering*, Vol. 9, No. 1), I find it particularly sad that when the term permanence is mentioned in British social work circles it tends to be seen as synonymous with adoption. In the average social work department that would be the first reaction of social workers when permanent placement was mentioned. The Select Committee on Children in Care (para. 191) commented:

> There is at the moment, considerable confusion over the significance of the search for permanence in a placement. It should not have become a synonym for adoption. The search for permanence, in our view, could be accomplished in many ways including custodianship, long-term fostering, or even in some circumstances a stay in a residential home or, of course, rehabilitation with a child's natural family.

By contrast, in America permanence planning and research into permanence are always seen as including rehabilitation with the child's natural family as a major permanence option. In this country we discovered the value of prevention and rehabilitation in the 1950s and 1960s and our belief in permanence achieved through working with a child in his own family was given legal sanction in Section 1 of the 1963 Act. Our permanency planning has been a two-stage affair, but we never got our preventive and rehabilitative act together properly in the 1960s. The research of Jane Rowe and Lydia Lambert, published in *Children Who Wait* in 1973, showed us how inadequate our work had been in that respect. We therefore moved over to the second limb of the permanency strategy, the strategy of placement in substitute new families preferably for adoption.

The Americans were actually behind us in discovering the importance of preventive and rehabilitative services, but when they got round to looking for permanence for children in care their strategy was a combined one of permanence with natural families and permanence with new families. The biggest difference one sees in practice is that in America permanence placement units employ workers who are specialists at working with natural families, whereas in this country, as far as I know, the units employ only specialists in adoption and fostering. Even so, they find that their skills do enable them to get children back to their own homes, although this as yet is a secondary role. I very much hope that we will soon move forward to see permanence units which employ staff equally for their ability to work at getting a child back with natural families as for their skills in working with substitute new families.

It is an interesting question whether the sort of workers who are good at getting children back with their natural families are different from those who are good at placing children with new families. It may be that we need to experiment with permanence units, some of which will specialise in achieving permanence through the return to natural families, and others in achieving permanence by placement with new families, and also having units which combine the two functions. The Americans do not seem to have had problems in setting up units which seek to provide permanence by offering specialist and intensive social work services both to natural families and to children joining substitute new families. Although many local authorities in their strategy documents state that they aim first at rehabilitation, I remain unconvinced that they are devoting the same resources in terms of skilled social workers with small caseloads and adequate financial support to natural families, as they do to finding and supporting new families.

Towards the end of the research on The Child Wants a Home project we noted more flexibility in the way in which placements were effected. This probably reflects a change in the children to be placed. In the early stages many of the children had been in residential care for periods of years, had little or no contact with members of the natural family and had lost all serious hope of returning there. Towards the end of the research most of the children referred had been in care for shorter periods of time and were still in more or less meaningful contact with members of their natural families. I would like to suggest that a rigid model of permanent placement and of methods of achieving it is no longer appropriate, given the much wider range of needs of children. I for one very much welcome the possibility of custodianship as yet another route to permanence for children in care, or at risk of coming into long-term care.

Routes into permanence

Thus, the routes to achieving permanence are numerous. I would suggest that, leaving aside permanence achieved by return home to the child's natural parents, relatives or close friends, and permanence in some cases achieved by residential care (and I think we should look very carefully at the work of the Children's Family Trust and at the Ockenden Venture, where results are extremely promising), there are sixteen different routes to achieving permanent family placement with substitute families. These are:

1 Secure fostering with the current foster family.
2 Secure fostering with a new foster family.
3 Custodianship with foster parents or relatives with whom the child is already living.
4 Placement before custodianship with known relatives or friends.

5   Foster placement with strangers with a view to custodianship if all goes well.
6   Foster placement with a new family with a view to adoption if all goes well.
7   Foster placement leading quickly to adoption.
8   Placement directly for adoption.

The eight routes can each be with or without contact with natural parents or siblings placed elsewhere, making sixteen routes in all.

So how does one decide which of these routes would be appropriate for which child? How does one assess the needs of the children? And what do I mean when I use the term 'permanence'? I am thinking of the child becoming part of a new family so that the new parents become the 'psychological parents', and thus offer a sense of security, a sense of belonging, of being loved, until the child reaches adulthood and beyond. It is what John Triseliotis has referred to as 'a family for life, with its network of support systems not only for them but also for their future children'. So what are the needs of children which we hope will be met by placement with new psychological parents? Security, a sense of belonging, family life, being loved and loving, are benefits which we hope a child will achieve through such placements and which will be put alongside the other important need to be met by any placement, the child's need for a sense of his or her own identity. We are aiming to provide these two sets of things for the child in care, not as ends in themselves, but in order that children may develop a sense of their own self-worth, and research tells us that we have to get the balance right between these two important sets of needs for this end to be achieved.

When we undertook our study we found that the categorisation usually made of the special needs of children was insufficiently detailed. We found that in each case it was necessary to think of three dimensions. Most often only the problems of the children were given as the significant handicaps to placement. However, we found that the age of the child was an important dimension and, perhaps most important of all, the nature of the child's previous relationships and the attitudes of the child and significant others towards the continuation or termination of those relationships.

There were two other important factors to be considered. First, the temperament of the child (. . .) and particularly the child's ability to withstand stress and uncertainty. And second, the attitudes and temperament of any family with whom the child is already living and where either the parents have already become the psychological parents or else the intention is that they should become so. There is an important parallel here with relationships between adults. For some adults cohabitation before marriage is unthinkable (in Asian families, for example); for others the idea of marriage without first living together to get to know each other is equally unthinkable. For some the strain of living together without legal ties leads to considerable anguish. For others there is no problem and complete trust in a verbal commitment. Some adults are more 'possessive' about their partners, whilst others are more willing to share. Similarly, some children and some substitute parents need the certainty of the legal tie of adoption. To others it is of little significance. They feel totally secure within a fostering relationship.

We are not here just talking about 'inclusive' or 'exclusive' families in Robert Holman's terms. Some families who need the certainty of legal adoption are none the less more than willing to allow their child to continue contact with members of the birth family. They may be more willing than some social workers. We found new families insisting on meeting and keeping in contact with natural parents, when social workers, especially from the referring authorities, were discouraging this.

Social care planning

The social care planning role requires workers to be familiar with the research findings which are beginning to appear not only on permanent family placement but on children coming into care, such as the cohort studies by Jean Packman (1984), the Dartington Group and the National Children's Bureau; Jane Rowe's study on long-term fostering (1984); and John Triseliotis and Russell's (1984); on adoption and residential care. Cumulatively these studies are telling a very similar story. What they seem to be saying about outcomes of adoption is quite positive but nevertheless we should be warned that the heady days of 'no child is unadoptable' are in the past. It would seem that it is particularly difficult for older children (over twelve), institutionalised children, or children with behaviour or severe learning difficulties, to settle in new families, at least without serious and lasting problems. It would also seem that the time before adoption for such children is quite long, that some for whom adoption was the plan will not be adopted even though they will stay with their new families, and that long-term support by specialist workers will be necessary for many of these children. Interestingly enough, the really hard to place child would appear to be not the young mentally or physically handicapped child, but the older child coming into care from a muddled family situation, possibly where child abuse or neglect have figured in his early life.

I think that we must still look cautiously at adoption without consent. The very positive research findings about children who have been adopted (including those described by Triseliotis who were placed later from disturbed backgrounds), are all largely about children who were adopted with their parents' consent. We do not, as yet, have enough long-term studies of the minority of children adopted without consent, especially if contact was artificially terminated and if the child was aware of a battle between the two sets of parents. Research studies, however, including (. . .) those of Wolkind and Kozaruk (1983) on children placed through the Adoption Resource Exchange, and Reich and Lewis (1986), and Macaskill (1985a) concerning the agency Parents for Children, indicate that children who have been placed against their parents' wishes seem to be settling quite well, but there are insufficient numbers, followed up for insufficiently long, for us to know what the impact of adoption of older children without consent is going to be in the long term. The requirement in the Adoption Agency Regulations to counsel the parents specifically about all the alternatives to adoption, and to make sure that their views about these different alternatives are placed before the court, together with the fact that guardians *ad litem* and reporting officers will also be scrutinising this element of the work, should lead to more careful practice at this stage. I hope that these factors, together with custodianship and more willingness to look at open adoption by the judiciary as well as by social workers, will diminish the number of occasions when adoptive placements have to be made against the wishes of the natural parents, and/or children.

Regarding work with the children and the new families, my plea for a more sophisticated approach in assessing the needs of children and finding the appropriate routes to permanent placement for each child leads me to the conclusion that the nature of the social work service to each child and family must vary according to their needs and their wishes. I am convinced by recent research findings in America and Britain that social work practice can either foster a sense of permanence or detract from it, and that in the past our treating permanent substitute families as if they were temporary has been a cause of insecurity. John Triseliotis has used the term 'constructed insecurity'. Jane Rowe's study of children in long-term foster care reinforces my view that social work practice often actually creates or increases a sense of insecurity.

In looking at routes to permanence I have already indicated that I believe that long-term fostering will be the best route for a number, albeit a diminishing number, of children in care. However, some children who will eventually pass out of care through custodianship or adoption will spend periods, sometimes periods of years, in care after moving to permanent new families. Social work practice with these families should concentrate on constructing a framework of security from the matching stage onwards, and this must mean delegating the maximum degree of responsibility to the new family to do things their way which the law allows.

It also means that it is extremely important to get the matching stage right because no amount of back-seat driving will persuade new parents to change their basic way of running their family. For example, if continued family contact is in the child's best interest, social workers should make sure at the matching stage that the proposed new parents really believe so too. Once a child has been placed, workers will need to be guided by the new parents and the child about the how and the when of contact and, of course, once adoption or custodianship orders are made, social workers no longer have the right to give directions, although they may have an important role, when asked, in providing a conciliation service between custodians or adopters and natural parents, if there are disagreements about contact. In other words, I argue that the social work service offered to permanent new families, whatever their initial or planned legal status, should be different from that offered to the majority of foster families. A rethink is needed at all stages from recruitment, training and approval through to the post-placement and post-adoption support. The specialist placement agencies have pioneered this work and certainly my own study, and those of research colleagues looking at other agencies, have shown that the model that they have pioneered is seen by the families and the children as appropriate.

These studies show us that many of the families who successfully parent hard to place children are not conventional, middle-class, two-child families. They sometimes have unusual parenting styles and some, though by no means all, find that having a social worker looking over their shoulder makes them feel uncomfortable and unnecessarily unsure of themselves. It is up to social workers and the legal system to find ways of supporting rather than hindering parents and children in the difficult task of building themselves into a new family. This does, I believe, mean that a rethink is urgently needed about the boarding-out regulations, reviews and some other aspects of social work practice, which are appropriate to social work with permanent new families. Essentially it is about increasing the authority of the new family and playing down the authority role of the social worker.

What then are the more detailed conclusions I came to about the nature of the social work service? I found myself constantly making a connection between what new families were saying to me about what they found most helpful from a social worker and what I as a social worker find most helpful from a team leader. Essentially they wanted a consultancy service from a social worker who was basically a colleague sharing their frustrations and difficulties but also their joys and successes and recognising their own expertise and greater knowledge of detail; a sounding-board off which to bounce ideas about how to solve a problem; someone concerned about quality control, providing an inspectorial service so that the child's interests could be safeguarded (but this aspect they saw as being of prime importance at the approval and matching stage). They acknowledged that the inspectorial role was always there, but wanted somebody who felt comfortable with this role, neither over- nor underemphasising it. A social worker, they felt, should have information available or at least provide access to good information systems which the family could itself use. They wanted advice but also to be free to decide whether it was or was not good advice. They wanted practical help without being forced to beg for it. If therapy was needed for the child, they wanted to share in the offering of help and particularly valued taking part with the workers in life-story work. If the family themselves needed therapy, again there are parallels with the relationship between the social worker and team leader. They needed the worker to care about them, to be willing to sit down with them and help solve a problem and be a good listener.

However, if more than that was needed and the family began to have more serious problems, then on the whole it seemed to be better to bring in an outside agency unconnected to the placement process. Family therapy techniques, emphasising as they do the role of the parents and the necessity for them being fully involved in solving their own problems, were considered helpful. However, there are dangers here. Families expressed resentment if they came to think that they were being considered as a 'problem' family, and were quick to point out that had it not been for the arrival of the new child, they would not have needed the services of the family therapist. The initial stages of negotiating the nature of the family therapy, and why the family needs it, must be extremely important. The use of family therapy techniques throughout the process of recruiting and training new parents, and preparing children for placement, helps them to be familiar with such techniques and to acknowledge their value when problems develop.

Work with children

All the children we spoke to stressed that the social worker from the placement agency was the family's social worker and not their social worker, and this was a position of which they very much approved. All the children we spoke to about reviews found them either an unnecessary irrelevance or else an extremely threatening or distressing event. When considering the form of review, it seems essential to differentiate between what is appropriate for a child in a temporary or therapeutic placement, and what is appropriate for a permanent family placement.

Finally, a plea to those preparing children for permanent placement, especially if they are older. Please do not talk in terms of adoption but rather in terms of finding a permanent, new family. We are beginning to see that even in those cases where the child and the new family intend the placement to be adoptive, adoption sometimes does not happen. When a placement does run into problems, Catherine Macaskill (1985b) has warned us of the dangers of thinking that adoption will solve the problems:

> A widely held opinion was that the security of adoption would ameliorate difficulties in the problematic placements. I searched in vain through the ensuing histories of children for any evidence to validate this belief. The more common response was a temporary lull in the onslaught of behavioural difficulties for a few months before and after adoption. As the formality of adoption receded into past history, leaving the same accumulation of problems, hope began to wane and problems took on a different perspective.

Some of the children in our study felt desperately disappointed that they had not been adopted, and yet they did have a home which would continue to be available to them in their adult life and had found a kind of loving, though perhaps not the all-accepting, all-loving parent of their dreams. In other cases, the 'will they or won't they adopt me' issue came to dominate the placement to the exclusion of all other considerations. If social workers continue to tell children that the only way of achieving permanence and security is through adoption, children will continue to believe this. In my view the challenge to us all is to find adoptive families for those children for whom this is appropriate and to offer security to those new families and children for whom adoption is not appropriate, and to convince them that they do have a secure future together.

References

HOLMAN, R. (1975) 'The place of fostering in social work', *British Journal of Social Work*, Vol. 9, No. 1, pp. 3–29.

MACASKILL, C. (1985a) 'Post-adoption support: is it essential?' *Adoption and Fostering*, Vol. 9, No. 1, pp. 45–9.

MACASKILL, C. (1985b) 'Who should support after adoption?' *Adoption and Fostering*, Vol. 9, No. 2, pp. 21–5.

MILLHAM, S. *et al.* (1985) 'Maintaining family links of children in care', *Adoption and Fostering*, Vol. 9, No. 2, pp. 12–16.

PACKMAN, J. *et al.* (1984) *Into the Net*, Colchester, University of Essex.

REICH, D. and LEWIS, J. (1986) 'Placements by Parents for Children', in Wedge, P. and Thoburn, J. (eds) *Finding families for 'hard-to-place' children; evidence from research*, London, BAAF.

ROWE, J. and LAMBERT, L. (1973) *Children Who Wait*, London, ABAA.

ROWE, J. *et al.* (1984) *Long-Term Foster Care*, London, BAAF/Batsford.

THOBURN, J. (1980) *Captive Clients*, London, Routledge and Kegan Paul.

THOBURN, J. *et al.* (1985) 'Routes to permanence: CWAH evaluation', *Adoption and Fostering*, Vol. 9, No. 1, pp. 50–4.

TRISELIOTIS, J. (1983) 'Identity and security', *Adoption and Fostering*, Vol. 7, No. 1, pp. 22–31.

TRISELIOTIS, J. and RUSSELL, J. (1984) *Hard to Place*, London, Heinemann Educational.

VERNON, J. (1985) 'Planning for children in care?' *Adoption and Fostering*, Vol. 9, No. 1, pp. 13–17.

WOLKIND, S. and KOZARUK, A. (1983) 'The adoption of children with medical handicap', *Adoption and Fostering*, Vol. 7, No. 1, pp. 32–35.

4   Transracial placements: conflicts and contradictions

John Small

Introduction

This chapter focuses on one of the most fundamental yet controversial areas of social work practice, namely, transracial placements. By this is meant placement of black children in white homes. The problems experienced by foster- and adoptive parents who are caring for black children are qualitatively similar. Consequently the arguments presented here in respect of adoption practices are equally valid for fostering.

This chapter includes an examination of the concept of race and uses several frameworks to demonstrate how racial identity confusion in black children is rooted in the family and society, and therefore cannot be separated from the power relationships within society in general and social work agencies in particular. Different groups of transracial adopters and their dilemmas are identified and the implications for their children illustrated. Gill and Jackson's research in 1983 will be critically examined, and in particular the failure to recognise the identity needs of black children in a racist society. If 'these black children have been made white in all but skin colour . . . have no contact with the black community and their "coping" mechanisms are based on denying their racial background' (p. 137), we must surely question Gill and Jackson's conclusion, that:

> they feel confident in using the term 'success' to describe the experiences of the majority of these families and children and there is little evidence that a group of similarly aged white children growing up with their natural parents would not include a number of children experiencing similar or greater difficulties'. (pp. 132–3)

Certainly white children in substitute white families, or their biological families, do not deny that they are white, nor want to be black. For them the vital issue of racial identity confusion does not exist.

Many white people do not understand the conflicts and the suffering experienced by those who are confused about their racial identity, and the following brief accounts illustrate the dilemmas.

Many transracially adopted children are aware that the darker their skin colour the more undesirable they are to white society; and many feel it is better to be white than black. One adoptive parent of a black child heard the child saying 'I'm glad I'm not black, the black children get teased; but I don't want to be brown either, because everyone notices me because I'm different.' Mother replied, 'But it is nice to be different; people are all different and it would be boring if we all looked the same.' Parents may understandably often try to deny the reality of their black children's unhappiness because they like to think that their children are secure and happy, thus reflecting their success as adopters. The denial of the reality of the visibility of the black child in a white family creates the preconditions for the phenomenon of identity confusion. Many, although black, will grow up believing or wishing that they are white. Yet 'they will be moving out into a society which is significantly racist in its attitudes and its distribution of opportunities. They will be moving towards establishing their own families and racial background will be an issue' (p. 136). These children will not always live in the protective arms of the family, they will have to make decisions about jobs, marriage, political and social commitments based on where in society they feel that they are able to find a place. Many of these children do not have skills to relate to black people and they will experience rejection by white society (Ladner, 1978).

Yvonne, placed transracially and now twenty-four years old, will never forget the day when she and friends were playing in the park and saw a black man passing by. The white youths began yelling 'Nigger, nigger, go back to where you come from.' The girls continued to play. One of the youths walked over to the group, looked at the black girl and said, 'By the way, you are a nigger too.' That was the first knowledge that Yvonne had of being black. 'I was devastated. I really did not want to be black because it was different to what my parents and the other children were. It was something totally new to me. I hated being black.' To tell the child that colour in this society does not matter is to ignore the racism in the society.

Transracial placements: a question of power

Transracial adoption, the adoption of children by parents of different racial origin, developed in earnest in the mid–1960s and has been on the increase since then. In part it was a response to the needs of childless white couples for whom white infants were no longer available for adoption. It gained momentum with the philosophy of the assimilation of the immigrant child into society. The black community thus became a 'donor' group for white society. This usually entailed placement at a very tender age, because it would be difficult for some parents to deal with the issue of race and colour if the child had developed a sense of racial identity and pride in his or her heritage. This could prevent the possibility of identification with, and integration into, the white family.

Transracial adoption was also encouraged by developments in child care practice designed to reduce dramatically the number of children living in institutions, of whom a disproportionate number were and still are black (Raynor 1975; Rowe and Lambert, 1970). There was too the erroneous belief that black substitute parents could not be found (ABAFA, 1976).

New Black Families has demonstrated unequivocally that black homes can be found for black children (Small, 1982b). The choice for the children trapped in the welfare system is therefore not solely between white families and a life of institutional care as we are led to believe; there are black families willing and capable of opening up their homes to these children, but there have been policies and practices which have prevented this development. Paradoxically, Gill and Jackson's book appeared at a time when there was a great deal of activity in the black community directed towards finding black families for black children, thereby making it progressively unnecessary for transracial placements to continue. Nevertheless, finding more black adoptive families will necessitate more black social workers in the key agency posts that determine policy, more black social workers involved in family finding and child placements, and recognition of the strengths of black families.

The one-way traffic of black children into white families begs fundamental questions of power and ideology. It raises questions as to the type of relationship which exists between black and white people and, furthermore, the type of society that those involved in the practice are creating. Transracial adoption encourages the phenomenon of racial identity confusion described in other contexts by Fanon (1968), Naipaul (1961, 1962) and Rushdie (1981). 'They did not . . . see themselves as black or show any real sign of having developed a sense of racial identity' (Gill and Jackson, 1983, p. 139). This often leads black children to deny the reality of their skin colour and to reject people of similar race and colour. White liberals have recognised the problem and made attempts to recruit black parents in the 1970s (ABAFA, 1976). The first black adoption agency, New Black Families, began to tackle the problem in 1980. While some workers believe that the best place for a child is within a family, and that it is better for a child to be placed transracially than to have no family, anxiety is increasing about the outcome of transracial placements.

It is of crucial importance that, while Social Services Departments, voluntary agencies, and professionals are adjusting their views and talking about issues relating to transracial adoption, the matter should be dealt with in a sensitive way. That is to say, when there is a shift from traditional methods in the placement of black children then careful consideration should also be given to the implications that this will have for black children, the black community and adopters. It is certainly not the intention of the black community to undermine the good work being done by current transracial adopters and foster-parents, who have opened their homes to black children.

Transracial placements and the social environment

The social context of transracial adoption raises several fundamental questions. First, is the best place for a child with a family? If the answer is yes, should it be a family similar to the child's racial and cultural origin? If the answer is again yes and such a family is not available, should the child remain in institutional care, or should the child be placed transracially?

If we believe that the child should be placed transracially as an alternative to institutional care, then social workers must resist the massive denial or evasion of the negative consequences of some transracial placements for black children when the substitute parents have not been prepared or perhaps are very unsuitable to care for a black child. Out of the multiplicity of factors influencing the development of the personality of the black child the following are the major influences.

The first is the estimation and expectation of others: the majority of society and the 'significant others'. The latter, who have the most profound impact on the personality or the self of the child, are those individuals with whom the child interacts most closely and who give him or her security. These 'significant others' over time actually become a part of the psychic structure of the child from which develops the concept of self. Reality is usually defined by parents, as the most important 'significant others'. Children will adjust their behaviour to meet parental approval. This may not include positive valuation of black people or different ethnic backgrounds. Thus, at least until adolescence, the black child is likely to share these values. The most recent findings have highlighted some of the fears of the critics of transracial adoption; 'These black children have been made white in all but skin colour' (Gill and Jackson, 1983, p. 137).

Curiously, Gill and Jackson are aware of the problem of identity confusion but believe that it can be avoided if black children are placed transracially when very young: 'it is possible that older black children may, by the time a placement has occurred, have already internalised a definition of themselves as being black and that this definition may jeopardise the possibility of integration and emotional identification within a white family' (p. 138). The argument seems to be that the world of reality and the concept of self are or should be structured by white parents and society. Thus children should be placed transracially at a very young age, so becoming 'white in all but skin colour'. If they already have a concept of themselves as black it will be too late to 'turn them white'. Bean, writing a year later in 1984, supported this view by saying that 'when the adopted child is an older child who has already acquired a cultural background and a set of cultural responses, these will have to be unlearned if he or she is to acquire a new cultural identity'. A crucial aspect of a child's interests is thus ignored. Jackson herself saw the danger in 1976: 'Unless you can accept a child's colour, you will always be rejecting a very important part of him' (p. 4). Sadly, this principle does not seem to have informed the later research.

As racial tension increases, social workers must adapt themselves to the prevailing racial climate. They must take a leading role in giving direction to families who have expressed interest in providing a home for a black child. For example, they must be helped to recognise that, in a society which is hostile and oppressively racist to black people, the black family has to develop coping mechanisms which allow the group to maintain dignity and self-respect and which help the family to survive in a psychologically healthy way. These survival mechanisms of the black family have to be extended to the black community generally in its economic life, education and social relations. These experiences are outside those of white society. Consequently most white families are ill-equipped to provide the environment to prepare the black child for the tremendous task ahead. It is these survival techniques which provide the cultural and psychological framework that gives energy and support to black children. The desperate wish to care for a child, however sincere, is not a guarantee that white adopters will provide such an environment.

If the black child is placed in an environment which is hostile, the inevitable consequence of this will be repeated attacks on the child's personality which will cause severe damage to his or her self-esteem. It should be clear that if a child is placed in an ethnically insensitive white community he or she will fail to develop the mechanisms necessary to survive in a racist society.

If Britain were not a racist society, transracial adoption would not be an issue; but as long as race relations continue their current path transracial adoption must be an area of concern. Since the aim of adoption must always be to provide a child without parents with an environment which will foster normal development, the commitment must be to the child, not to the parents or to the agency.

The characteristics of transracial adopters

The limited systematic study of transracial adoptive couples in Britain shows some general characteristics. First, transracial adopters tend to belong to relatively high socioeconomic groups. Second, they often live some distance from the black communities and so their black children tend to be socially isolated from immediate relatives and from other black people. The literature further suggests that transracial adopters are often very self-confident people with a resilience to stress. They often approach agencies that have a policy for placing children transracially; they may prefer children who are racially different from themselves. Their motivation to open homes to black children appears often to have a strong moral and ethical base (Fricke, 1965; Roskes, 1963). These values, held usually with great sincerity, deserve examination because they may have unintended harmful implications.

Some parents only want to adopt a child of two black parents, that is of African, Afro-Caribbean or Asian origin. The rationale behind this decision may be to make it abundantly clear that the child is not the product of the adopters' relationship with each other or with anyone else. These adopters often see themselves as helping the 'poor blacks' with the fantasy or rescue mission born out of collective guilt. It is as though they are saying 'Look at us, we are not like others because we even adopted a black child.' They may feel responsible for the racial injustice which other white people have inflicted on blacks, and see these injustices as entailing all manner of pathology for the black community, with its strengths and survival denied or not recognised. These assumptions will be detrimental to the black child if he or she is seen as being rescued from a life of misery. Embracing such a cause does not ensure a black child's welfare and may, unwittingly, damage it.

This group of adopters may include those whose motivation is largely intellectual or political. They cannot become emotionally involved, and if faced with difficulties they withdraw their interest because their motivation and commitment are often very superficial. It is possible too for some adopters to attempt to improve their self-image if they believe, perhaps subconsciously, that 'having a black child in the family confirms our self-worth because they are much less than we are'. Others may adopt because it is a dramatic way of rejecting what their family and society stand for.

A second group are the adopters who are prepared to adopt a child of two black parents or a child of one white and one black parent, and to accept the child as he or she is, recognising the difference in racial and cultural origin. Some of these parents may also wish, through adoption, to protect children against the social order, but they are 'real' parents in that they are prepared to go beyond their own concerns and hold the child's interests as their priority. (The guidelines towards the end of this chapter can be used to identify this group of parents.) Many such adopters are anchored firmly in their beliefs; they are open-minded and not contented with stereotypes or a superficial view of society. They are also very confident people with a secure sense of their own identity, and are able to resist the various pressures brought to bear on them by friends, relatives and society. They eventually become black families in white skins.

A third group are the colonialists and the neo-colonialists with experience of colonial societies. They often feel they know it all and tend to give the impression that they are 'experts' on blacks. They are often the most difficult to assess since their experience usually lies outside that of social workers, who may be suspicious of such applicants' knowledge but uneasy about rejecting their apparently confident experience.

Some transracial adopters will only adopt a child of 'mixed race'. These adopters do not want society to say that they have a black child, that is, a child of two black parents. A child of 'mixed race' is therefore seen by them as not black and not white, but closer to white than black. They perhaps feel that since there is a degree of whiteness in the child they will be able to identify with that. Some of these families may never be able to accept the blackness of such a child, but, at the same time, they know that he or she is not really white. It is often the children of such families who have the most profound racial identity crisis.

Colour and identity

If a healthy personality is to be formed the psychic image of the child must merge with the reality of what the child actually is. That is to say, if the child is black (reality), he or she must first recognise and accept that he or she has a black psychic image. There are several black children who have grown up in children's homes with purely white staff, and others who have been placed with white families who are isolated geographically and have no contact with black people (Gill and Jackson, 1983, p. 134). Some of these children are saying that they are not black or that they do not want to be associated with other black people. What seems to have happened is that they have internalised the negative images that are attributed to black people and do not feel that they should identify with them. This can happen when an institution or family is racially sensitive, in the white sense, but ethnically insensitive to the child's background and needs. This may sometimes be the result of lack of information and reluctance on the part of the carers to take measures to correct this. Many families often feel that assisting the child to reinforce his or her identity in terms of colour and ethnicity will probably render the child unable to form a healthy attachment to them; the child may feel that he or she should belong to a black family. Many people also feel that there is no necessity to deal with racial issues since the child is seen as part and parcel of the family and 'a child is a child'.

Within my own practice, I have never met a white child who says he or she is not white; neither have I met a black child growing up in a black family saying that he or she is not black. It should therefore be clear that there are factors operating within the family and the society which contribute to this pathological state.

Gill and Jackson had the ideal opportunity to demonstrate how the phenomenon of identity confusion could be understood through the process of racial discrimination in society, a path whereby children of minority groups tend to internalise the values of the dominant society, and internalise derogatory values about themselves. Milner (1975) has summarised and contributed to the long history of research which demonstrates black children's denial of their colour (Clark and Clark, 1947), and their preference for white identity (Goodman, 1964). Social workers must recognise, therefore, that in racist societies they are working with a potentially vulnerable group. But that is not the end of the story. As black communities became aware of the effect that society was having on their children, they forged a conscious approach to provide a buffer between racism and the self-esteem and self-worth of their children by raising the level of consciousness of the strengths of black traditions and family life. They have fought against the pressures to make black people invisible and their efforts have, in part, been recognised by wider society (Milner, 1981, 1983). Black people have thus carved a social and political path more conducive to the psychological well-being of their children, who do not now misidentify their ethnic origins. They have a sense of worth anchored in positive racial identity although they still perceive, correctly, that whites are the most favoured social group (Davey *et al.*, 1980). It is curious and extremely unfortunate that this evidence has been ignored and the significance of racial identity minimised.

Fundamental dilemmas in transracial placements

The acknowledgement of differences?

Transracial adopters face the profound problems of defining their position as a family and in society. Should they see themselves as all other parents in the general population, or as different? If they decide on the former, then they may deny differences between themselves and their child but they must, in the interests of the child, differentiate the child and his or her natural parents from themselves in terms of race, colour and sometimes culture. Recognition of differences and the acknowledgement of attachment struggle together and are major difficulties. There are several ways in which this dilemma could be resolved.

The family may choose to minimise differences and emphasise the need to attach and integrate the child within the family network, perhaps from the moment the child enters the family, as part of the love, warmth and attention which a young child needs and which is the hallmark of good parenting. Others may try to steer a middle passage. Then there are those families who emphasise differences by their awareness of the racial origin of the child. Thus they try to help the child to develop a concrete sense of identity based on the child's race, colour or ethnic origin. All of these approaches involve acute dilemmas for the families.

Some families wonder whether they should request information about the background of the child and, if this is supplied, how it should be used. Should it be taken seriously, or should it be ignored? If the family should choose the first method, for example, ensuring that a life-story book is provided, then the child has the option of an identity outside his or her adoptive family. If they choose to ignore the historical background of the child and feel that thus they will be better able to identify with him or her, then in times of crisis the child will have no solid racial and cultural identity and the family may not have the information to help the child in these crucial times. Some transracial adopters may prefer to isolate themselves from the cultural background and ethnic origin of their child because it is easier in the short run to escape conflicts.

Then there are others who are satisfied with superficial information because they feel that if more is revealed then conflict could arise in the family. In cases where a child is born out of wedlock, these families may struggle with their conception of what a normal family should be and various moral issues. Families with such children are sometimes in a moral trap. They fear damaging the child within their secure family relationship. Their dilemmas are similar to those of many adoptive families but are exacerbated by the racial and ethnic issues already discussed. When it is difficult for the family or the child to attach themselves to each other, then at the end of the day the child will leave the family and become attached to the black community.

The 'closed' family system as a contributory factor in racial identity confusion

Most transracial families operate a closed family system (Gill and Jackson, 1983, p. 104). They are closed in the sense that the black child is cut off from the black community and all interaction takes place within a white social structure. In such a setting, all lines of authority descend from white society, all interaction takes place between members of the white society and there is no interaction which would enable a bicultural existence (p. 134). To protect the black child we need to develop strategies to enable the white family to become open so that there can be reciprocity between white and black society. The child's psychic structure must not only be that of his or her white parents and of white society. If a child does not know any other black people, he or she does not value them; all his or her values descend from the adoptive parents. The child may rationalise the situation by saying that the family is the only family he or she knows and thereby acquire a psychic balance. Creating links with the black community may not be easy, and some families will try to maintain their original form by blocking out positive responses from black people to the child and other members of the family. These positive responses are desirable and would indeed change the nature of the family and would be in the best interests of the black child and his or her parents, but may not be seen in this light by the white family.

To adopt or foster a black child means that the family is no longer white, if the interest of the black child is considered paramount. They can no longer live as a middle-class white family geographically isolated and alienated from other black people. The families cannot remain within the confines of the white world without serious psychological damage to the black child:

> White parents who adopt black youngsters must also be willing and able to identify not only with their black children but also with black people generally. They cannot be permitted to isolate their child and view him or her as different from other blacks; rather they must perceive their child to be an extension of other black people. (Ladner, 1978, p. 288)

Fortunately, some transracial adopters are able to speak for themselves and are therefore able to correct in some ways the folly of others:

The black culture will have a significant, if not dominant, place in your family perspective because every other influence will be portraying and reinforcing the white culture – hence a token attempt with a few books and the occasional embarrassed conversation will not combat it. Think how it feels to be a black child looking at books, advertisements, films, TV, and hardly ever seeing a similar face – the message that comes across is that there is no place for black people in our society. (Parent to Parent Adoption Service, 1983, p. 3)

Mixed race: its meanings and implications

The concept of mixed race, which has become part of conventional social work language, is misleading because it causes confusion in the minds of transracial adopters. It can lead them to believe that such children are racially distinct from other blacks. Consequently, they may neglect the child's need to develop a balanced racial identity and thereby a well-integrated personality. The term 'mixed race' should therefore not be used by administrators or professionals, and should be discouraged among people who want to provide homes for black children. Many black people find the term derogatory and racist because they feel it is a conscious and hypocritical way of denying the reality of a child's blackness. Certainly, mixed race children are regarded as black by society and eventually the majority of such children will identify with blacks, except in instances where reality and self-image have not merged (Bagley and Young, 1982). Indeed, Gill and Jackson (1983) found no difference in racial identity between so-called mixed race and black children. It is therefore more appropriate to use the term 'mixed parentage' instead of 'mixed race'.

The term 'mixed race' is also inaccurate. The majority of the people from the Caribbean, and to a lesser extent from Africa, are of 'mixed race' although they are not regarded as such by professionals and trans-racial adopters. Their various racial mixtures, for example, African and Chinese, Indian and African, white and African, are the result of misce-genation under slavery and colonialism. Out of this process come the different shades of black people's skin colour which we see on the streets of London. These people and their children differ from the so-called mixed race children only in terms of time, and are only a few generations removed from the point at which the mixture occurred. If there is a need to ascertain the race of the parents of the child then this can be done by describing each parent.

For some prospective adopters, the lighter the skin, the more powerful the attraction; the darker the skin the more powerful the repulsion. We should constantly be aware that when most people use the term 'mixed race' they do not mean a child of Indian and African parents, nor a Chinese and a person of African descent, they generally mean the child of a white person and any other person who is not white. Nevertheless, in this society any child who has the slightest taint of black is seen by the majority as black. This is indeed unfortunate, but in a society where race and colour has been made into such an issue, for those children there are no 'in-betweens'. 'Mixed race' children are cemented in their blackness.

Many families who are misled into believing that 'mixed race' children are not black will go on to think that their children are capable of becoming culturally assimilated colourless Europeans. As a consequence, the child will be given a white mask (Fanon, 1968). The child in such an environment is given maximum protection from exposure to his or her real self, or from those who will act as a mirror to reflect the child's racial image. But can the child transcend the blackness and wear the white mask with pride? I would suggest that in this society it is not only impossible but psychologically dangerous.

> It may be that those parents do not consider colour to be important, but such a blind attitude towards the role of group differences in the society is unwise. It is possible that parents do convey to their children that they themselves do not judge and relate to people on the basis of their skin colour, but they should also tell the child that many people in the society do. Failure to do this will obviously leave the child unprepared to understand and deal with the first time he or she is called 'nigger', or some other racial slur. (Ladner, 1978, p. 125)

The trauma of experiencing racism is inevitable, and this experience will result in a sudden and rapid disintegration of the white mask with all the consequences that depersonalisation brings. The majority of these children have not been given the tools to function as black people. Consequently, they are likely to be equally rejected by some black people who may say that they are not black enough, not in the colour sense of the term but in culture and attitude. Some children may therefore adopt a black mask which they wear fiercely but weakly. Professionals must recognise this process.

The development of positive identity

It is possible, but rare, for black children in white families to form a positive identity. Gill and Jackson (1983) found that five of the thirty-five children were to some degree proud of their colour but only a small minority of the children had positive feelings about their colour. The parents of these five children had made some effort to give the children pride in racial background. No such efforts had been made for the children who preferred to be white or by those parents who brought up their children 'entirely white'.

Gill and Jackson go on to identify eight 'black and mixed race couples', seven 'mixed race' children and three black children, and use this sample to demonstrate that racial identity confusion, as they found it in the transracially placed children, could also be found in black children in black families and 'mixed race' children in 'mixed race' families: 'They provide an interesting comparison . . . because . . . same race placements are increasingly regarded as the ideal by social workers . . . and it is in the black and mixed race couples that (it is said) the child will come to develop a strong racial identity' (p. 129). They report that, like the transracially adopted children, none of this sub-group used the term 'black' when referring to racial background. The parents did not have a policy of stressing racial pride or identity and these children did not identify with the black community. They regarded themselves as 'coloured' or 'half-caste' and at least one wished to be white; they had no sense of racial pride. Consequently, they are roughly equivalent to the transracially adopted children.

This argument highlights flaws in the study as a whole. First is the difficulty of depending substantially on parents' responses. Green and Shapiro (1974) caution: 'parents [are] usually the persons best informed about their [the children's] behaviour – [but] are also the most emotionally involved and usually the most biased in their favour. Case records, social workers' reports and teachers' evaluations all have inherited biases and limitations' (p. 90). Second, the instruments used for white middle-class parents may not be equally appropriate for black parents because they may fail to take account of different subjective experiences and racial and ethnic backgrounds. Third, this sub-sample of seven parents is an inadequate basis for Gill and Jackson's major claim. Only three of the couples were black, and five of the children were 'mixed race' thus further complicating the analysis. Fourth, the two researchers were white and so handicapped in their assessment of black families and children. It is poss-ible too that the black couples who were allowed to adopt in the period of the study were 'white parents in black skins'. The resistance then to black families adopting makes it likely that successful selections in the 1960s and 1970s depended heavily on identification and involvement with white society, with the neighbourhood, the school and friends being pre-dominantly white.

Towards the interests of the black child

Given our understanding of the dynamics of transracial placements what should be the essential ingredients of any substitute home for black chil-dren? In addition to the ingredients necessary to enhance the normal development of any child, such placements should be capable of:

(a) enhancing positive black identity;
(b) providing the child with the 'survival skills' necessary for living in a racist society;
(c) developing cultural and linguistic attributes necessary for functioning effectively in the black community;
(d) equipping the child with a balanced bicultural experience, thus enhancing the healthy integration of his or her personality;

(e)   providing continuity of experience based on the reality of British society;

(f)   minimising alienation from the black community;

(g)   enriching the environment of the child's cultural heritage by balancing the black community response to its heritage.

Many transracial adopters find it difficult to refer to the child as black, and moreover they feel, as we have seen, that telling the child about his or her ethnic origin is potentially dangerous (Gill and Jackson, 1983, p. 130). It is indeed the fear of those families which contributes to negative self-concepts in the children.

They should be helped to recognise that racism is a reality in society and that, although they cannot protect the child from it, they can prepare him or her to deal with it when it is encountered. Consequently, helping the child to develop a positive racial identity and pride in being black is an essential component of good parenting in a transracial setting. It is crucial to good self-concepts and for the healthy integration of the child's personality.

White families who have adopted or who are currently fostering black children should be given training. These training sessions could be conducted along the lines of pre-adoptive and foster care classes (Small, 1982a).

The outline presented below is in note form with issues which could be used in training.

Guidelines for selection and preparation

1   The geographical location of the prospective family must be considered carefully since it is important for the child to see black people:
    (a)   to reduce the feeling of isolation;
    (b)   to mirror the blackness of the child;
    (c)   to provide black role models;
    (d)   to protect the child from racial attacks and abuse.

2   The family should be sensitive to the prevailing race relations climate and be cognisant of the possible effect of this on the child's identity formation.

3   The family should have clear concepts of what a multiracial society is, or should be, and should be willing and able to provide the child with a balanced view of the different races.

4   The family must be prepared to have black friends to demonstrate to the child that blacks and whites do have common interests and can interact harmoniously.

5   The family must be prepared to develop contact with the black community in order that the child does not feel that he or she is being

cut off from his or her roots, which often creates the condition whereby negative images emerge.

6　The family must be willing and able to carry the child's past into the present and sustain it into the future, thus linking the child with its ancestral past in a positive way.

7　The family must be able to accept the child as a black child in a positive way and not dismiss the child's colour as insignificant, because in society generally the truth is the opposite.

8　The family must be prepared to find ways and means of linking the black child with other black children.

9　The family must demonstrate that it has the capacity to work with its conscious or unconscious feelings of threat from blacks.

10　The family must be prepared to foster an awareness of the child's religious background.

Lifestyle of the family

1　Reality for the child is defined and controlled by the family. Consequently, the neighbourhood they live in, the interests they have, the lifestyle of their friends and colleagues, will necessarily determine what is reality for the child. These issues must be confronted.

2　The attitude of the extended family and friends towards black people and to a black child being part of their family, must be ascertained.

3　The family must be able to demonstrate its willingness and ability to differentiate between different lifestyles, race and colour without inferring the inferiority of one and the superiority of the other.

4　The motivation for wanting a black child should be carefully examined. Is it ideological, is it guilt, is it to fight a political battle, or to make a political statement? Is it religious, or is it out of pity? Is it concern for overpopulation? Is it to resolve curiosity about black people, or is it an experiment? Is it a second best, or in line with current fashion?

5　Every effort should be made to discover whether the family have the ability to put themselves in hypothetical situations and conceptualise and deal with the difficulties that are likely to arise with the black child, particularly during adolescence. What, for example, is the prevailing attitude in the family towards the black child dating the neighbour's daughter? Can they deal with what may appear to be sexual threats, and the reality of mixed marriage?

6　If there are no institutionalised support systems, particularly in relation to adoption, can the family, friends and local community help the black adolescent to overcome these difficulties?

7　Can grandparents accept that they have black grandchildren which will change the nature of their family?

Identification with white adopters and the black community

1   Can the family provide the environment for bridging the gap in the interests of the child's personality?
2   Can the family accept what may not be the attractive child in terms of race and colour that they initially wanted?
3   Can the family help or allow the child to develop a black personality without feeling that a wedge is being driven between the family and the child; does the family expect the child to be a white person in a black skin?
4   Can the child or children of the prospective family accept and relate meaningfully to the black child?

Socialisation outside the family

1   The attitude of neighbours and parents to black children mixing with their own children should be ascertained.
2   What opportunities exist for relationships as either boyfriends or girlfriends?
3   What opportunities exist for socialising with two cultures?
4   What is the attitude of friends, neighbours and the community to mixed marriages?

Adaptation of family and child to existing and future conditions

1   Can the family deal with conflicts about colour within and without the family? Is the family aware of the stresses and strains that will be brought about for the child and family if the child should experience rejection on the basis of colour; can it deal with this type of problem?
2   Can the family provide the child with the skills that the black person learns in the black community: the skills to cope with racism? Can the family provide the cultural and linguistic skills necessary for the child to relate to, and be accepted by, black people?
3   Can the family accept the fact that not all people in the UK are white, and those who are not white are, by definition, black?

The school environment

1 Is the school multiracial? If not:
2 What is the prevailing attitude of teachers towards black people generally?
3 What expectations do teachers have for black children?
4 What concept does the school have of a multiracial society?
5 What is the attitude of pupils in the school towards black people?
6 What is the attitude of families towards black children attending the same school as their own children?

Acknowledgement

This chapter is an extension of 'The crisis in adoption' which was originally published in the *International Journal of Social Psychiatry*, Vol. 30, Nos. 1 and 2, Spring 1984.

References

ASSOCIATION OF BRITISH ADOPTION AND FOSTERING AGENCIES (1976) *The Soul Kids Campaign*, London, ABAFA.

BAGLEY, C. and YOUNG, L. (1982) 'Policy dilemmas and the adoption of black children', in Cheetham, J. (ed.) *Social Work and Ethnicity*, London, Routledge and Kegan Paul.

BEAN, P. (1984) *Adoption Essays in Social Policy, Law and Sociology*, London, Tavistock.

CLARK, K. and CLARK, M. (1947) 'Racial identification and preference in Negro children', in Newcombe, T. and Hartley, E. (eds) *Readings in Social Psychology*, New York, Holt.

DAVEY, A. G. *et al.* (1980) 'Who would you most like to be?', *New Society*, 25 September.

FANON, F. (1968) *Black Skin, White Mask*, London MacGibbon and Kee.

FRICKE, H. (1965) 'The little revolution in social work', *International Adoption*, Vol. 10, pp. 92–7.

GILL, O. and JACKSON, B. (1983) *Adoption and Race: Black, Asian and Mixed Race Children in White Families*, London, Batsford.

GOODMAN, M. E. (1964) *Race Awareness in Young Children*, London, Collier-Macmillan.

GREEN, L. J. and SHAPIRO, D. (1974) *Black Children, White Parents: A Study of Transracial Adoption*, Child Welfare League of America, New York.

JACKSON, B. (1976) *Adopting a Black Child*, London, ABAFA.

LADNER, J. (1978) *Mixed Families*, New York, Doubleday.

MILNER, D. (1975) *Children and Race*, Harmondsworth, Penguin.

MILNER, D. (1981) 'The education of the black child in Britain: a review and a response', *New Community*, Vol. 9, No. 2, pp. 289–93.

MILNER, D. (1983) 'Children and race: ten years on', *New Society*, 18 June.

NAIPAUL, V. S. (1961) *A House for Mr Biswas*, Harmondsworth, Penguin.

NAIPAUL, V. S. (1962) *The Middle Passage*, Harmondsworth, Penguin.

RAYNOR, L. (1970a) *Adoption of Non-White Children in Britain*, London, Allen and Unwin.

RAYNOR, L. (1970b) *Inter-racial Adoption*, London, ABAFA.

RAYNOR, L. (1975) *Adopting a Black Child*, London, ABAFA.

ROSKES, E. (1963) 'An exploratory study of the characteristics of adoptive parents of mixed race children in the Montreal area', thesis submitted to the Institute of Psychology, University of Montreal.

ROWE, J. and LAMBERT, L. (1970) *Children Who Wait*, London, Routledge and Kegan Paul.

SMALL, J. (1982a) 'Black children in care: transracial placements', in *Good Practice Guide for Working with Black Families and Black Children in Care*, Lambeth Social Services, unpublished.

SMALL, J. (1982b) 'New Black Families', *Adoption*, Vol. 6, No. 3, the New Black Families research report in preparation.

5 Professional/client relationships: creating a 'working alliance' with people with learning difficulties

Ann Brechin and John Swain

Introduction

Relationships between professionals and people labelled as having a mental handicap have their origins in past and present social structures and attitudes. Within this broad context of changing patterns of social organisation, social and professional constructions of mental handicap have led to particular attitudes and practices being adopted. In the Western world, two approaches have come to dominate in the course of the past 50 years: a medical approach and an educational approach. The growing consumer movement, reflected in this instance by the burgeoning of self-advocacy, and the advent of the normalisation movement has impinged very little as yet on these strongly established professional traditions. Reactions to change have tended to involve attempts to encompass new approaches within existing frameworks of practice and thinking.

Yet the concept of self-advocacy and the parallel emergence of normalisation, demand a radical revision of professional roles and approaches. Assumptions about the nature of the professional/client relationship will have to change significantly, if professionals are going to keep pace with the changes which are coming increasingly from sources beyond their control.

In this chapter, we shall be exploring the nature and implications of existing professional approaches, and the growing awareness of the importance of professional/client relationships. We shall be considering how new styles of relationship might be defined and generated; relationships which would be more in tune with the increasingly influential changes in philosophy and policy, and which can support, in turn, the development of new professional attitudes and practices.

Historical perspectives

Various constructions of people with learning difficulties have existed down the ages as society has attempted to define and make sense of patterns of behaviour which differ from the norm. Wolfensberger (1969) provides a useful review of historical perceptions, as does Kurtz (1981), and Ryan and Thomas (1987). Concepts of people with learning difficulties as sub-human; as a menace to society and to the genetic make-up of the race; as eternal children; or as objects of pity, are all beliefs with a long history which still have some currency today. It is worth noting that these accounts do not include any history of the views of people with learning difficulties themselves. In general, the documented history has concentrated on changes in legislation, buildings, numbers of people and terminology.

A part of the history of perceptions of people has been the changes in the labels that have been used over the years.

The terminology adopted in this chapter, 'people with learning difficulties', is a reflection of an increasing readiness to attend to the views of the people themselves. Self-advocacy groups, particularly, have laid emphasis on potential to learn rather than status-quo labelling, and on differences between people, of degree rather than kind. Such terminology will undoubtedly continue to change as social constructions of disability evolve.

Before examining the more recent developments in self-advocacy and normalisation, however, we need to consider the two approaches which have been prominent and have dominated the emergence and style of professional practice over the past 50 years: the medical and educational approaches.

The medical approach

From the medical perspective, the problem, if it is a 'problem', is seen as located in the individual, its origin lying in an innate physiological disorder which brings it into the realm of medical jurisdiction. Thinking and practice impose what has been called the 'sick role' (Tuckett, 1976) on people with learning difficulties.

The assumptions and implications of this have been exhaustively written about, (e.g. Mittler, 1979; Ryan and Thomas, 1987) in relation to mental handicap, and on a broader front on medicalisation in general (Illich, 1977; McKnight, 1977; Kennedy, 1981). In essence, the effect of medically conceived interpretations and solutions has been to provide institutional care settings and services, often taking over pre-existing custodial arrangements, in which basic nursing care, supervision and protection have been provided, with drug therapy as the major planned 'intervention' or treatment. Decisions about management, life-styles and living arrangements, even about educational capacity have been taken by doctors with a consequent decrease in the power of individuals and their families to plan and control their lives. The impact of such approaches on relationships has been essentially to increase dependency with stereotyped perceptions leading to self-fulfilling prophecies (Edgerton, 1976; Ryan and Thomas, 1987). People labelled as 'mentally handicapped' have been perceived as sick and incurable, as dependent, and as ineducable. In return, they have, not surprisingly, behaved in ways which confirmed these perceptions.

Essentially, the medical approach has painted a pessimistic picture.

Retarded development, disturbed patterns of behaviour, inability to form relationships or to be self-sufficient have been seen as resulting from disease or physiological abnormality. Yet, although this defines the individual in 'a sick role', no cure is available. A counsel of despair was offered for many years, which, in effect, said, 'put them away and forget them'. Against such a background of hopelessness, compounded by living circumstances which were at best dreary and unstimulating for patients and staff alike, and at worst a contravention of basic human rights and dignity, individuals had no opportunity to develop any other picture of themselves. The picture was provided for them in terms of medical explanations with patterns of behaviour, development, and any personal or emotional problems accounted for by their medical condition. Diagnosis and treatment were in the hands of the medical experts who held the franchise on knowledge. Professional/client relationships were thus inevitably one-sided with all the power and knowledge (at least that which was perceived as relevant) resting with the medical profession. At best the relationship was paternalistic, at worst it was authoritarian and dehumanising.

The educational approach

A second major influence which has had a dramatic effect in the second half of the century has been the educational approach. Interestingly, though, the close ties with and influence of medicine have meant that only recently has an educational approach begun to emerge which is freed from the decision-making power of the medical profession, and from the diagnostic and treatment framework. With improvements in educational technologies, more detailed understanding of how behaviour is controlled and developed, and a greater focus on curriculum planning has come a flood of new opportunities for people with learning difficulties. The recognition that, given appropriate opportunities, time, and carefully devised teaching strategies, even people with very severe learning difficulties can make progress has led to a new commitment. The aim of this approach is not so much to offer care and protection, but to help people to reach their 'full potential'.

While this has only relatively recently become widely influential, affecting policies and services across the board and not just in the formal educational sphere, Ryan and Thomas (1987) point out its longer history. They quote Seguin, for example, as saying as far back as 1846:

> While waiting for medicine to cure idiots, I have undertaken to see that they participate in the benefit of education.

The educational regimes apparent in early asylums pay tribute to the humanitarian spirit which existed at the time. Ryan and Thomas quote from a description of Earlswood Asylum, opened in 1855, where 'everything is done that can make learning enjoyable'.

With the growth in numbers in asylums, however, and the take-over by medical men rather than educators, the early conviction that education could lead to improvement and a return to the community was eroded and replaced by the more pessimistic approach reflected in the oppressive institutions of this century.

The re-emergence of interest in the potential of education coincided with the development of more effective teaching strategies, and the inclusion of all children within the education system, although even here Ryan and Thomas suggest:

> Psychologists in the last 20 years have had to rediscover much of what was already known and practised by the 1860s.

The opening up of educational strategies and opportunities has had to include, of course, a broadening of the more traditional educational curriculum, with a recognition that the development of basic social skills, including methods of communication, may be the important focus.

Such new developments have led inevitably to new kinds of relationships. Not only in school contexts, but in hospitals and day centres and at home, the new relationship has become a teacher/pupil one.

Successful teaching requires that learning should take place. This provides a valuable feedback loop, in one sense, which forces the 'teacher' to seek more appropriate methods or goals if the first strategies are not successful. In another sense, though, it also puts an onus on the individual with learning difficulties to accept the role of learner in the relationship – perhaps for life (Tomlinson, 1985). Opportunities for continuing education in adulthood are increasingly recognised as desirable, but when people are put in a position of having an obligation to learn with no prospect of ever quite passing the test and graduating to full citizenship, this may not be so desirable.

There are some within education who quarrel with an approach which, with an emphasis on objectives and skill development, appears to require little more than continuing compliance from pupils. Goddard (1983), for instance, argues that education should involve setting in motion a 'process' of active development which can enable 'the individual child to unfold his or her unique personality'.

Nevertheless, the enthusiasm for developing skills grew. It was quickly recognised that effective learning could most easily take place when opportunities were created frequently throughout each day, in a relaxed familiar setting and with a trusted companion. Parents and direct care staff were the answer and 'parents as teachers' became the byword of many teaching programmes. The ideal environment has come to be seen as one which offers continual opportunities to maximise learning, and succeeds in engaging the attention and motivation of the individual for as near to 100 per cent of his/her time as possible. Anything less involves wasted potential and the limiting factors are seen as the time and energy of the carers.

The incentive and justification for all such activity is the goal of 'independence'; independence which is presented as the state to which we all aspire. Leaving aside for now the question of whether independence is appropriate as the ultimate goal for us all, it is important to recognise the inherent difficulty and contradiction in trying to achieve or work towards independence through a teacher/pupil relationship which remains essentially a dependent one.

Of course, that is not in essence what education is intended to be about. The 'leading out' implied by the name strikes a better chord. Unfortunately, in the realm of education, particularly for people with learning difficulties, attitudes and practices mitigate against this happening. In general it seems that the greater the learning difficulties, the more didactic is the approach and the more controlling the relationship. The aims, the curriculum and the methods used are predicated upon, on the one hand, assumptions of incapacity and unsatisfactoriness, and, on the other hand, assumptions that the only worthwhile goal is 'independence'. This is then defined in a normative sense which must therefore inevitably exclude these pupils from its attainment. If these arguments need rehearsing, they are most thoroughly explored and exhaustively referenced in a recent book (Wood and Shears, 1986). The authors argue:

> We are not suggesting that the tasks and skills children with severe learning difficulties are taught in schools under the new orthodoxy are of no value, or that they may not be useful to the children, either now or in later life. What we are suggesting is that such an education does not add up to learning to be independent, to participating in and contributing to one's own community, either as a child or later as an adult, as the aims of education purport. Rather the objectives/skills analysis curriculum actually teaches dependence, in that it does not teach the children to challenge the system they are in and the places they will graduate to. The curriculum is not seen in terms of constant amelioration of handicapping conditions, but rather in terms of making up for deficiencies which are constantly imputed to the child. The curriculum, as it is, functions to make children with severe learning difficulties as near normal as possible – the means to the end – not to enhance who they actually are. (Wood and Shears, 1986, p. 40)

Such contradictions are integral to educational relationships with other adults also. Under the tutelage, very often of the psychologist, nurses, care staff, ATC instructors and parents acquire the new educational methodologies which enable them to develop a more effective teaching role. What this usually means in practice, however, is that they can more effectively control and manipulate the behaviour of their 'pupil'.

Parallels between the medical and educational approaches

In one sense the educational approach is the polar opposite of the medical one, in directing attention to the possibilities of improvement and change, rather than to the physiological account of permanent impairment. In another sense, however, the approaches stand alongside each other. Both assume that existing social constructions of normality define the goal to which people with learning difficulties must aspire; both define and understand the 'problems of mentally handicapped' people in such a way as to indicate clearly the impossibility of ever achieving that goal (the best hope being to build up patterns of skills which approximate to 'normal' behaviour); and both create a professional/client relationship which enshrines the professional in a world of exclusive and privileged knowledge, and consequently entombs the individual with learning difficulties in a fundamentally dependent role.

Self-advocacy and normalisation: impact and implications

Against this backdrop of professional attitudes and practices, the self-advocacy and normalisation movements have struggled to emerge. Both movements are concerned ultimately with individual human rights, but their origins and protagonists are different.

On the one hand, the self-advocacy impetus has grown with the increasing emphasis on consumer sovereignty and an awareness of the potential power and influence of self-help pressure groups. The professional role has been minimal, and, where it has been relevant has been facilitative rather than directive or initiating.

Normalisation, on the other hand, has been a largely profession-led push towards service revisions.

The two developments have emerged in parallel, developing separately, but inevitably influencing and interacting with each other. It will be argued here that their aims can and should converge. Self-advocacy is in essence about a process of self-actualisation. It is about people coming to identify and express personal feelings, wishes and circumstances and coming to understand what contributes to the positive and negative of their existence. It is about opening up ideas about the range of choices which could and should be available to them.

Any professional approach that does not concern itself with supporting and facilitating these same processes of growth for people with learning difficulties must be seriously open to question. Similarly, approaches which seem to imply a pre-knowledge of the aims and goals of other people's lives, and lack the willingness to retain an open mind, to live with uncertainties, possibilities and transitions – these too must be seen as professional approaches with little to recommend them.

When we look at the normalisation movement we can see that it has implications for professional approaches, but it will be argued that the concept itself has been open to more than one interpretation leading to differential impact on professional practice. These interpretations can be reviewed and considered in the light of the aims of the self-advocacy movement, with the question being posed – does this interpretation of normalisation and the implications for professional practice appear to support and facilitate the open-ended processes of growth emerging from the advocacy movements? We are suggesting, in effect, that this can be used as a kind of litmus test of appropriateness against which professional approaches can be measured.

The early voices expounding and refining the idea of normalisation and its implications came from Denmark, Sweden and the United States (e.g. Nirje, 1969, 1980; Bank-Mikklesen, 1969; Wolfensberger and Glenn, 1973; Wolfensberger, 1980). These were quickly taken up and written about in the British context (e.g. Thomas *et al.*, 1978; O'Brien and Tyne, 1981).

One of the earliest definitions of normalisation at an international symposium saw it as 'making available to the mentally retarded patterns of everyday life which are as close as possible to the patterns of the mainstream of society' (Nirje, 1969). Nirje's more detailed definition included reference to the importance of normal rhythms of life, daily, weekly and yearly; normal developmental experiences such as leaving home in adulthood; and normal respect and understanding (Nirje, 1980).

Wolfensberger in the United States has focused attention specifically on the implications for service delivery and has developed an assessment procedure aimed not at individuals, but at the quality of services. PASS (Programme Analysis of Service Systems; Wolfensberger and Glenn, 1973) evaluates services in terms of how far they comply with appearances, practices and settings which would be valued by the rest of society. Again, this has been taken up in this country with workshops on 'PASS' and 'PASSING' being widely networked largely through the energies of CMHERA.

Within the movement, definitions have shifted over time. A critical account of such shifts (Baldwin, 1985) suggests that this has made evaluation of the concept particularly difficult to achieve.

We are suggesting here that normalisation, over and above these many attempts to define it coherently and carefully, is open to different interpretations in practice. In our view, two common interpretations of the term are unfortunate and probably unintended by at least some of the protagonists of the concept. The third interpretation seems to us to be the one which is in line with the philosophy of valuing and supporting each individual, reflected in the growing advocacy movement.

The first, and perhaps commonest interpretation of the term, is the one which takes it to be about normalising people, i.e. making people as close an approximation of normal as possible. A clear example of this was presented in the recent critique by Sinha (1986) of the goals of psychology. Contrasting practices of differentiation, 'preserving the "normal" through the exclusion of the deviant', and the newer approach of normalisation, he sees normalisation as 'predicated upon the changing of the subject so classified, towards normality'. Moreover, he suggests that 'the predominant model for the implementation of normalisation practices utilises behavioural pedagogies and objectives-based curricula'. Sadly, he may well be right. Professionals do tend to see normalisation in terms of practices designed to change the individual.

It is perhaps not surprising that such an interpretation should come to the fore in the implementation of normalisation. It is precisely in line with the common professional assumptions outlined earlier and fits comfortably within the existing style of professional/client relationships.

In particular, the straightforward application of goal planning or Individual Planning approaches (Schachter *et al.*, 1978; Blunden, 1980; Humphreys *et al.*, 1985), as if their underlying assumptions were in line with the principles of normalisation, highlights the apparent feeling amongst professionals that all that is necessary is to change the name and call what they are doing 'normalisation' and all will be well. The authors have argued elsewhere (Brechin and Swain, 1988) that the skill-development focus of goal planning and Individual Planning can be at odds with an approach that emphasises an individual's right to be valued for what he/she is, and to have opportunities for an ordinary life made available unconditionally.

The second kind of interpretation is perhaps the extreme of the position that Wolfensberger espouses. Seeking to ensure that people are seen to live in pleasant, ordinary homes, are seen to drive in ordinary vehicles (not Sunshine buses, for example), go on ordinary holidays (not with large groups of other people who also have handicaps), wear attractive clothes, have attractive hairstyles, receive the same kind of support services as other people, and now, with social role valorisation (Wolfensberger, 1983) be seen to have appropriate, valued roles in society; seeking all this begins to sound dangerously close to a marketing strategy. The product, i.e. the person in this case, becomes secondary to the packaging and to the image that is projected and promoted.

In the midst of this sales hype, what rights does the individual retain to be as he/she wishes to be? Must the individual bend to comply with (usually) middle-class value systems in order to achieve some kind of acceptance? Normalisation in this sense begins to sound like superimposing a currently fashionable veneer without any attention to the detail of what lies underneath.

In terms of the professional/client relationship, how easily this translates into the professional working to make the individual with learning difficulties socially acceptable – again on other people's terms.

Both these interpretations of normalisation seem to be in danger of losing sight of the individual at the centre of things. The relationship which is implied between professional and client by these assumptions still tallies with the traditional relationship. It remains inherently dependent from the client's point of view. Behaviour, development, appearance, social role, etc. are still judged against a 'given' of social norms accepted as appropriate goals by the professional and the task is to bring the 'deviant' individual into line as far as possible, by modifying or repackaging or both. 'Success' inevitably remains elusive by definition unless the individual escapes the label altogether.

This account sounds extremely critical of professional practice, and it should perhaps be made clear that such approaches have, paradoxically, contributed to considerable progress. Finklestein (1980) described this same paradox in relation to people with physical impairments. In the field of mental handicap the growth of the self-advocacy movement reflects the ability of a spirit of self-determination to emerge in the face of *and* (paradoxically) with the help of, an oppressive and dependency inducing style of professional help.

Many professionals, of course, struggle to escape from this difficulty. Others fail to recognise its existence. In the remainder of this chapter, we shall try to outline:

- firstly, the interpretation of normalisation which seems to us to be in line with the sense of direction of the self-advocacy movement recognising that people with learning difficulties need to be seen as autonomous individuals with their own rights of self-determination;

- secondly, our reading of the way that professionals and people with learning difficulties are working towards recreating the relationship between them, including an outline of a support structure developed recently by the authors (Brechin and Swain, 1986, 1987) designed as a tool to help shape a more equal relationship, or 'a working alliance' as it has been described elsewhere (Deffenbacher, 1985; Egan, 1986);

- thirdly, some principles of professional practice which may be drawn up on the basis of these discussions.

A preferred interpretation of normalisation

We have referred earlier to a third interpretation of normalisation which we see as being in line with the spirit of much that has been written, particularly in the earlier days. More recent summaries of these earlier statements are available (Bank-Mikklesen, 1980; Nirje, 1980). This account of normalisation focuses on opening up a range of life-style opportunities which are available to the rest of the population but which have tended to be closed to people with learning difficulties.

Some inherent problems remain in a concept premised on the desirability of normality, in whatever sense it is interpreted. If it is used, however, to highlight commonly experienced deprivations and restrictions, and stimulate a move away from those towards a range of service provisions and life-styles which would normally be seen as more adequate, more acceptable, and even more desirable – which would, in short, be valued by most of that society – then normalisation must offer some hope of a breakthrough.

Such an emphasis shifts the focus away from modifying or repackaging the individual on to a concern to minimise the restrictiveness of opportunities. As such, it is not at odds with the 'litmus-test' of self-advocacy, seeming to support a view of people as potentially autonomous and with a right to self-determination within a less restrictive social milieu.

What it does not do, of course, is to prescribe an appropriate style of professional practice. The principles of normalisation relate to a style of living towards which people with learning difficulties and their supporters can aspire. It does not suggest how their relationships with each other may have to change as part of the process. The tendency is, then, for professional/client relationships to continue in the existing mode – even, as suggested earlier, pushing their interpretation of normalisation principles into line with their established practice in order to reduce the dissonance they might otherwise experience. It seems essential to look explicitly at the implications of the interpretation of normalisation for professional styles of working.

Towards a working alliance

What are the alternatives to the more traditional professional/client relationship? Are there alternatives to the modifying or repackaging strategies which aim to reduce deviance? What measures of success might there be if the goal of changing client behaviour in some way is no longer centre stage?

It is too simplistic to suggest that by offering improved opportunities in a less restrictive setting, individuals with often severe learning difficulties, frequently additional disabilities, and histories of damaging experiences, will thereby have *access* to improved, more satisfying life-styles. Access requires more than just the existence of possibilities. Professional roles in offering support both directly and indirectly through other helpers will remain important in facilitating this process of accessing opportunities. But how can this role be described?

It has been suggested that the self-advocacy movement offers a model of growth and development against which professional assumptions and approaches can be tested. This is not to argue that professionals should try to replicate the process of supporting self-advocacy, but it is to suggest that the aims, mode of operation and the nature of the professional/client working relationshp should, at the very least, not be in conflict with the emergence of self-advocacy.

Williams and Shoultz (1982) set out their view of some of the processes at work in self advocacy, and the following account is built around their observations.

Gains from self-advocacy	*Features of support offered*
1 Growth and confidence	Enhancing mastery and control
2 Trust	Learning to be on their side in seeing problems
3 Self valuing/pride	Learning to enjoy and know people
4 Identity	Believing in people
5 Determination	Commitment
6 Responsibility	Accentuating positive qualities
7 Ability and knowledge	Shared skills and information
8 Sensitivity to others	Monitoring own communication
9 Developing a voice	Learning to assist without control or power.
	(from Brechin and Swain, 1987)

Such skills as are implicated in those two lists are essentially relationship skills and are arguably as relevant to individual professional/client relationships as they are to work with self-advocacy groups.

In exploring what this may mean for professional practice, it may be helpful to look at other attempts to reconstrue the nature of professional activity. Models do exist which move away from the tendency to pathologise the individual.

Perhaps the most useful body of literature and experience to look at is that which addresses approaches to counselling. Stemming largely from the work of Carl Rogers (e.g. Rogers, 1951, 1978), a school of thought has grown up emphasising both the centrality of the relationship between professional and client and the concept of personal growth – a growth which is essentially self-defined and personally experienced. Others such as Maslow (1973) had proferred similar views about the potential of human development given appropriate nurturing opportunities for growth.

Such ideas have been extended and broadened (see, for example, Egan, 1986; Murgatroyd and Wolfe, 1982) to encompass the notion of 'helping skills' or even 'human relationship skills' (Nelson-Jones, 1986). The term 'working alliance', (Deffenbacher, 1985) also seems to lay an appropriate emphasis on the concept of partnership.

Though they seem to have great relevance here, approaches to 'counselling' have tended to emerge and operate mostly in the context of more able, verbal and reflective groups in society. Working with people whose verbal skills and ability to conceptualise may be limited or sometimes non-existent, offers a particular challenge. Elsewhere the authors have explored in more detail the nature and relevance of such approaches to people with learning difficulties (Swain and Brechin, forthcoming). Here we shall move straight to looking at how such principles may be extended to encompass this challenge.

In practice settings, those involved are often struggling to find ways of resolving the dilemmas they face. Established methods and approaches are often the products of outdated assumptions, and professionals are forced to invent, adapt, adjust on a day-to-day basis. Few guidelines, other than very broad statements such as 'the use of culturally valued means to enable people to lead culturally valued lives' (Wolfensberger, 1980) exist to translate the new expectations into styles of working practice.

Shared Action Planning (Brechin and Swain, 1986, 1987) is an attempt to take up this challenge. A method or approach to working together has been devised with the explicit intention of creating a relationship and setting in motion a process which supports the moves towards normalisation whilst still tallying with the emergence of self-advocacy. The process which is generated becomes in effect an end in itself, creating as it does a working alliance within which both partners develop a shared approach to identifying and tackling goals and problems. Pitt (1987) describes succinctly the incorporation of the approach and its direct relevance to the broad aims of normalisation and self-advocacy within a developing community support service.

A radical approach to shared assessment, which emphasises the importance of getting to know and understand each other; the identification of aims in terms of what people would like to see happening; and a process of considering plans for action which recognises the existence of different perspectives, moves the focus away from the usual concern with the individual and how he/she should change, to focus instead on the role of other people and wider circumstances. The professional as mediator is frequently the picture which emerges. But, whatever the plan for action arrived at, it is the process of travelling, and the nature of relationships generated on the journey which is of prime concern in Shared Action Planning. Interestingly, Egan's discussion of the concept of a working alliance makes a similar point (Egan, 1986). He cites Deffenbacher (1985) as suggesting that many of the outcomes of the helping process such as the development of goals and plans, happen inadvertently, with the most important focus being the client/helper relationship.

Drawing out principles of professional practice

We have been concerned here with the need for consistency in the principles underlying different movements, attitudes and approaches. The assumption tends to be made that principles of normalisation, the self-advocacy movement, and professional/client relationships will somehow remain in tune with each other. The reality seems to be somewhat different. Interpretations of normalisation are too easily made to fit with long-established assumptions and practice.

If this pitfall is to be avoided, it is suggested that careful attention is needed to the way in which normalisation is being interpreted. New methods and structures may be needed to help practitioners develop new relationships and styles of working. Finally, attention to the nature of relationships and the aims of self-advocacy may serve as a litmus-test to measure the appropriateness of other approaches.

Out of this, we can arrive perhaps at some principles of practice which can be seen to be both compatible with normalisation (in our preferred sense) and supportive of self-advocacy.

Six principles of practice

We would suggest that *from the perspective of people with learning difficulties*, a working alliance with professionals should seem:

1 to be an entitlement rather than an imposition;
2 to promote self-realisation rather than compliance;
3 to open up choices rather than replace one option with another;
4 to develop opportunities, relationships and patterns of living, in line with their individual wishes rather than rule of thumb normality;
5 to enhance their decision-making control of their own lives;
6 to allow them to move at their own pace.

Such principles of professional practice, measured as they are in terms of the client's perspective on the relationship, are, on the face of it, clear and straightforward. Abiding by them, indeed trying to find ways of moving towards them, is, however, infinitely more problematic.

This chapter has explored some of the issues and challenges involved in helping such process of change to take place.

References

BANK-MIKKLESEN, N. E. (1969) *Changing Patterns in Residential Services for the Mentally Retarded*, Washington, DC, President's Committee on Mental Retardation.

BANK-MIKKLESEN, N. E. (1980) 'Denmark' in FLYNN, J. and NITSCH, K. (eds) *Normalisation, Social Integration and Community Service*, Baltimore, University Park Press.

BALDWIN, S. (1985) 'Sheep in Wolf's clothing: impact of normalisation teaching on human services and service providers', *International Journal of Rehabilitation Research*, 8, pp. 131–42.

BLUNDEN, R. (1980) *Individual Plans for Mentally Handicapped People: a draft procedural guide*, Cardiff, Mental Handicap in Wales Applied Research Unit.

BRECHIN, A. and SWAIN, J. (1986) 'Shared Action Planning: a skills workbook' in *Mental Handicap: patterns for living*, p. 555, Milton Keynes, Open University Press.

BRECHIN, A. and SWAIN, J. (1987) *Changing Relationships: shared action planning with people with a mental handicap*, London, Harper and Row.

BRECHIN, A. and SWAIN, J. (1988) 'A share of the action for consumers', *Community Living*, 1(6), pp. 20–1.

DEFFENBACHER, J. L. (1985) 'A cognitive-behavioural response and a modest proposal', *Counselling Psychologist*, 13, pp. 261–9.

EDGERTON, R. B. (1976) 'The cloak of competence: years later', *American Journal of Mental Deficiency*, 80, pp. 485–97.

EGAN, G. (1986) *The Skilled Helper: a systematic approach to effective helping*, 3rd edn, California, Brooks/Cole.

FINKLESTEIN, V. (1980) *Attitudes and Disabled People*, Monograph 5, New York, World Rehabilitation Fund.

GODDARD, A. (1983) *Processes in special education* in BLENKIN, G. and KELLY, A. (eds) *Primary Curriculum in Action*, London, Harper and Row.

HUMPHREYS, S. *et al.* (1985) *Planning for Progress: a collaborative evaluation of the individual planning system in NIMROD*, Research Report No. 18, Cardiff, Mental Handicap in Wales Applied Research Unit.

ILLICH, I. (1977) *Disabling Professions*, London, Marion Boyars.

KENNEDY, I. (1981) *The Unmasking of Medicine*, London, Allen and Unwin.

KURTZ, R. A. (1981) 'The sociological approach to retardation' in BRECHIN, A., LIDDIARD, P. and SWAIN, J. (eds) *Handicap in a Social World*, London, Hodder and Stoughton.

MASLOW, A. (1973) *The Farther Reaches of Human Nature*, London, Penguin.

MCKNIGHT, J. (1977) 'Professionalised service and disabling help' in I. ILLICH *Disabling Professions*, London, Marion Boyars.

MITTLER, P. (1979) *People Not Patients: problems and policies in mental handicap*, London, Methuen.

MURGATROYD, S. and WOLFE, R. (1982) *Coping with Crisis: understanding and helping people in need*, London, Harper and Row.

NELSON-JONES, R. (1986) *Human Relationships Skills*, Eastbourne, Holt, Rinehart and Winston.

NIRJE, B. (1969) 'Towards independence' in 11th World Congress of the International Society for Rehabilitation of the Disabled, Dublin.

NIRJE, B. (1980) 'The normalisation principle' in J. FLYNN and K. NITSCH (eds) *Normalisation, Social Integration and Community Services*, Baltimore, University Park Press.

O'BRIEN, J. and TYNE, A. (1981) *The Principle of Normalisation: a foundation for effective services*, London, Campaign for Mentally Handicapped People.

PITT, M. (1987) 'Client choice and self determination', *Care in the Community Newsletter*, No. 7, pp. 7–8, PSSRU, University of Kent at Canterbury.

ROGERS, C. (1951) *Client Centred Therapy*, London, Constable.

ROGERS, C. (1978) *Carl Rogers on Personal Power*, London, Constable.

RYAN, J. and THOMAS, F. (1987) *The Politics of Mental Handicap*, revd edn, London, Free Association Books.

SCHACHTER, M. *et al.* (1978) 'A process for individual program planning based on the adaptive behaviour scale', *Mental Retardation*, 16, pp. 259–63.

SINHA, C. (1986) 'Psychology, Education and the Ghost of Kaspar Hauser', *Disability, Handicap and Society*, 1(3), pp. 245–59.

SWAIN, J. and BRECHIN, A. (forthcoming) 'Giving psychology away' to people with learning difficulties and key people in their lives.

THOMAS, D. *et al.* (1978) *Encor: a way ahead*, CMH Enquiry paper 6, London, Campaign for Mentally Handicapped People.

TOMLINSON, S. (1985) 'The Expansion of Special Education', *Oxford Review of Education*, 11(2), pp. 157–65.

TUCKETT, D. (1976) (ed.) *An Introduction to Medical Sociology*, London, Tavistock.

WILLIAMS, P. and SCHOULTZ, B. (1982) *We Can Speak for Ourselves*, London, Souvenir Press.

WOLFENSBERGER, W. (1969) 'The origin and nature of our institutional models' in *Changing Patterns in Residential Services for the Mentally Retarded*, Washington, Presidents Committee on Mental Retardation.

WOLFENSBERGER, W. (1980) 'Overview of normalisation' in FLYNN, J. and NITSCH, K. (eds) *Normalisation, Social Integration and Community Services*, Baltimore, University Park Press.

WOLFENSBERGER, W. (1983) 'Social role valorisation: a proposed new term for the principle of normalisation', *Mental Retardation*, 21, pp. 234–9.

WOLFENSBERGER, W. and GLENN, L. (1973) *Program Analysis of Service Systems: a method for the quantitative evaluation of human services. Vol. 1, Handbook*, 2nd edn, Toronto, National Institute on Mental Retardation.

WOOD, S. and SHEARS, B. (1986) *Teaching Children with Severe Learning Difficulties: a radical reappraisal*, Beckenham, Croom Helm.

6 Effective co-operation in child protection work

Wendy Stainton Rogers

Children and young people have a right not to be mistreated, and are entitled to expect that adults will intervene to help them if they are being abused or neglected. But they also have a right to the love, support and long-term commitment that their families are usually best able to provide. And children facing troubles have a right not to be subjected to the 'system abuse' that may arise because of clumsy or inadequate professional intervention which – however well intentioned – can make them feel even more vulnerable, manipulated or 'kept in the dark'.

To fulfil their obligations to children and young people, it is not enough for individuals who are concerned with protecting children to do their own jobs properly. It is equally important that their different roles and functions are properly co-ordinated with each other, so that the participants in the process are mindful of all of the child's needs and rights, that they keep each other well informed, ensure that nothing gets 'left out' and yet avoid duplication. And in all this, as so eloquently argued by Lord Butler-Sloss in her report to the Cleveland inquiry (DHSS, 1988a), children must always be treated as people, not as mere objects of professional concern.

Therefore, possibly more than in any other work concerned with children and young people, it is in the sphere of child protection that all of the people involved – whether they are professionals, volunteers or the child's parents and wider family – need to be able to work together. Sadly, it has been all too often the case that it is precisely in this area that individuals and agencies have found it most difficult to co-operate.

In the inquiries into the deaths of children like Maria Colwell, Jasmine Beckford and Kimberley Carlile (DHSS, 1982; Blom-Cooper, 1986, 1987) the observation has been repeatedly made that children who were known to be 'at risk' were failed by those given the statutory duty to protect them, because of poor communication, mistakes about knowing who was (or was not) responsible for undertaking particular tasks, and, it has to be admitted, professional rivalries and jealousies. Similarly, with regard to the recent events in Cleveland (DHSS, 1988a), it was not the good intentions of individual professionals that were criticised so much as their inability – or unwillingness – to operate as a team with a common purpose.

It is easy to assume (as some politicians have done) that the mistakes were simply due to professional bungling or individual pigheadedness. A more thorough analysis suggests that, although professional incompetence and 'personality conflicts' were certainly involved, in every case there were also some very genuine reasons why it proved so difficult to work harmoniously together. In this chapter I shall argue that such problems are rooted in a variety of differences in values, practices, perspectives and professional ethos, arising out of a range of social, cultural and historical processes. To tease out their effects, I will begin by briefly outlining the procedural and organisational framework intended to promote interagency co-operation. Next, I will examine some of the reasons why this co-operation is so hard to achieve. And finally, I will explore some suggestions about how such problems may be overcome.

The procedural and organisational framework

Roles and responsibilities

Three main agencies share the primary responsibility for the protection of children – the police, social services and health authorities. In addition the National Society for the Prevention of Cruelty to Children (NSPCC) alone amongst the voluntary organisations has statutory powers in this area. (This is not the case for the Royal Scottish Society for the Prevention of Cruelty to Children, RSSPCC.) Each has particular duties with regard to preventive work, investigations, monitoring and support. Other agencies (such as the education service) and organisations (such as the Family Rights Group and self-help groups such as OPUS, the Organisation for Parents Under Stress) also serve important functions. Table 6.1 sets out the main responsibilities of different professionals within the main agencies.

Table 6.1 The roles and responsibilities of the agencies primarily involved in child protection

Worker/agency[1]	Overall responsibility	Prevention responsibility	Investigation responsibility	Protection responsibility
Social worker	General promotion of child's well-being	Providing services to help families care for children	A statutory duty to investigate all allegations of abuse or neglect General assessment of child and family Gathering information about possible abuse or neglect	Lead agency in co-ordinating protection plan Overall monitoring of child's safety in family Providing services for children 'in care'

Worker/agency[1]	Overall responsibility	Prevention responsibility	Investigation responsibility	Protection responsibility
NSPCC worker	Identification and prevention of child abuse	Providing services to help families care for children Educative role with other professions	Similar duties and roles as social workers	May act on behalf of social services Providing specialist preventive services (e.g. Family Centres)
Health visitor	General responsibility for child's health and well-being	Monitoring the child's healthy development	Assessment of child's overall health and development	Monitoring child's well-being and supporting family
General practitioner	Specific and general responsibility for child health in the community	Alert to possible abuse or neglect within general care of child and family	Assessment of child's general health and well-being; route to specialist medical services where needed	Monitoring child's progress, and supporting family
Paediatrician	Medical treatment at casualty or following referral from GP	Alert to possible abuse or neglect whenever dealing with children	Specialist assessment (e.g. for sexual abuse or non-accidental injury)	Monitoring child's progress after assessment and treatment
Police	Prevention, investigation and prosecution of crime	Work in the community with families and children	Investigating alleged abuse or neglect by gathering evidence about the alleged abuser	Providing support to other agencies enabling them to monitor 'at risk' children
School teachers and Educational Welfare Officers (no EWOs in Scotland)	Overall responsibility for children's welfare within education system, as well as their educational development	Alert to possible abuse or neglect whenever dealing with children; educative role in empowering children	Providing reports about child's welfare and circumstances in educational setting	Monitoring children in their daily contact, and offering them support

[1]All these professionals will have common responsibilities (e.g. to engage in policy making, attend case conferences, attend Area Child Protection Committees). Other workers will have similar roles (e.g. childminders and nursery officers similar to teachers) and some others (e.g. child psychologists and

probation officers) will have more specialist roles to play. In Scotland the role of the Reporter is crucial, and within the Scottish legal system, he or she occupies a role unlike any of the above. It is the Reporter who must be informed about any suspected abuse, who decides whether to call a children's hearing, and who oversees that its decisions are implemented.

It is the Social Services Departments (Social Work Departments in Scotland, and Health and Social Services Boards in Northern Ireland) that have the principal statutory duty to protect children. Where children are considered to be 'at risk' within their families, the social service agencies have a statutory duty to monitor their continued safety, and to co-ordinate services to help their families look after them properly. Where the risk is considered too serious for the children to remain in their family, they have a duty to provide alternative care, in foster homes or other forms of residential care (and there is a duty to monitor children's safety and well-being in these situations also).

The other agencies and bodies are expected to carry out their particular functions under the co-ordination of the 'lead' social service agency. More detailed information about the roles and responsibilities of the different workers, agencies and organisations can be found in Dingwall *et al.* (1983) and Osborne (1989).

The machinery of interagency co-operation

There are three main ways in which interagency co-operation is organised. These are: Area Child Protection Committees, case conferences, and Child Protection Registers.

Area Child Protection Committees (formerly Area Review Committees)

Area Child Protection Committees (ACPCs), based upon the boundaries of local authorities, are intended to provide a forum for developing, monitoring and reviewing child protection policies in a particular locality. Although there is some variation from area to area, each committee is made up of representatives of the key agencies who carry sufficient authority to act on their agency's behalf. Those would normally include:

- social services;
- NSPCC (in some areas only);
- health authorities, including health service management, medical services, (e.g. paediatricians), psychiatric services (e.g. child psychiatrists), and nursing;
- family practitioner services, including GPs and health visitors;
- education services, including the education authority and teachers;
- police;

- probation service;
- armed forces (where appropriate).

More specifically the roles of the ACPCs are to establish and review local interagency guidelines about procedures; tackle significant issues that arise, and establish good practice; offer expert advice about the handling of cases in general; make policy and review progress about prevention; and oversee interagency training. Work is often delegated to specific working groups, which frequently co-opt specialists and experienced fieldworkers.

Case conferences

Case conferences are the main procedure by which interagency co-oper-ation is initiated and maintained at case level. Whenever child abuse is suspected, a conference will be held at an early stage in the investigation and decision-making processes. For efficiency and confidentiality, the con-ference is expected to have a clear set of objectives, and to be restricted to those people directly involved with the child and the family concerned, and those who need to know about or have a contribution to make to the tasks involved.

The formal duties of the conference are to decide whether or not to place a child's name on the *Child Protection Register* and, if so, to appoint a 'key worker' who then assumes the main responsibility for overall co-ordination of any subsequent work with the child and the family. This may not be the person with the most frequent face-to-face contact with the child or family, but he or she has the task of ensuring that the statutory responsibilities of the social service agency are fulfilled towards the child, including the regular reviewing of the case, the completion of assessments and the provision of services.

As well as these formal duties, case conferences have three further functions in relation to interagency co-operation:

1   Providing a forum for discussing and sharing information about the child and the family, and in particular the allegations or suspicions of abuse. The aim is to assess what has happened, and to decide whether the child needs protection.

2   Promoting collective planning and decision making to devise an overall protection plan for the child, which integrates the work of the agencies concerned and divides up tasks in an economic and functional manner. The plan should include: (a) ensuring the child's immediate safety; (b) assessing the child's situation and likely needs in the future; and (c) providing the services needed by the child and family.

3   Recommending actions, tasks and responsibilities to each agency. While it remains (in theory at least) the prerogative of each agency to decide whether to co-operate with the overall plan, they are at least

expected to notify the key worker if they intend to deviate from what has been agreed.

The key worker is responsible for monitoring the plan worked out to protect the child, and for co-ordinating all interagency activity in order to make sure it is carried out.

Conferences are normally convened and chaired by social services, or (in some parts of England and Wales) by the NSPCC on their behalf, but may be requested by any of the other agencies. If the child in question is placed on the Child Protection Register, review conferences must be held regularly to monitor the child's safety and to review his or her registration.

However, case conferences are not just a forum for professional decision making. Department of Health guidelines (DHSS, 1988b) suggest that they should also offer parents an opportunity to have their views and wishes heard and that parents should be invited, where practicable, to attend part, or if appropriate the whole, of the case conference. Until recently this has been a rare occurrence, but increasingly local authorities are devising strategies to involve parents in case conferences, despite professional reluctance in some areas and the genuine problems that this poses.

At the very least parents should be kept fully informed about the purpose of the case conference, and arrangements made to ensure that their views, and accounts of what happened, are heard. This includes making sure parents know the reasons for professional concern, the statutory powers, duties and roles of the agencies involved, their legal rights, and any changes in the family which the agencies consider necessary in the interests of the child. They must always be informed afterwards, in writing, about the outcome of the conference.

Child Protection Registers

The Child Protection Register provides a central record of all children in a given area who have been identified as abused, or who are considered to be at risk of abuse, and who therefore are currently the subject of an interagency plan to protect them. The intention is to offer a speedy point of enquiry for professionals from different agencies who may be worried about a particular child.

The register is held by social services or, in a few areas, by the NSPCC on their behalf. Information is kept separately from other records, in conditions which safeguard its confidentiality. Registration is reviewed at least every six months. Department of Health guidelines (1988b) suggest five categories of registration, which are not necessarily exhaustive or mutually exclusive:

- neglect
- physical abuse
- sexual abuse

- emotional abuse
- grave concern (e.g. where another child in the household has been identified as abused)

The register is managed by a 'custodian', an experienced social worker with appropriate knowledge and skills in child abuse work, who is available to provide advice to professional staff making enquiries. Custodians are expected to inform each other immediately when children are moved from one part of the country to another, and the child's name should be immediately registered in the new locality, pending a case conference. If at any time the whereabouts of a child on the register are not known, it is the custodian's specific responsibility to set in hand immediate action to try to trace the child. The key worker should regularly check that the child's whereabouts are known, and inform the Child Protection Register's custodian immediately if the child goes missing.

Reasons for poor co-operation

There are four main explanations for the failure of this machinery for co-operation, and for the conflicts and dissensions that often emerge between the different agencies and organisations with a duty to protect children:

- the differing functions allocated to the different agencies, and the ways in which these may clash or compete with each other;
- the differing – and often conflicting – values, ideologies, cultures, ground-rules and practices of the various professions and groups involved;
- a lack of clarity in the boundaries and lines of authority and decision making between one agency and another;
- the consequences of historical prejudices and more immediate inter-professional jealousies between groups and individuals.

Different functions

Each of the participating agencies has a different job to do, a different area of activity, and different interests and concerns. Some have a focused role at a particular stage (e.g. the role of the paediatrician during an investigation), whereas others have a more diffuse role that spans all the stages (e.g. the NSPCC). Similarly, within any stage, different agencies may need to focus on different aspects. For instance, during an investigation, the police must concentrate upon collecting adequate and appropriate evidence for a possible prosecution, whereas social workers are concerned to gain much broader information about the child and the family's situation and resources.

Traditionally these different functions and objectives have been regarded as somewhat incompatible. The police, for example, might worry about consulting too closely with social workers in case the validity of the evidence they gained might be threatened. Doctors have been concerned that requests for repeated medical examinations, while justified for the purposes of forensic evidence, might be detrimental to their primary responsibility for the child's health and well-being. Increasingly, however, the professionals concerned are finding ways in which they can do their own jobs properly, while working together for the child's benefit. For example, police surgeons and paediatricians are learning to conduct medical examinations in partnership, and social workers and police officers are being trained to conduct joint interviews with children where sexual abuse is suspected. The need for good teamwork is now being recognised as essential.

Different perspectives

Professionals involved with child protection define and explain it in different and sometimes conflicting ways, and adopt quite different stances about the way it should be undertaken (Stainton Rogers and Stainton Rogers, 1989). For example, they differ in whether they consider all adult–child sexual relationships as abusive, and in their judgements about the relative effects of different kinds of abuse. Some take a highly individualistic approach, regarding child abuse and neglect as primarily the actions of particular persons; others adopt a broader perspective, seeing poverty, disadvantage and exploitation to be just as abusive as individual cruelties. Some people stress the need to protect innocent children from the misuse of adult power; others see the way forward as one of liberating and empowering children, even if this places them at risk. Some seek to keep the family together at all costs; others, particularly in relation to sexual abuse, argue for the exclusion of the abuser from the home.

Some of these conflicts can be identified with particular ideologies. Feminists, for example, are highly critical of some family therapists. To them, seeking to explain and treat the 'problem' in terms of the dynamics within a family is morally indefensible – it lets the abuser 'off the hook' and blames the child, or more usually the mother, for colluding with or even encouraging the abuse (see, for example, Nelson, 1987; MacLeod and Saraga, 1987). Given that these viewpoints and value bases are so antagonistic, and yet rarely made explicit, it is not surprising that different groups find it so hard to trust and respect each other.

Even outside these types of confrontation, the very differences in language and traditions can lead to a breakdown in communication. Fred Sedgwick, a teacher, captured this recently in an article describing a case conference he attended (*Guardian*, 28 January 1989). His account has the doctor describing the mother in question as a 'silly girl who ought to have her tubes tied up', the social workers 'dressed in natural materials' and concerned to achieve 'a caring situation for the whole family' and the policemen 'all in matching fawns and beiges' talking in language 'clipped yet verbose, impersonal and jargony'. Teachers, he admitted, are no better: 'How committed to learning we are. How clever our sarcasm is.'

Lines of authority and decision making

As well as government guidelines (DHSS, 1988b) most professional bodies (e.g. General Medical Council, 1987) instruct their members to share information about allegations of abuse. However, given that only social workers have a legal responsibility to investigate allegations, and other professionals (e.g. priests) may be under an obligation to protect confidentiality, social services face the dilemma of undertaking the 'lead agency' role, while having no authority to insist that other professionals pass on information to them. Similarly, while there is a growing willingness by agencies like the police to be guided by a case conference in decisions, they can, if they choose, act independently.

Even within agencies, the aims and approaches of people at different levels of the professional hierarchy are often at odds. Peter Dale (1989) talks of 'defensive practices' where managers may choose to play safe in order to avoid criticism 'if anything goes wrong', whereas their staff, more closely in touch with children and families, may prefer to employ a strategy of rehabilitation.

And behind all the distinct and conflicting perspectives described earlier, underneath all the rhetoric about 'working together', are barely hidden power and status differentials. Doctors, health visitors, social workers and police – even parents – may sit round a table at a case conference ostensibly discussing a 'team decision' which is 'in the best interests of the child'. But they are far from equal in their ability to achieve the outcome they want. Case conferences do not have the status of a court of law and so parents have no right to challenge decisions that are made. A single voice, if it comes from somebody sufficiently powerful, can overturn the consensus arrived at by the rest (Sedgwick wryly ends his article by saying that the child's name was put on the 'register', the doctor having used his influence to overturn the decision made by the rest).

Professional prejudices and jealousies

The different approaches necessarily adopted by professional groups may give rise to stereotypical 'cardboard' images of each other. The other day a friend described another woman to me as 'a typical social worker, you know, all Freud and knitted lentils'. Stereotyping can be dangerous when it allows us to distance ourselves from others, and to fail to see the individual through the distorting lens of our own prejudice. It can be used defensively to convince ourselves we do not need to take their ideas, understandings and values seriously, and to reinforce our own superior knowledge. This is all the more true when we share our prejudices with our colleagues and friends, competing with each other to paint ever more rude or ridiculous portraits of whatever 'out group' we have chosen as our prey.

Of course, the motivation for playing this game is all the stronger when we have reason to resent the 'out group' for being more powerful or better resourced than we are, or not subject to the strains, pressures and tensions we face (of course, because they *are* an 'out group' we know little about the problems that they have and we do not). This is as true of child protection work as of any other field, and indeed perhaps the very danger-ousness of the work (for professionals and clients alike) and the appalling nature of some of the cruelties and neglects make such professional jeal-ousy and prejudice all the more likely.

Improving co-operation

Very little research has been conducted to discover how the barriers to effective co-operation might be knocked down. Specifically in terms of child protection, the best-known British work has been carried out by Hallett and Stevenson (1980). Stevenson herself has written more recently (Stevenson, 1988) reviewing the main themes that have emerged, and is well worth following up.

Drawing upon her work I would suggest the following guidelines for improving co-operation:

- Clear and agreed definitions of the functions and tasks of each agency and each worker need to be identified, and agreed boundaries estab-lished so that all workers know their own roles and responsibilities and understand each other's. Everybody should know the boundaries of their own competence, where and how their activities touch on those of others, and in what circumstances they need to consult others or keep them informed.

- Specific individuals need to be identified within each agency who are willing, competent and have the resources to make their work with child abuse and neglect a major commitment. These people need to be enabled to act as representatives for their agencies and as link-persons with other agencies.

- Regular, well-organised and properly established channels of com-munication between the different agencies need to be set up and maintained, both on a case-by-case basis and at a higher managerial level. Work needs to be done to agree how these forms of communi-cation will operate, and to ensure they are maintained and followed, despite crises and other pressures. The people concerned need opportunities to develop the necessary competencies to ensure effective intra- and interagency communication.

- Ways of overcoming ignorance and prejudice about each other's functions, ways of working and training, need to be found, both by the sharing of information and by such endeavours as joint training schemes and regular forums for discussion and debate.

- Common goals, common commitment and common terminology need to be defined, while respecting and valuing differences in values, approaches and specialist language and skills.

- Procedures for tackling problems when they emerge must be specified, so that they can be dealt with before they become intractable. This involves a willingness to acknowledge that co-operation can be difficult and that mistakes will occur, and a commitment to making the solving of problems a priority, rather than allowing them to fester.

- Opportunities need to be made for individuals to develop good working relationships with others from the different agencies, at all levels from grass-roots workers to senior managers.

- Ways must be found to ensure that all professionals involved in child abuse work are fully informed about the local arrangements for interprofessional co-operation, and are regularly kept up to date with new developments.

These principles are easy enough to state, but much more difficult to accomplish. They will not merely 'happen' but need to be put into action by deliberate planning and the creation of active programmes of work and staff development. The problem is, of course, that child abuse work is all too often conducted under enormous time and resource pressures, and may at times have to be done under the glare of unwelcome publicity or in the aftermath of an incident that has aroused public concern. It is in these situations, particularly following a public inquiry into a case where a child has died, that poor co-operation tends to be most exposed. This tends to make invisible the enormous amount of good co-operative work that is already being done. We hear very little about those localities where people are working away quietly with encouraging results, and about the many examples of excellent collaboration that protect so many children.

However, it does highlight a major problem that we have so far not considered – some would argue it is *the* major reason why interagency co-operation is so difficult – and that is lack of resources. At a recent conference for teachers, a great deal of anger was expressed about a DES circular. It specified a large number of actions to be taken, including the appointment of teachers in each school with, among other duties, a responsibility for interagency liaison. But the document commented that the recommendations 'had no resource implications'. 'How', the teachers asked, 'are we to be trained and to find the time to do the job, without any extra resources?'

A point that is often forgotten is that effective co-operation is not just a matter of professionals working with each other. Professionals need also to work together with parents and other carers of children. Tunnard (1989) makes some excellent suggestions about ways this can be achieved, including: improving ways of providing emergency protection for children at times of crisis by drawing upon the support of the extended family and local community; involving parents in decision making, providing parents' representatives and encouraging the development of local support groups; improving what happens after separation by offering children and families choices about what can be done, and ensuring contact is promoted and maintained; dealing with sexual abuse cases in ways that help non-abusing parents to avoid taking a defensive position and that give them the resources and support they need to be able to protect their children. Her article is clearly argued and worth reading in full.

And finally, we must always remember that the most essential form of co-operation must be that between the 'helpers' and the 'helped'. Adults who seek to protect children and act as their advocates need to work *with* and not just 'for' children and young people. They have a duty to make sure that the best principles of co-operation are applied to all they do in relation to each child in the name of the 'child's best interests'. Children and young people are entitled to the same levels of respect, consultation and competent practice that we advocate for ourselves as professional workers.

References

BLOM-COOPER, L. (1986) *A Child in Trust*, London, London Borough of Brent.

BLOM-COOPER, L. (1987) *A Child in Mind*, London, London Borough of Greenwich.

DALE, P. (1989) 'What happens next?' in Stainton Rogers, W., Hevey, D. and Ash, E. (eds) *Child Abuse and Neglect: Facing the Challenge*, London, Batsford.

DHSS (1982) *Child Abuse: A Study of Inquiry Reports, 1973–81*, London, HMSO.

DHSS (1988a) *Report of the Inquiry into Child Abuse in Cleveland*, Cmnd. 412, London, HMSO.

DHSS (1988b) *Working Together: A Guide to Arrangements for Inter-agency Co-operation for the Protection of Children from Abuse*, London, HMSO.

DINGWALL, R., EEKLAAR, J. and MURRAY, T. (1983) *The Protection of Children: State Intervention and Family Life*, Oxford, Blackwell.

GENERAL MEDICAL COUNCIL (1987) *Annual Report*, London, Goric.

HALLETT, C. and STEVENSON, O. (1980) *Child Abuse: Aspects of Inter-professional Co-operation*, London, Allen and Unwin.

MACLEOD, M. and SARAGA, E. (1987) 'Abuse of trust', *Marxism Today*, August, pp. 10–13.

NELSON, S. (1987) *Incest: Fact and Myth*, Edinburgh, Stramullion.

OSBORNE, A. (1989) 'Interagency work in child protection', in Stainton Rogers,

W., Hevey, D. and Ash, E. (eds) *Child Abuse and Neglect: Facing the Challenge*, London, Batsford.

STAINTON ROGERS, W. and STAINTON ROGERS, R. (1989) 'Taking the child abuse debate apart', in Stainton Rogers, W., Hevey, D. and Ash, E. (eds) *Child Abuse and Neglect: Facing the Challenge*, London, Batsford.

STEVENSON, O. (1988) 'Multi-disciplinary work: where next?' *Child Abuse Review*, Vol. 2, No. 1, pp. 5–9.

TUNNARD, J. (1989) 'Supporting parents suspected of abuse', in Stainton Rogers, W., Hevey, D. and Ash, E. (eds) *Child Abuse and Neglect: Facing the Challenge*, London, Batsford.

7 In defence of residential care

Lorraine Waterhouse

'We put them to bed, we wake them up, we laugh and we cry with them'
(Berridge, 1985, p. 54).

Introduction

Research findings of decision making in child care have revealed some
disturbing features in contemporary practice. Social workers demonstrated
a professional preference for children remaining with their natural families, and regarded admissions to care as tantamount to failure. Residential
institutions were doubly punished: admission to care was bad enough, but
admission to residential care was even worse. In this paper the unfairness
of this professional attitude is argued and encouragement given to the
need for residential care to be seen as part of a continuum of services for
children in care. The idea of partnership between residential workers and
fieldworkers is offered as one means by which a spirit of mutual respect
and co-operation can develop between them. The consequences of two
critical changes in child care policy and practice for day-to-day work in
residential homes are discussed. A final section outlines three policy and
practice themes arising from recent research which could point the way
ahead.

Changes in child care policy and practice

The past fifteen years have seen critical changes in child care policy and
practice with important consequences for the balance between residential
and other forms of child care. *First*, there has been a notable increase in
the use of fostering, and a slight decline in the use of residential care
(DHSS, 1982). *Second*, there has been a definite increase in the proportion
of older children admitted into care, and a decrease, although less marked,
in the number of very young children admitted.

These outcomes were the result of new policy initiatives and practice
methods in child care. A policy of normalisation to ensure that the circumstances of children in care should be as near to those of children not in
care, to be achieved through planning for permanency, was formulated;
and a practice of finding alternative families for children as the first choice,
using residential care mainly as a brief transitional experience, was
implemented.

The initiative was taken first in relation to young children, and an almost universal policy was adopted to prevent the reception into residential care of young children under five. This changed not only the nature of provision for young children, but also the use made of residential care and the patterns of referral to it. Young people approaching the age when they would no longer be the formal responsibility of the local authorities became the primary consumers of residential care for several reasons: first, many had been placed with a family and temporary readmission to residential care was needed when such placements broke down; second, some did not wish to join a new family and preferred group living amongst other young people and appointed caregivers; and third, some were admitted to a residential setting for help with specific problems or as part of a strategy to prepare them for independent living. Children's homes, therefore, were left to care for an older group of children, many of whom were experiencing severe problems and anxieties about their future, and showing serious emotional and behavioural symptoms. The care staff in such homes understandably felt inadequately trained to respond to this new pattern and were no longer certain about their roles, so clearly defined in the past as parental. While previously residential care had been seen as the *solution* for many young children, it was now considered as part of the *problem*.

The move away from residential to alternative family care shaped the form of subsequent endeavours to help children. Social work intervention concentrated on *planning* for children in care, and *resource finding* focusing on families and not institutions. In practice the solution was to find the right placement for the children, rather than try to help the parents, child or care staff to adjust to each other. Casework with parents, therapeutic work with children in care, and skills training for residential workers and field workers were now of secondary importance.

What consequences follow from these two main changes for day-to-day work in residential homes? Two issues in particular stand out which may pose serious dilemmas for residential workers in caring for children and young people. *First*, the fact that those in residential care are young people not children; *second*, that the main emphasis in child care work has been on the discussion of personal family relationships and in working towards the return of children to their own families or placement with another family.

Practice issues in the residential care of young people

Young people, not children

Residential workers have been left to care for troubled young people just as professional interest in residential communities was declining. The composition by age of children in children's homes had always included some adolescents, but they had never been together in such large numbers before. While these changes were taking place, I had the opportunity to visit a number of local children's homes. Staff in these homes, particularly those who had committed much of their working lives to children in children's homes, were distressed and confused by these changes. As one residential worker remarked: 'I wouldn't mind if only they weren't adolescents.' This observation is critical. Daily encounters in residential settings underwent a major change because the needs of young people are different from those of children.

The needs of young people

Young people have conflicting needs. Like children, they require a sense of security, of belonging, and of their own importance to others, yet as young people they need also a sense of growing independence, of self-assertion, of occupational skill and of responsibility. They share this psychological conflict in growing up with other young people, not in public care. Just as parents sometimes feel caught in the middle of competing demands which arise from this conflict, so also do residential workers, often in more extreme ways. Why is this? Packman *et al.* (1986) found that young people admitted to care had experienced and continued to experience during the admission highly disturbing and unpredictable family relationships. Many young people have more than one admission to residential care and many moves between settings (Millham *et al.*, 1986). Although adolescents are not as vulnerable as young children to the effect of parental separation, contact between young people and their parents becomes less frequent the longer they remain in care (Millham *et al.*, 1986). Residential workers are faced with youngsters who are not only anxious and resentful about family events, but may also be mistrustful of those who try to help them. Field social workers visit children and young people in care less frequently over time and then only briefly (Millham *et al.*, 1986). In consequence residential workers may become the main caregivers for young people in residential care.

Because of what has gone before, young people coming into residential care need security and a sense of belonging, neither of which they may have experienced in great measure before. To expect them to stride manfully towards independence is rather like asking them to dive before they have been taught to swim. And yet, to try and care for them, to protect them, is to touch a sensitive wound. Fisher *et al.* (1986) and Morgan Klein (1985) describe convincingly the conflict which young people in residential care experience between longing for their parents to provide for them and the growing realisation that this may only ever be partial. Residential workers have the difficult task of finding a balance between guiding young people forward, perhaps before they are ready, and caring for them in a personal way which does not threaten loyalty to their parents. As a result the tension which this conflict inevitably creates makes it difficult and sometimes impossible to get close to young people in residential care.

An illustrative case

John, 13, who lived with his young mother and maternal grandmother in a small sparsely furnished council flat on a large housing estate, was seen by a student training to be a social worker. The student described an overwhelming sense of poverty and decay. John's father left the family when John was seven, although he had spent long periods away when John was younger. The health visitor referred John to a voluntary family agency in the city because of his non-attendance at school and his increasingly aggressive acts at home. The student found John big for his age, stoney faced and sullen. The family were visited at home until John was admitted into a local residential home. During the visits to the flat, the student fully expected to establish a relationship with John. The student was to be disappointed. He tried different approaches: he tried going out with John; talking with him; sitting with him; even designing a game for him based on football which the student knew interested John.

The student wrote of his experience:

> At each attempt John invariably left the home having completely ignored what I was saying. This in fact became very difficult for me, personally as well as professionally. In my, albeit limited, experience of working with clients, I had never before been unable to establish any kind of empathic relationship. I felt frustrated that I was not able to offer real hope or solutions. The situation at home was fast deteriorating as my relationship with John worsened. One incident stands out in particular as a point when I felt there was little more I could do:
>
> I had called round at the house early in the week to check on how things had gone over the weekend. I found John to be, as usual, watching the television, and after getting no response I sat and chatted to his mother. Suddenly John stood up, kicked me on the shins and walked off to his bedroom bemoaning the fact that he couldn't get 'peace' to watch the television. I decided to follow him to his bedroom to confront him with this unacceptable behaviour. He swore at me to get out. I stayed, nonetheless, and tried to reason with him. I said that I accepted that maybe he hated me and that he wanted nothing to do with me. However he knew, as well as I did, that the behaviour was not on, nor could he avoid school for evermore. Unfortunately, I said the longer he chose to ignore me and others who were trying to find out what was making him so unhappy, the more chance there was that decisions about his future might be made regardless of his willingness to discuss his situation. This was greeted by yet another rush of insults. He pushed past me and ran out of the house.

John's behaviour seriously deteriorated. He tried to burn himself. After a long search a place in a local residential home for young people was found. The residential staff helped John, his mother and the student to see the move as positive. John responded well to the admission. He became communicative for the first time. The student was cautiously optimistic for the future.

Discussion

Three points arise from this example. *First*, the student thought that no communication existed between himself and John because the encounters were negative. Yet there *was* communication, albeit of an unhappy quality. It is possible to speculate that John's anger may have stemmed from the student turning his attention to the mother; but whatever the explanation, John responded and reacted to the student. The problem for the student, which residential workers may also face, was to know how to shift this embryonic relationship into a form which was less disturbing to both. *Second*, the student wanted to appeal to the rational side of John, to that side of him which could see the futility of his actions. None the less, he was aware of John's vulnerability and John's need to be protected by adults against his destructive impulses. Appealing to rationality fuelled John's anger; protective overtures won disdain. The student bravely and patiently spoke with John throughout the contact. He had to content himself with the fact that it was mostly a one-way affair. The student's willingness, however, to involve John and to try and behave fairly towards him were acts which potentially respected both his rationality and his vulnerability. *Finally*, the student questioned whether he had helped John. There is no simple answer but I think he may have halted a destructive spiral.

John's extreme aggression to himself and others was a sign that he was no longer responsive to self-control or the standard of protective control which his family could offer. Although John's overt behaviour was sometimes violent, it seems likely that it masked a pervasive sense of anxiety, although the precise nature of the anxiety was not clear. The student found it easier to curb his own aggressive feelings to John when he defined John's anger as a partial manifestation of anxiety. In practice the student endeavoured to respond not to the aggression but to the idea that this big, angry and intimidating young man was probably the more frightened of the two of them. The student was not capable of protecting John in his family, but the recognition of this need was brought to fruition in the planned admission to a residential home. This admission to residential care restored some external order in John's life, which in turn may have helped to re-establish a view of himself as someone capable of personal relations with others.

It is important, however, to bear in mind that the student responded to John's distressed and distressing behaviour when he was reasonably satisfied that he, as a student social worker, was neither provoking the behaviour nor sufficiently able to help John's mother and grandmother look after John. Had the student acted without regard to either of these considerations, then the act of admission to residential care might have come to represent for John an aggressive act against him rather than one which was intended to be supportive.

Residential workers may also be uncertain whether they have helped the youngsters in their care. Morgan Klein (1985), in her study of Scottish youth in residential care, concluded from her interviews with young people that they do want help, are often puzzled when communication fails to occur, and are bereft when it is abandoned. Such help is more complex than has been conveyed by my observations of the student's work with John. Residential workers significantly contribute to the psychological development of young people in their care when they stand by them in the face of the young person's opposition or retreat, and when they continue to strive to know and understand them. Even if residential workers are not able always to succeed, then at the very least young people may come to see these efforts as an indication of their own importance for others.

The emphasis on family relationships and restoration to the family of origin

The emphasis in child care practice on families before institutions has contributed to a definition of the aims and the means of helping young people which accentuates personal, family relationships. Residential workers were expected both to prepare young people for joining a new family and to respond to them if and when these new family relationships failed. This deliberate emphasis on the young people's unreliable and hurtful past relationships poses a dilemma for residential workers. Should they concentrate mainly on enabling youngsters in their care to manage family relationships, or should they endeavour to help young people develop cultural and social interests and to further their practical competence in preparation for future citizenship? If the focus of helping young people in residential care were redefined to identify *the development of personal self-worth as a primary aim*, then it would be possible to achieve this by including both dimensions, neither to the exclusion of the other. To illustrate:

A former social work student, after completing her training, went to work in a residential unit for adolescents. Most of the young people had suffered several foster placement breakdowns, and some had been in trouble with the law. I interviewed the student after she had worked in the residential unit for one year. She described her working experience as 'worse than anything I had ever imagined'. The reason for this was the violent behaviour of the young people to the staff, and sometimes of the staff to the young people. Weekends and weekday evenings were the most difficult to manage; times when the young people were unoccupied. The student described an aimlessness. Sometimes group outings were arranged, but often they were cancelled when the young people behaved badly; sometimes the young people went out alone; often nothing happened. The young people became restless; angry exchanges amongst them and between them and the carers erupted; occasionally the police were called. The cycle began again.

The student found that it was not uncommon to regard the young person's stay in residential care as temporary. Because the emphasis was on family placements, residential workers and families expected other plans to be made. These plans did not always materialise and even when they did, they happened only slowly. The student observed: '*If only we could stop waiting and do something.*'

I think she has a fair point, even if there were better times in this home and altogether better times in other homes. If it were possible in the residential care of young people to replace their sense of failure in personal relationships with successes, small or big, in other aspects of their lives, then the experience of residential care could be seen as beneficial in its own right, whatever the outcome of work to restore family relationships. This might create a balance in the day-to-day encounters of young people and carers between, on the one hand, issues concerned with the young person's feelings and behaviour towards others and, on the other hand, the appreciation and learning of skills associated with a range of activities and interests. This balance is more in keeping with the needs of young people and takes into account the low self-esteem of many of those in public care. A greater emphasis on cultivating young people's interests and creative activities in art, music, literature and sports could lessen their self-doubt in residential care, further their competence, and create a sense of achievement.

In recent years there has been a move to teach young people in residential care practical skills such as cooking and budgeting which they will need when they leave care. To take this initiative and extend it to include a range of interests which they can use, whether or not they are employed in the future, might help them to be on a more equal footing with their peers who have not been in public care. Should their personal and family relationships remain or become negligible, then they might leave residential care supplied with skills and interests which they did not have before coming into care. This in itself would constitute a major achievement and would give recognition to the important contribution of residential workers in preparing young people for citizenship. At the same time, it would provide variety in the work of residential carers, and give purpose to the daily encounters which would be less demoralising for all concerned. I do not wish to suggest that helping young people with personal family relationships is unimportant; far from it! I wish only to encourage the development of an already existing trend which recognises that personal self-worth depends not only on relations with others, but also on the development and mastery of creative, intellectual and physical interests. I do not see why these opportunities should be less available to young people simply because they are in public care. Nor do I see why caregivers should be expected to sustain a focus on personal relationships which would not ordinarily exist in the encounters between young people and adults.

This raises the more general question of the overall policy and practice likely to influence the nature and scope of residential social work in years to come. The final section of this chapter deals briefly with some recent research studies and identifies the main policy and practice themes arising from these, as a pointer towards the future work of residential social workers.

Recent studies in decision making in child care

Between 1981 and 1986 nine major research studies (Adcock, 1983; Berridge, 1985; Fisher *et al.*, 1986; Hilgendorff, 1981; Millham *et al.*, 1986; Packman *et al.*, 1986; Rowe *et al.*, 1984; Sinclair, 1984; Vernon and Fruin, 1986) funded by the DHSS and the ESRC, broadly concerned with social work decisions in child care, were completed. These studies were based on observed patterns of practice from 1979 to 1982, in forty-nine local authorities in England and Wales, and included approximately 2,000 children (DHSS, 1985). Although, with the important exceptions of Berridge (1985) and Fisher *et al.* (1986), the studies are primarily concerned with fieldwork practice, a number of findings emerge which are highly relevant to residential services for children and young people. It is these which I will emphasise.

It is important, however, to remember that the studies, whilst representing a considerable achievement, were not comprehensive on two counts: first, they did not include Scotland or Ireland; second, the principal informants were field social workers and not residential care staff (DHSS, 1985). Finally, the findings are not necessarily consistent with each other, although substantial areas of correspondence exist.

Policy and practice themes in the residential care of children and young people

The themes to be discussed are: admission into care: the last resort; the compulsory nature of most residential admissions; and the relationship between field and residential workers.

Admission into care: the last resort

Residential care continues to form a major part of the experience of children and young people in care. It performs important functions in times of crisis, both when children enter care and when foster placements break down. Millham *et al.* (1986), for example, found that of the 450 children coming into care in five local authorities in England and Wales, residential care accounted for 51 per cent of all admissions (p. 80). Despite this, Fisher *et al.* (1986), Millham *et al.* (1986), Packman *et al.* (1986) and Vernon and Fruin (1986) all found that field social workers, and sometimes residential workers, associated the provision of care for children and young people with failure, and thought that good social work practice meant avoiding the use of care, especially residential care. Consequently, field social workers delayed the decision to admit young people to care, and, subsequently, were forced to do so when events had overtaken them (Vernon and Fruin, 1986).

Social workers appear to expect few benefits to accrue from residential care. They do not, for example, expect that young people might be helped by residential workers to become better people, to develop new interests and to learn new skills.

Nor are social workers' preconceptions changed by the experience of using residential placements. Fisher *et al.* (1986) followed fifty-five children admitted to care, most of whom were young people in residential care. They found that field social workers were on the whole critical of the residential experience. They complained of frequent staff changes resulting in a lack of consistency between residential workers and inadequate control of the youngsters.

Why is residential care looked on with special pessimism by social workers? It is not mere chance that admitting children into residential care is seen as a last resort by field and residential social workers, but it is, I wish to argue, the logical outcome of what has gone before. The research of Rowe and Lambert (1973) undoubtedly led to a major reform in child care policy and practice by documenting through its research findings the plight of children in care, of whom more than 50 per cent were accommodated in residential settings. They found that a large proportion of the children had already spent the greater part of their lives in care. The children had little contact with their parents, and the longer they remained in care the less contact they had. There was little planning by field social workers for the children's futures.

Whilst Rowe and Lambert took exception to the then prevailing view that children should, and more important could, be returned to their own families, they were strongly committed to family care as the main form of substitute care for those children who could not return home. Rowe and Lambert concluded that residential care was of value for some children, but not usually for young children except very briefly. The fact that at least half of the children who waited in long-term care were in children's homes became the more powerful message. That children also lingered in foster homes without any definite plan for their future care was taken seriously, but the indictment was levied more against the former than the latter. Findings of successful residential care were given little attention.

It is possible to argue that the research of Rowe and Lambert was influential for the growth of an ideology about the supremacy of the family as the basis for alternative public care of children and young people. Rowe and Lambert, in describing the aspirations of social workers in child care before 1970, thought that the failure to plan for children in public care stemmed in part from a rejection by social workers of state care for children as a permanent alternative to care by the natural family. Hence, an illusion that the children would sooner or later return home was sustained, mitigating the need to plan for another outcome which, in any case, was considered inferior and likely to do as much harm as good. To trace the thread further, Rowe and Lambert not only articulated the prevailing ideology of the need and right of children to belong to families, but also asserted their support for it. They knew from their own and others' research that there was a diminishing prospect for children returning home once they had been long in care. A compromise was needed. Permanent family placements for children in care would provide such a compromise. Family placements offered a context for growing up in care that was consistent with their belief in the children's psychological need to belong to families. Many of the children in care were young, and unless positive steps to plan for their future were taken, they would continue like the older children in their sample to wait for lengthy periods in care.

The momentum engendered by the moral and political appeal of 'a family for every child' was very strong. Residential institutions lost favour and became associated with, if not blamed for, the lack of professional vision and determination to plan for the long term future of children.

But other factors also prevailed. There was a political will in Britain and in the United States to reduce spending on institutional care and to promote cheaper community-based services, not only in child care but also in other sectors of public care such as mental health and mental handicap. Professional aims and social and economic policies were in alignment with each other. Yet Mary Ann Jones, author of the major American study *A Second Chance for Families* (1976), ruefully remarked: 'The money which should have been saved from the reduction in institutional care was never transferred to support the financing of the new community services.' It is now recognised that the costing of community-based care to take account of the wider back-up services on which it must depend is a complicated calculation which was not available with any degree of sophistication at the height of the movement away from institutional care (Knapp, 1986).

Apart from considerations of cost, the changing forms of family life also supported a move to substitute family care rather than institutional care. Whilst at one time the personal characteristics of children, and the circumstances in which they were received into care, set them apart from other children not admitted into care, the norms of family life for children inside and outside of public care could no longer be regarded as so different from each other. Just as some children in public care had experienced the break-up of their parents' marriage, or other family changes, so also had many children not admitted into care. That the family was no longer a single entity, but included a variety of arrangements for caring for children, allowed extension of the net for suitable placement for children in public care. If children outside of public care could be brought up, for example, in single-parent families, then so too could children on the inside. The need for institutional care was diminished. Residential care for children and young people became a last resort.

How fair is the view of residential care as a last resort? There is no doubt from the studies of Millham *et al.* (1986) and Packman *et al.* (1986), that social workers since 1973 have pursued family placements for children in care, although not exclusively. It is also clear that family placements are no panacea. They frequently break down, dealing, as Berridge (1985) argued, a very personal blow to the children and young people; they are difficult to find; they demand, if they are to work, levels of support which field social workers cannot guarantee; and some young people, and some children, do not want them.

Furthermore, there has been a tendency to ignore the value which children, young people and their parents place in residential care. Some young people in care have voiced for a long time their preference for residential rather than fostering care (Page and Clark, 1977). Some, but not all (Triseliotis and Russell, 1983), find residential care less intrusive and less disruptive to their relationship with their parents. Others prefer residential care because they are more likely to be placed with their brothers and sisters and friends, whilst in foster care solitary placements are more often the norm.

Parents too appear to prefer residential care (Aldgate, 1978) and are more likely to visit their children in residential care than in foster placements (Packman *et al.*, 1986; Rowe and Lambert, 1973). Less rivalry and conflict appears to develop between parents and residential workers than between parents and foster-parents. Parents regard residential workers as professionals working on behalf of an institution; foster-parents are seen as no different from themselves (Morgan Klein, 1985). Finally, Fisher *et al.* (1986) discovered that parents understood and expected care to mean residential care, and that both they and the young people were cautiously optimistic that some good would come from the admission.

When the views of those who have experience of residential care are taken into account, and when the finding that fostering does not necessarily prove a permanent solution for young people in care is assimilated, then residential care is at least equal in its advantages to foster care. There can be little justification in the pursuit of a child care policy which relegates the residential care of children and young people to second best and a last resort. Nor can it be concluded that this state of affairs is anything other than unfair to residential workers and the institutions they serve in order to help young people. Not only must they care for distressed and disturbed young people, but they must do so under a cloud.

The compulsory nature of residential admissions

Packman *et al.* (1986), in their study *Who Needs Care?* examined child care decision making in two English local authorities which involved 361 children from 266 families, all of whom were considered for care during

1980–1. They found that 161 of the children were admitted, and for the remaining 200 children the initial decision was that they should not come into care although subsequently a significant proportion did. Outcomes for the children and young people were analysed according to the legal route which was taken as the basis for the child's admission into care. Of the 161 children admitted to care, 90 were compulsory admissions and 71 were voluntary (p. 74). Of particular importance for the residential sector was the fact that 75 per cent of the children admitted compulsorily were placed first in some form of residential care, with half of them in observation and assessment centres or in reception homes (p. 162).

The practical importance of this legal bias for parents' and children's readiness to co-operate with residential staff and make use of the placement is clarified by Packman when the association between compulsory admissions and emergency admissions is made. Compulsory admissions were also emergencies. Emergency admissions to residential care were unplanned with no chance of preparation for the child or of pre-placement visits by the child and his or her family. Restrictions on the visiting of parents and relatives to the children were common, with 71 per cent of the parents subject to limits on the frequency and timing of contact (p. 163). The limits were instigated by the social worker or the residential staff, but were not a condition imposed by the court, and they remained largely unchanged over time.

This trend towards compulsory admissions of young people to residential care is the reverse of that intended in the Children Act 1975, which stresses the importance of considering the child's wishes and feelings, having regard to his age and understanding (Children Act 1975, Ch. 5.3). The precipitate nature of the admissions and the legal imposition which propels them means that residential staff are faced with outcomes of decisions in which they and the families played little or no part. If field social workers define child care services mainly in terms of planning and resource finding (for better or worse), they may well consider their main work ended once the children enter care. The quality and quantity of contact by field social workers with the children and the families quite quickly begins to fade, and residential workers are left alone to care for the children. Although the pressing need to plan for children in care is now well documented (Millham *et al.*, 1986), and whilst most social workers would accept this need, the sense of failure which surrounds admissions, compounded by the instigation of compulsory measures of care, depletes any expectation that good might come from the admission. No doubt this is what Vernon and Fruin (1986) are referring to when they characterise the outlook of fieldworkers, once children are in care, as one of 'wait and see'. But the repercussions for residential workers, because they are not involved administratively in decision making (Packman *et al.*, 1986), is that they too must 'wait and see'. This is precisely what the student referred to earlier in this paper identified while working in residential care.

Parents and children are acutely vulnerable under circumstances of compulsion and emergency which are regular occurrences in residential admissions. The residential staff are presented with an unenviable task. Not only do the social workers regard the admissions as a failure, but the parents may be poorly informed about the purpose of the admission, its duration and the expectations which it places on them. The children, at least the younger ones, become bewildered and distraught. It is not a prepossessing start, as the following example from my past experience as a social worker suggests.

A young boy, *Michael*, was admitted to compulsory care against the wishes of his parents and placed in a group home. The father had punched Michael, then three, and caused bruising to his face. The father, so angered by the compulsory admission, became threatening and abusive to residential staff. Restrictions were imposed on the father, allowing him regular but infrequent access. Contact between Michael and his parents became erratic and unhappy. Michael was fostered when he was six, only to have it break down, much to his devastation. I saw Michael on a regular basis in the children's home to which he returned. The residential workers found him evasive in the account he gave of his actions and feelings. He was destructive of the other children's toys and refused to have any personal belongings in his shared room in the home. When I played with him he enacted pretend battles between warring camps of soldiers. The side which lost were reprimanded for their weakness; the side which won could have anything they wanted from new horses to new leaders. Michael, I suspect, considered himself to be on the losing side and probably wished he was on the winning side.

He said, on repeated occasions, that he did not want any more families. Those who cared for Michael gently encouraged him to accept his toys and belongings again. Further attempts at fostering were not tried, and the residential workers saw themselves as the main people in Michael's life. In time Michael too came to accept their centrality, although for a long time he asked when he could go home to his parents.

There are aspects of practice in Michael's case which probably would not happen now. It is unlikely that he would have gone to a children's home in the first place and stayed for as long as he did before fostering was tried. One attempt at fostering would not have sufficed and now, no doubt, more attempts would be made. The compulsory and emergency nature of the initial admission, however, is no different from the trend in current practice. A question remains about the impact of this forceful intervention on the family and the caregivers and its significance for the subsequent course of events in Michael's life.

The relationship between field and residential workers

One underlying theme which runs throughout the accounts of child care practice in the recent DHSS studies is the complex and largely unsatisfactory nature of the relationship between field and residential social workers. Whilst the problematic nature of the traditional pattern by which responsibilities have been divided between them is well recognised, there is little evidence which can be used to evaluate what would happen if other arrangements were tried. Furthermore, unless the exclusive control for the welfare of the children and young people is transferred to the residential sector once they are received into care, then some division of labour is inevitable and necessitates decisions about when fieldwork ends and residential work begins. The underlying assumption identifies fieldwork with the job of linking with the family and through this contact planning for the children's future. It is based on the hope that the fieldworker will provide continuity of care for the young people before and after admission. The residential workers are traditionally on the receiving end, responsible for the immediate and daily care of the children and young people, but having less involvement in planning, discussions with the family and contacts with other services. Berridge (1985), for example, describes the considerable isolation of residential workers, not only in a personal sense, but also professionally. Apart from the Heads of Units, they rarely have contact with other similar services. Organisationally the residential workers work as part of a team in a place which is separate from fieldworkers, who are members of another separate and distinct team. For residential and field social workers to work together a bridge has to be found.

Several specific, and probably longstanding, complaints by the residential workers of field practice were graphically documented in the DHSS studies. Residential workers are not involved in decisions as to whether, when and where to admit children into care; fieldworkers fail to provide basic information about the personal histories of the children and young people admitted to care; young people are admitted to care precipitously, without warning or preparation; fieldworkers sometimes fail to keep in touch with the young person and the residential staff once the child is admitted; discharge for the young people can be as sudden as their arrival.

These complaints define, for a start, some of the problems which have to be overcome. Surprisingly, no mention of the role of the key worker is made in the studies, and the conclusion must be drawn that this arrangement is either not very common or, if it is used, has done little to resolve the problems for which it was intended, many of which are listed above.

The reasons for these difficulties are complex. Some undoubtedly arise from attitudes, and others are a function of organisational structures (Newman, 1975). In the first case, fieldworkers may have wished to retain certain functions, such as working directly with children and young people, as their prerogative, because they considered themselves to be better trained to undertake these tasks, albeit with limited time at their disposal and with, in some instances, limited skills. They may also have had misgivings about the power and influence of residential staff over children, and the potential abuses which could and sometimes do occur.

Secondly, the organisational model which until very recently has characterised the residential sector has been a centralised one, in which most administrative decisions are taken by the management staff in the headquarters of local authority social work departments. Residential staff and fieldwork staff operate under different auspices within the same local authority. Residential admissions are taken from a wide geographical area, rather than locally.

For changes to occur, field social workers have to form a partnership with their residential colleagues, so that together they can make available as comprehensive a service as possible to families in need of help with and for their children. Residential workers need to take part in the decisions as to whether to admit children to care, and, if so, when and on what basis. In order for this to happen a decentralised partnership between residential workers and social service teams is required, which ensures joint partici-pation and influence in child care decisions.

A decentralised model was adopted in the psychiatric department of a children's hospital in which I worked. Nursing staff from the in-patient unit experienced many of the same problems towards the out-patient teams as residential workers had in relation to fieldworkers. Representa-tives from the out-patient teams, together with representatives from the in-patient unit, formed a new and supplementary in-patient team. The remit of the in-patient team was to oversee admissions and discharges, and to devise and carry out treatment plans in hospital for the children and their families. Individual nurses took responsibility for particular func-tions, for example securing adequate historical information about the children, monitoring treatment progress and liaising with teachers and parents. Representatives from out-patient teams played a more active part in stressful daily decisions about child care management. Tensions continued but the opportunities to discuss and resolve them were improved by regular and closer collaboration.

This was a small initiative. The outcome was positive in so far as nursing staff who looked after the children were happier about the admissions themselves, and were clearer about the purpose of the admission. Out-patient representatives understood better the daily issues of residential care and were able to convey these to their colleagues. Nursing staff, on the other hand, began to participate in out-patient team discussions and contributed at an early stage to identifying children and young people who might benefit from hospital admission. The precipitous discharge of some young children, I think, was avoided.

Conclusions

The research findings here reviewed suggest that residential work con-tinues to be a vital part of child care. It is certainly much more than 'the chilly anteroom to a warm foster family' (Millham *et al.*, 1986, p. 82) that the attitudes of some field and residential workers would suggest. Moreover, the residential sector serves the important functions of obser-vation, assessment and containment of some of the most troubled young people in care. Nearly 80 per cent of the children and young people in

Millham *et al.*'s study (1986) had experienced residential care during a part of their admission to care. How should the residential task be pursued?

First, there is a need for a continuum of services in which residential care is positively included for children and young people who may be or who are in need of public care. Residential care should not be used as a last resort. *Second*, there is a need for partnership between residential and field social workers, which is reflected in decentralised structures where joint participation in child care decisions is possible. *Third*, the move towards compulsory admissions to residential care should be discouraged in favour of voluntary and planned admissions. *Fourth*, residential workers should concern themselves with the personal self-worth of young people as future citizens, thereby giving equal value to the encouragement of intellectual, creative and social skills on the one hand, and success in personal and family relationships on the other. *Finally*, residential workers have an important part to play not only in standing by young people, but also in communicating with them about their experiences and in helping them to explain and discover meaning in their lives.

Finally, it is clear that neither residential nor foster care is a 'perfect' institution. Both have their critics, and justifiably so. But parents, children and young people do not regard coming into residential care as an admission of failure. Nor should they; nor should field and residential social workers. For some young people it is the preferred option.

Acknowledgement

I am very grateful to Douglas Hardie and Fiona Hodge for allowing me to quote from their student notes.

References

ADCOCK, M. (1983) *The Administrative Parent: A Study of the Assumption of Parental Rights and Duties*, London, BAAF.

ALDGATE, J. (1978) 'The advantages of residential care', *Journal of Adoption and Fostering*, Vol. 92, pp. 29–33.

BERRIDGE, D. (1985) *Children's Homes*, Oxford, Blackwell.

DHSS (1982) *Children in Care in England and Wales*, London, HMSO.

DHSS (1985) *Social Work Decisions in Child Care: Recent Research Findings and Their Implications*, London, HMSO.

DRUCKER, N. and WATERHOUSE, L. (1980) *Child Welfare Services in Philadelphia: A View from Outside*, Edinburgh University, from an interview with Mary Ann Jones in New York, 1979.

FISHER, M., MARSH, P., PHILLIPS, D. and SAINSBURY, E. (1986) *In and Out of Care: The Experience of Children, Parents and Social Workers*, London, Batsford/BAAF.

CASCADES/CYGNETS

NAME. _____

DAY & TIME OF LESSON _____

BADGES ALREADY ATTAINED.

HILGENDORFF, L. (1981) *Social Workers and Solicitors in Child Care Cases*, London, HMSO.

JONES, M. A. (1976) *A Second Chance for Families: Evaluation of a Program to Reduce Foster Care*, Child Welfare League of America.

KNAPP, M. (1986) 'The field social work implication of residential child care', *British Journal of Social Work*, Vol. 16, pp. 25–48.

MILLHAM, S., BULLOCK, R., HOSIE, K. and HAAK, M. (1986) *Lost in Care: The Family Contact of Children in Care*, Aldershot, Gower.

MORGAN KLEIN (1985) *Where am I Going to Stay?* Edinburgh, Scottish Council for Single Homeless.

NEWMAN, N. (1975) *A Roof over Their Heads*, Edinburgh University, Department of Social Administration.

PACKMAN, J., RANDALL, J. and JACQUES, N. (1986) *Who Needs Care? Social work Decisions about Children*, Oxford, Blackwell.

PAGE, R. and CLARK, G. (1977) *Who Cares? Young People in Care Speak Out*, London, National Children's Bureau.

ROWE, J. and LAMBERT, L. (1973) *Children Who Wait*, London, ABAA.

ROWE, J., CAIN, H., HUNDLEBY, M. and KLINE, A. (1984) *Long-Term Foster Care*, London, Batsford/BAAF.

SINCLAIR, R. (1984) *Decision Making in Statutory Reviews on Children in Care*, Aldershot, Court.

TRISELIOTIS, J. and RUSSELL, J. (1983) *Hard to Place*, London, Heinemann.

VERNON, J. and FRUIN, D. (1986) *In Care: A Study of Social Work Decision Making*, London, National Children's Bureau.

8 Are links important?

Spencer Millham, Roger Bullock, Kenneth Hosie and Martin Haak

[*Editorial note*: This chapter forms part of a major research study, *Lost in Care*, in which Spencer Millham and his colleagues describe and analyse the 'care careers' of 450 children. Among many other findings, Spencer's team established that the longer a child remains in care, the less likely it becomes that he or she will be reunited with his or her family. Hence the importance of work done to maintain family links. You will notice several references to this study during the course of the chapter.]

In daily life we give little thought to the complex process by which we maintain contact with family, kin and friends. We reach for the telephone, gossip with our families, remind our children of mother's birthday and annually make out a list of Christmas cards without the guidance of a sociometric test. Like most human games, we have long since learned the rules of maintaining contact with others so that the strategy largely remains unconscious.

Nevertheless, even the shortest separations can add a problematic dimension to maintaining links with our families and inject unfamiliar anxiety. When our needs for contact are frustrated, with ill grace we desperately trudge round vandalised telephone boxes or wait, in agonies of frustration, for the arrival of the Automobile Association, momentarily obsessed by distance and isolation. To cope with longer separations we have developed a wide range of reassurances and rituals which protect us and others from the yawning abyss of feeling unwanted. Thus, we undertake or receive wearisome and regular hospital visits, clutching symbolic fruits and eau-de-Cologne. We write daily letters to absent sailors and, on return from long separations, mime passionate and inappropriate Hollywood embraces. Indeed, it takes much effort to maintain links with the separated, in which time and money, energy and inclination, are prerequisites. Unfortunately, some of these attributes are sparse among the families scrutinised in this study and many of their children in local authority care are still learning the rules of keeping in contact with parents and the wider world. Many of the rules they will learn may preclude the possibility of forming adequate and consistent links in the future. Thus, we shall find as this study develops that maintaining links between parents and child presents many problems.

There are many ways in which we can link with those from whom we are separated. First of all, we can visit or be visited with a frequency that reflects the depth of our attachment, feelings of obligation and which meets the expectations of others. With children in care many of these visits will be carefully regulated and under scrutiny. Naturally, visiting patterns will vary considerably, affected by culture, by class and by age, although they will have some common features. Interestingly, an event as familiar as a visit has received more attention from novelists and anthropologists than from sociologists and psychologists. Visiting rules have been little explored. Yet managing a visit, either as a guest or a host, is a complex interaction.

Apart from instrumental visits such as to the dentist or the supermarket, which are relatively straightforward, visits with an expressive dimension, such as those to family or friends, are more difficult. Rules closely govern our behaviour: there are norms on when to arrive, when to leave, what role to adopt during the visit, what topics of conversation to avoid, and what currency to use in the interaction. The rules that govern our visiting behaviour may be unwritten but they are clear, and gross violations are long remembered. For example, few even of one's closest family would brim with welcome at an unexpected dawn visit, and you usually spare great-aunts the company of transvestite friends. Care must always be taken when managing a visit.

Visiting those we know intimately in strange contexts and before unfamiliar audiences is a particularly fraught experience. We only reluctantly pay visits to hospital, although the cool, neutral ethos of the ward and the specific role of the visitor make arrival easier. We take soap and clean pyjamas and desperately try to look pastoral. Visiting our offspring at school or summer camp is particularly difficult. We feel superfluous, uneasily aware that our loved ones are different and cannot incorporate us into those alien settings. Thus wives rarely visit husbands at work, or vice versa, neither do parents, however anxious, brave the disco, looking for their liberated adolescent offspring. The more separate the contexts and the more specific our role within them, the less easy it becomes to move from one situation to another. For example, it makes the transition from working colleague to bosom companion lengthy and difficult.

By now it should be obvious that a lone parent whose child lingers in the care of strangers in unknown territory, to whom the care intervention is a violation, a parent who is bereft of a meaningful role and is unversed in the rules of this unfamiliar game, will find visiting difficult. These barriers to contact are compounded by the complex feelings of guilt, powerlessness, anger and mourning that most parents experience on the removal of their children to care. No wonder that to ease the interactions of a visit and win indulgence for their unwitting violations parents, like the Wise Men, usually take their children inappropriate gifts.

Yet, for us all, seeing is only part of belonging. Apart from the fact that those who do not visit us, those whom we dislike, can be among the keenest reminders of home, we need the reassurance of familiar territories; to see our house, flat, garden and neighbourhood. So we tour our homes on return from a long holiday, checking that everything is in place, like a family of bears fearing the violation of Goldilocks. Frequently, those long separated from home ache for such reassurances quite as much as for familiar faces. [. . .]

Equally, children find contact with their immediate neighbourhood very important: it provides a sense of belonging, whether they experience the delights of Kensington Gardens or the welcoming chippy and warm launderette. Unfortunately, these aspects of belonging rarely impinge on our planning for separated children. We rarely, if ever, consider returning them on a brief visit to the reassurances of their neighbourhoods. Indeed, to a child, family members removed from familiar contexts take on an almost unreal, surrealist quality and a parental visit can lose much of its impact. Children have very limited perceptions of time, space and appropriate behaviour, and adults seen out of context generate great surprise. [. . .] Several children illustrated this disorientation in the intensive study: 'It didn't seem like my mum somehow, she had a new coat on, sitting in a room at social services, she could have been anyone's mum' (boy aged twelve, foster home). And, more ambitiously, a fifteen-year-old girl in an assessment centre mused, 'I wish we all lived in a bus, then my mum could drive up with the dog and the budgie and everything else, we could row over who does the washing-up, it would be nice, just like it was before.' Both these children illustrate the need for parents to be seen in familiar contexts, and incidentally remind us of the importance of pets, the absence of which is keenly felt.

In addition, the neighbourhood in which we live provides endless reassurance and reinforcement of our family links. When we go out or shop there are chance meetings with wider kin, with brothers and sisters, with friends, one's whole social network, and we endlessly channel, sift and embroider family information. To the child, the familiar warning, 'Watch out or I'll tell your mum' is not only a sanction but also a reminder of a powerful presence.

For many children in care it is likely that a return to the sagging tents of the Saturday market or an hour spent amongst the debris of a familiar, disused railway siding would be as therapeutic as an hour spent in pastoral care. One of the problems of maintaining links between children absent in care and their families is that linking is a part of an elaborate package of belonging, each aspect of which reinforces the others. Preoccupation with access, particularly parental access to children, should not blunt our realisation that belonging for the absent child is a much wider and more complex experience.

Again, failure to be on the scene regularly can make return very difficult for children. Not only have they little in common to talk about to visitors but writing of reconstituting families Burgoyne and Clarke comment, 'New partners systematically work through past events, they reconstruct personal biographies which they feel are internally consistent and, above all, form a manageable basis from which to develop new relationships.'[1] Such a strategy on the part of parents involves lies and half-truths; thus reconstituting families move home, abandoning familiar neighbourhoods which undermine their new image. Not only are absent children a threat to these fresh parental constructs but, on return, children often have to face unfamiliar localities.

Links are also maintained with home in other ways. On departure, we take things with us – photographs for our locker doors, slippers for anonymous hotel bedrooms; we pack children's toys for a trip as much to give them a sense of continuity as to bring comfort and amuse. On return we bring back odd T-shirts and inappropriate camel stools or assegai for the living room – trophies which, by their very incongruity, reinforce homeliness. [. . .]

Links also have another aspect: a power dimension. Children need not regularly be in contact, be visited, and receive letters or phone calls to feel in touch with parents and wider family. Security and a feeling of belonging can come from the knowledge that someone at a distance is watching over you with power to intervene. Just as an anchorite in the desert belongs to the deity, so awareness of parental power can link an absent child with his or her family. We have seen in other studies that boarding school children rarely express anxiety about maintaining links with their parents; indeed they feel more isolation from their siblings and pets than they do from significant adults.[2]

Hall and Stacey, in their study of hospitalised children, show how important socialisation for absence and awareness of parental competence can be in ameliorating for children the stress of separation.[3] Links between parents and absent child can be quite strong when maintained by reversed-charge phone calls, when there is a 'hot-line' to the security of father's office. Naturally, the power of parents to intervene will depend on their resources and the young person's situation, but whether on a kibbutz or a cadet ship, children value a return ticket, and letters from home are particularly welcome when they contain a cheque. Sadly, almost by definition, this power dimension is little enjoyed by parents of children in care, even in situations where children have entered care voluntarily and can be unilaterally removed. Indeed, the sense of isolation that must be experienced by both parents and children who are largely powerless to change a situation must be severe.

We can see that there are many aspects to the problem of maintaining links between parents and a child absent in local authority care. Parents' successful accomplishment of regular visiting is only a small part of maintaining links with children. Contact by telephone, letters and through other people such as the wider family, siblings or friends are also very important. We have noted that return to the neighbourhood also reinforces the child's sense of belonging. In addition, links between parents and absent child have a power dimension, an anchor provided by parents who can do something about their child's situation how and when they see fit. [. . .]

Some aspects of links, such as parental power, will be less significant than others. Nevertheless, the ways in which families maintain contact with absent members are varied and it would be wrong to assume that links between parents and children in care should be nurtured in every case. Some parents are uncaring and indifferent, some are dangerous, and some by their actions will have forfeited the rights they might once have had over their children. Similarly, some injured children or older adolescents may not be anxious for frequent contact with their parents; they will have seen quite enough of them already. We have seen how complex many care situations are and that the arrangements concerning access and other aspects of contact between parents and child will be very much an individual social work decision. Guidance can only be at a very general level.

The significance of parental contact

Some of these issues were very much in mind during the framing of our research design. We were discouraged from exploring whether strong links were beneficial to absent children or from examining such controversial issues as blood ties or psychological parenting. Such a mammoth task, for which we are ill-fitted, would have diverted our efforts. Nevertheless, some brief review of these issues and the light cast on them by this study is appropriate, although it should be re-emphasised that our investigation is not about the consequences of separation for children or the psychological impact of long careers in local authority care.

Through the 1960s and early 1970s the DHSS received conflicting messages from a variety of child care authorities and from research on the importance of maintaining links between children in care and their parents.[4] Though few studies had actually explored the issue of contact between absent children and their parents, disturbing evidence on the effects of separation was accumulating, much of which seemed relevant to children in care. In addition, a number of scandals had revealed that social workers, mindful of the trauma of separation and its long-term consequences, were often reluctant to remove children from high-risk homes.[5] Some clarification of the role of parents in children's care experience was clearly needed.

The Curtis report (1946) which gave some unity to child welfare was both influenced by and implemented in an intellectual climate that stressed the child's need for stable, continuous parenting. No doubt mindful of the turbulence and disruption experienced by children during the war, the emphasis in much writing at that time was on stability in parenting, on the importance of the mother's early interaction with the child and on the traumatic effects of separation. These aspects of child rearing were stressed in the work of Bowlby, Winnicott, Burlingham and Freud, Isaacs and many others.[6] Some authorities, such as Rutter and Kellmer Pringle, pointed out that it was as much the quality of substitute care as its stability that was crucial in child development.[7] While authorities differed both then and now on the extent to which they view the psychological consequences of a disrupted childhood as irredeemable, there is a general consensus of what should be avoided, particularly separation in early childhood and a rapid succession of caring figures. [. . .]

While these authors stress that such perspectives on child rearing are general, they also point out that children in local authority care poignantly highlight the issues of continuity of parenting and the effects of separation. Indeed, over three decades a mass of evidence and even more theorising accumulated on separation, while the equally fraught problem of return was and remains little explored. [. . .]

The situation of children in local authority care was of particular concern because evidence was accumulating that some children stayed long in local authority care and many of these were in residential institutions. For example, Rowe and Lambert had highlighted that the rapid turnover of children in care concealed the problem of those who 'lingered long' and for whom coherent plans either were thwarted or failed to materialise.[8] Walton and Hayward also drew attention to the numbers of children in long-term care, an issue emphasised by both Boss and Parker who suggested that short-term admissions to care received greater social work attention than those who remained long.[9] In 1974 Kellmer Pringle stressed the damaging effects of instability and change on children in care.[10] She writes:

> He has no single person who shares his own, most basic and important memories, no one to confirm whether these memories are in fact correct or figments of his imagination, no one to polish up the fading memory before it was too late. Such deprivation is so damaging, I am not at all sure that we can make up for it artificially.

Nevertheless, the difficulties of providing substitute care, which were reiterated by Trasler and Parker in their studies of fostering, did not discourage local authorities from seeking to provide family placements for children and quasi-family experiences in residential care.[11] This emphasis continues to be very much in evidence in the five local authorities we have studied and in our recent studies of residential settings.

The vision of the nuclear family and the need to keep it together was reiterated in numerous reports, as was the need to substitute a family experience for those children deprived of normal home life. [. . .]

Nevertheless, this emphasis on the importance of the nuclear family and the role of stable, warm parenting within it has led to certain unintended consequences. It means that the failure of preventative work with families and the consequent separation of children on entry to care are viewed as signal defeats by social workers. We have seen that this affects the way in which they subsequently view children, dividing them into short- and long-term cases. Consequently, the family is seldom viewed as a resource. [. . .]

Research would suggest that the consequences for children of separation from parents is a more complex issue than the protagonists of particular viewpoints will allow. Indeed, Rutter, in his exhaustive and balanced reassessment of literature on maternal deprivation, suggests that the concept has outlived its value: 'It is evident that the experiences included under the term maternal deprivation are too heterogeneous and the effects too varied for it to continue to have any usefulness'[12] [. . .] and since that time several studies of particular relevance to the problems of maintaining links between children in local authority care and their parents have supported the views of Rutter, the Rapoports, Parker and others. These studies come to very different conclusions from those which advocate psychological parenting and the severance of links between child and family.

The importance of family links in social work literature

Much social work literature differs considerably from many government reports, legislation ànd research studies in that it also stresses the needs of parents, social workers, foster-parents and residential staff as well as those of the children. Many authorities emphasise that the benefits of contact between parents and absent child affect the family as a whole.

We have seen that the majority of children who are accepted into care have at least one parent alive and ongoing contact with their wider family. Many social workers have expressed concern for the separated child's emotional health if contact with the natural parent is not maintained. Indeed, social work literature implies that the interaction between child and parent allows for a more realistic awareness by the child of their relationship. Victor George writes of the need for parental contact: 'Even if reunion is unlikely, parental visiting is considered conducive to the child's emotional health and he tends otherwise to feel rejected, disloyal or to view his parents unrealistically.'[13] Peter Righton also stresses that, even where there is little or no expectation of a return home, the children's parents continue to matter emotionally.[14]

There are a number of studies in foster care which emphasise the importance of a link between parent and separated child. Robert Holman in several articles has suggested that self-knowledge is not a guarantee of success in a foster home but that it greatly helps the foster-child.[15] By self-knowledge, Holman is referring to the foster-child's awareness of his or her family background and of the reasons why he or she no longer lives with his or her parents. While his study is based on a scrutiny of only twenty children, he suggests that the rates of success in fostering were highest for those children with most self-knowledge.

Exploring the self-image of the foster-child, Eugene Weinstein shows that the well-being of the child in the foster home is closely related to the awareness of his or her origins and position as a foster-child.[16] Rosamund Thorpe in her study of 160 foster children also found that there was a relationship between an awareness of background and the foster-child's happiness.[17] She also points out that contact with the natural parents enabled the foster-children to create a more satisfactory picture of their family background and the reasons for their entry into care. Indeed,

Thorpe's findings support the suggestion of Weinstein and Holman that foster-children with parental contact were significantly better adjusted than those who did not have contact with their natural parents. In a very recent study of children in long-stay foster care, Rowe failed to find an association between continued contact with parents and the well-being of the child.[18] But she does emphasise that any firm conclusions are precluded by the fact that so few of her children had really regular parental contact at any time during their stay in care.

Social work literature is also concerned for the natural parent who relinquishes a child. Olive Stevenson, writing about reception into care and its implications for the natural family, emphasises that a continuing relationship with natural parents is necessary for parents, however inadequate, because of the feelings of gratification that parenthood gives.[19] Both the Rapoports and Wallerstein and Kelly reiterate this viewpoint, that the child and parent have a reciprocal relationship and that the development of each is interrelated. Juliet Berry also emphasises the importance of parents being encouraged to contact their children and the dangers of misinterpreting parental behaviour:

> It is only too easy for parents to adopt an all-or-nothing attitude, to opt out completely, to clamour possessively, to interfere obstructively, to appear like a bad fairy at the most awkward moment, to disappear when wanted (e.g. to sign some consent form) and generally to show themselves incapable of carrying through consistent plans.[20]

Berry suggests that social workers, by underestimating parents' distress, tend to encourage their passivity and subsequently use this as evidence of parental indifference to the child. Nevertheless, Berry joins Holtom, Righton, Mason and Thorpe in pointing out that foster-parents and social workers find the stress of linking children with their natural parents very difficult.[21]

It is important to highlight five recent studies which are particularly relevant to this issue of maintaining links between parents and child in state care. Three of these studies come from the United States while two others concern separated children in the United Kingdom.

While there have been few longitudinal studies in the United Kingdom of the relationship between children in local authority care and their parents, the USA has provided several major contributions to knowledge. Naturally, as with the deployment of many transatlantic imports, there are dangers in relying too heavily on findings which spring from very different child care contexts. Nevertheless, the findings of several investigations are of particular relevance to our task.

In the late 1950s, Maas and Engler in the USA studied children in the care of nine communities and showed the virtual isolation from family contact of those who stayed long in care.[22] They also highlighted that repeated movements between placements were common while in state care, and that these had a deleterious effect upon children's development and their contacts with their natural families. Stimulated by this study and

the work on separation of Bowlby, Freud, Solnit and others, David Fanshel and Eugene Shinn, again in the USA, began in 1966 a longitudinal
scrutiny over ten years of both children in care and their parents, looking
at 624 children in all.[23]

The children's adaptation to their care experience was assessed through
aspects of educational functioning and through careful psychological testing, and these were related to children's contact with their natural parents.
Their study, *Children in Foster Care* (1978), has been more recently supplemented by Fanshel's study, *On the Road to Permanency* (1982), which
looks specifically at the parental visiting of children in state care. The
studies also explore those factors which influence a child's length of stay
in care.

Fanshel's studies differ significantly in emphasis from our investigation.
[. . .] Nevertheless, Fanshel's painstaking and illuminating studies highlight certain important features of a child's career in care. He notes the
increasing isolation of children who stay long in care: 57 per cent of his
group were unvisited by parents and virtually abandoned after five years.
He emphasises the child's need for continuity of care and the poor level
of social work planning and support. He clearly demonstrates that the
children's well-being on a wide range of criteria is influenced by parental
visiting and that frequent contact with parents is the best available predic-
tor of the child's eventual rehabilitation with the natural family. Many of
these findings will be repeated in the study which follows; indeed, the
correlation between parental contact and exit from care is even stronger
in our study than in Fanshel's investigation.

Fanshel suggests that much of the responsibility for the withering links
between the natural family and the child lies with the caring agencies who
fail to appreciate the significance of parental links or to encourage contact.
He also highlights the pejorative perspectives on natural parents enter-
tained by caregivers and social workers. The study emphasises that,
although children might be distressed by contact with parents in the short
term, on all enduring criteria of adjustment association with a natural
parent is beneficial. In subsequent studies Fanshel has highlighted aspects
of contact and visiting which cause problems between caregivers and
visiting parents. He concludes:

> In the main we strongly support the notion that continued contact with
> parents, even when the functioning of the latter is marginal, is good for
> most foster children. Our data suggest that total abandonment by parents is
> associated with evidence of emotional turmoil in the children. We can think
> of no more profound insult to a child's personality than evidence that the
> parent thinks so little of the relationship with him that there is no motivation
> to visit and see how he is faring. Good care in the hands of loving parents or
> institutional child care staff can mitigate the insult but cannot fully compensate
> for it. It is our view that the parents continue to have significance for the
> child even when they are no longer visible to him.
>
> At the same time, we are saying that continued visiting by parents of
> children who are long-term wards of the foster care system, while beneficial,
> is not without stress. It is not easy for the child to juggle two sets of relation-

ships and the case workers report that some children show signs of strain in the process. We maintain, however, that this is a healthier state of affairs than that faced by the child who must reconcile questions about his own worth as a human being with the fact of parental abandonment. In the main, children are more able to accept additional, concerned and loving parental figures in their lives, with all the confusions inherent in such a situation, than to accept the loss of meaningful figures.

Stein, Gambrill and Wiltse develop Fanshel's suggestions of the need for a database for children in state care and explore predictive indices for early return of children to their parents. Their study, *Children in Foster Homes*, provides a recent and comprehensive review of the literature related to parental participation in child care in the USA and offers a code of good practice in many areas of social service delivery.[24] This study of the Almeda project in California demonstrates that, where intensive services are offered to parents and efforts are made to rehabilitate children, rapid exit from care is greatly facilitated. An important aspect of intensive work with families and children was the nurturing of contacts between the two, the seeking out of significant kin and friends, and the encouraging of the participation of both caregivers and parents in the child care task. However, the writers stress that rehabilitative work with families does not have high priority with social workers, that care plans are infrequently made, and that parental links are insufficiently valued or nurtured by caregivers and social workers. They also stress that shared care and rehabilitative work takes a great deal of social workers' time. [. . .]

Closer to home, Ivis Lasson concerned herself with a group of seventy-two children in care in Birmingham who had lived in residential care for at least three years.[25] Her study explores those caregivers who become important to these children over time and whether the links that the children enjoy with their family influence other relationships and experiences. It identifies those children who have retained links with their natural families and examines the differences between children who are visited and those who are not. Lasson shows that acceptance by and continued contact with a parent does have a positive effect on children while they are away in care. Her study, in a more modest way, echoes the findings of David Fanshel in New York. She shows that parental contact had a beneficial effect on children's behaviour within the residential home. She concludes:

This study, as with studies of foster children, confirms that visited children are more settled in their placements than unvisited children. This confirms Thorpe and Weinstein who were able to show a greater degree of settledness in the foster home when visiting was frequent.

The sample children who have never known their natural parents are shown to express less trust in caring adults, to know fewer families in the community and have less involvement with other families outside than all the remaining sample children.

Analysis of the data does, however, suggest that if the sample children are to be helped towards making a wide range of social relationships and to enjoy a wide range of social experiences, contact with natural parents, particularly with mother, will facilitate this.

Lasson stresses particularly the importance of contact with relatives and friends and the need to encourage the participation of the wider family:

> These findings would indicate that children who have no contact with a parent or relative tend not to go out of the home and make substitute relationships to the family. The reverse position takes place – those children with contact with their natural families go out and make additional relationships to the natural family. Yet, children without contact with their natural family, appear to be inhibited in their contacts with other family groups and individuals. It does seem to be a situation where the children who already have something go out and receive while those without turn inwards and receive less.

Finally, another significant contribution to understanding the needs of children in care for parental contact lies in Hall and Stacey's *Beyond Separation*.[26] Although this study relates the distress of children in hospital to the discontinuities which attend the experience, it has considerable implications for children in local authority care. They found that children differed considerably in the degree of suffering they experienced in hospital, although they were undergoing the same illnesses and treatments. The authors illustrate that these differences were related to the social background of the children, their position in the family, the style of parenting they had experienced and the ways in which they had learned to behave at home.

Hall and Stacey also emphasise that the suffering of children experiencing separation was closely associated with the meaning to them of the hospital experience. They stress the discontinuity of experience provided by the hospital ward and address themselves to the organisation of the hospital and its unnecessarily alien environment. They also highlight the important negotiating, arbitrating role of the visiting parent. Their study is particularly valuable in that it explores the impact of the hospital not only on young children, but upon adolescents. They conclude, 'We should be aware of the distress arising from separation, not just in the pre-school child, but in children of all ages, indeed probably also in adults.' It would be possible to explore further the implications of these studies for our research but space has not permitted more than a cursory glance. Indeed, when we began our investigation three years ago we erred in believing that the controversy between the child's rights to stable substitute parenting and a contrasting viewpoint which emphasised the value of parental links would pose us with considerable problems. As this study develops, it will be apparent that the dispute neither helps nor reflects the realities of the child's care career. Indeed, the problems as they emerge for the majority of children in care lie not in fraught decisions on the severance of family links, but in the difficulties of nurturing parental contact in unpropitious circumstances.

This study and the 'links' controversy

Can this study throw any light on the dispute between the blood tie and substitute parenting which has been outlined in the previous pages? We can see that, in recent years, research evidence would suggest that maintaining contact between the majority of children in care and their parents is desirable. This study, as it develops, will support such a viewpoint for reasons which lie outside issues of psychological and social well-being for the child. The findings do offer some answers to the blood tie controversy.

We have seen that Fanshel, Lasson and others have demonstrated that children absent in state care are happier and function better when contact is maintained with their parents or with the wider family. Fanshel also highlights that those children who have contacts with home are likely to leave care more quickly than those who do not. The pages which follow amply support such conclusions. For example, we have analysed carefully those factors which influence the length of stay of children in care and, after controlling for other variables, find that a weakening of parental links is strongly associated with declining chances of the child returning home. Indeed, a carefully controlled correlation exercise which, because of its complexity, is to be published separately, illustrates that contact with a parent most clearly correlates with an early exit from care.[27]

Naturally, parental links are not a sufficient condition to ensure exit from care, because love and the ability to care may not go hand in hand. Nevertheless, links with the family are a necessary condition for exit because without parental links, apart from the few for whom adoption is a likelihood, children without family contacts will stay in care, however much they improve in health, behaviour and functioning.

Most writers assume that a long stay in care is harmful to the child, forgetting that relying on fitful parental support may not be a less detrimental alternative to separation. Thankfully, it is not our task to arbitrate on this issue. But if early exit from care is an acceptable goal, then the maintenance of strong parental links is a very good way of facilitating departure. Unlike so many variables in the family and care situation of these children, all of which defy social work interventions, keeping links going is well within social workers' capabilities.

Secondly, it will become clear as this study develops that transfer and breakdown of children in placements selected by social workers are common. [. . .] This propensity to disruption is only slightly less common among young children than adolescents and is as likely to occur in foster as in residential care. Residential settings also face the additional problems of considerable turnover in care staff, although there is evidence that this movement has declined recently. Consequently, it is very difficult to ensure that some children deprived of normal home life receive a stable, caring, substitute home. In these circumstances parental and wider family links, however unsuitable they may seem on other grounds, may be the only enduring relationship the child enjoys. Indeed, in advocating the denial of access to the children of uncaring and ineffectual parents, Goldstein, Freud and Solnit nevertheless emphasise that:

> Even if grounds for modification or termination [of parents' access] could be established, there would be no justification for initiating an action if the state knew beforehand that it could not offer a less detrimental alternative. If the state cannot, or will not, provide something better, even if it did not know this at the time the action was initiated, the least detrimental alternative would be to let the *status quo* persist, however unsatisfactory that might be.[28]

It will clearly emerge from our study how difficult it is to ensure that some children experience a less detrimental alternative to the inadequacies of their own families' care.

Thirdly, the majority who enter and stay in care will be older children and adolescents. They enter care with well-forged links between themselves, their parents, their wider family, their friends, schools and neighbourhoods. These young people wish to maintain many of these relationships and, as we have suggested, such bonds are mutually reinforcing, providing a sense of belonging.

This and many other studies indicate that children resent their parents' roles being usurped in care situations and the inevitable decline that separation brings to many other relationships. We have already noted that fathers in particular get scant consideration, especially from social services and in the child care legislation. It will also be seen that, while many children enter care with siblings and considerable efforts can be made to keep them together, sometimes this is unsuccessful and separation occurs. Yet little thought is given to the nurturing of compensatory relationships with the wider family. Many children do not seek a replacement family experience, nor is the diminution of the role of natural parents and wider kin advisable, for it is to the family and/or immediate neighbourhood that the majority of children return on leaving care.

Fourthly, the number of young children who enter and stay long in care is small and those children who through neglect or risk of injury need to be isolated for long periods from their parents are even fewer. It is not disputed that these children need to be in stable alternative family situations and that adoption or long-term fostering seems most appropriate. It was not our task to explore this issue. But we have already seen that poverty, exacerbated by isolation and ill-health, puts intolerable pressure on some families and that the juxtaposition of many pressures precipitates their children into care. It would be unwarranted to limit the access of such parents without very cogent reasons, punishing them for poverty. One could hardly think of an action more likely to add to the periodic depression of many lone mothers. Indeed, some mothers fail to seek medical care for both physical and mental problems, haunted by the prospect of losing their children and the unequal fight to get them back. In such cases, severance of parental contact to facilitate replacement parenting is not the answer. For such children, foster homes with elements of shared care, however difficult this is to manage, would seem most appropriate.

In addition, we have already noted that wider family networks do exist and need to be tapped. On those rare occasions when parents are absent or dead, the wider family needs to be involved as children in long-stay care have a right to know their family and care circumstances. Many authorities have suggested that for psychological well-being and a sense of belonging we all need to have unbroken personal histories and a map of our lives.

Fifthly, it will become increasingly evident as this study progresses that parents feel frozen out by the care process. The decline in contact between children who stay in local authority care and their parents may in part reflect the indifference of some parents, but it also reflects their powerlessness to intervene, their lack of role and their feelings of guilt and inadequacy. We know from research, particularly that of Jenkins and Norman, Thorpe, Aldgate and Rowe, that these feelings on the parts of parents hinder contact with absentee children.[29] It is also likely that social workers misinterpret natural parents' behaviour at the time of admission. [. . .] They seem unaware that in grieving and mourning for their lost children, parents will oscillate between aggression, anger and rejection, and passivity and indifference. Indeed, the widespread comments made by social workers on parental indifference, ambivalence and rejection may reflect parents' outward stance rather than their inner feelings. Rowe comments:

> We were frequently dismayed and sometimes angered by the ways in which social workers so often failed to provide the necessary support and encouragement to maintain visiting. Sometimes they set up a 'no win' situation for the natural parents, first discouraging visits to let the child settle and later saying that, after such a long gap, renewed visiting would be upsetting.[30]

Finally, there is an assumption that, regardless of whether children seek such contacts or not, the child care scene is literally overflowing with adults aching to provide unconditional love; many longing to sit up at nights worrying about hedonistic and graceless adolescents or anxious to find deep fulfilment in chasing absconders and bailing out the delinquent. While social work probably has more than its fair share of saints, evidence would suggest that it is far easier to write of substitute parenting and the severance of parental links than it is to provide constant adult support and unconditional love. Indeed, Parker, in reviewing ten years of Seebohm, noted the ways in which the professionalisation of social workers has diminished the status of tending skills.[31]

As this study develops, we shall illustrate that children who stay long in care receive only a perfunctory scrutiny from social workers as time progresses. After some initial activity in the months immediately after reception, social work activity declines. Several studies, such as those by Lasson, Berridge, Rowe and Fanshel, have suggested that caregivers do not perceive themselves as replacement parents.[32] Indeed, Rowe's recent study of long-term fostering shows that, in spite of facilitating legislation, many foster-parents do not wish to shoulder the responsibilities of adoption and guardianship.[33] Our study will also demonstrate that many children experience long stays in residential care which, whatever its considerable and usually unrecognised strengths, finds it difficult to replicate family life.

Consequently, substitute parenting and an enduring relationship are not easily constructed for a child. As a result, the advisability of maintaining parental and wider family contact should be self-evident, particularly as it prevents the child being 'forgotten' while in care. The loneliness and homelessness of many young people who have been in care spring from the low priorities given to parental links by social workers and their failure to appreciate the barriers that parents and children face in maintaining contact. The isolation of adolescents who have long been in local authority care reflects not only their lack of social skills but also our short-term perspectives, a devotion to child care as opposed to adolescent or young adult care. Had these children been lucky enough to be born in other social classes, they would still, as young adults, be making considerable demands on parental love, time and purse.

For these reasons, which will be developed as this study unfolds, the maintenance of links between family and child in local authority care should have priority. They amply justify the focus adopted at the outset of our investigations which was to explore the barriers to contact that parents, children and others face.

Conclusions

We have seen in this chapter that maintaining a link between parent and child has many dimensions. For the child, contact with home is part of a wider package of belonging. We have also explored the ways in which experts differ in the significance they accord to parental links with absent children. We have suggested that aspects of the care situation, particularly the difficulty of providing stable, substitute parenting, makes home and contact very important to the child. This is reinforced by the fact that a child's withering relationships with the family make an early exit from care highly unlikely. [. . .]

The maintenance of links between separated child, parents and wider family is important because:

- Research evidence suggests that the absent child is happier and functions better when parents remain in contact.
- Frequent contact with home is the clearest indicator that the child will leave care quickly.
- The majority of very young children who enter care do not stay long, thus long-term substitute parenting is not a dominating issue.
- Stable, alternative care placements for children are very difficult to

ensure, thus the parents and family, while unsuitable on many criteria, may prove to be the only enduring relationships the child has.

● Increasingly, older children and adolescents tend to enter and stay in care, and they have well-forged family and friendship links which they wish to maintain. They often resent the conflict of loyalties that the care situation can bring, particularly in foster homes. Nevertheless, fostering is preferred by social workers and is believed to encourage family links.

● We can see that parents are beginning to feel frozen out by the care process and to feel that they are expected to be passive bystanders with little to contribute to the well-being of their children.

Notes

1   Burgoyne, J. and Clark, D. (1982) 'Reconstituted families' in Rapoport, R., Fogarty, M. and Rapoport, R. *Families in Britain*, London, Routledge and Kegan Paul.
2   Lambert, R. and Millham, S. (1968) *The Hothouse Society*, London, Weidenfeld and Nicolson; Lambert, R., Millham, S. and Bullock, R. *The Chance of a Lifetime?* London, Weidenfeld and Nicolson.
3   Hall, D. and Stacey, M. (eds) (1979) *Beyond Separation*, London, Routledge and Kegan Paul.
4   Rowe, J. and Lambert, R. (1973) *Children Who Wait*, London, ABAA; Goldstein, J., Freud, A. and Solnit, A. (1973) *Beyond the Best Interests of the Child*, New York, Free Press; Pilling, D. and Kellmer Pringle, M. (1978) *Controversial Issues in Child Development*, London, Elek; Fanshel, D. and Shinn, E. (1978) *Children in Foster Care*, Columbia, Columbia University Press; Maas, H. and Engler, R. (1981) *Children in Need of Parents*, Columbia, Columbia University Press; Lasson, I. (1981) *Where's My Mum?* Birmingham, Pepar Publications; see also publications of the Family Rights Group and the Children's Legal Centre.
5   *Committee of Inquiry into The Care and Supervision Provided in Relation to Maria Colwell* (1974) London, HMSO.
6   Bowlby, J. (1952) *Maternal Care and Mental Health*, Geneva, World Health Organisation; Winnicott, D. (1965) *The Family and Individual Development*, London, Tavistock; Freud, A. and Burlingham, D. (1973) 'Infants without families', in *The Writings of Anna Freud*, New York: International University Press.
7   Rutter, M. (1972) *Maternal Deprivation Reassessed*, Harmondsworth, Penguin; Kellmer Pringle, M. (1975) *The Needs of Children*, London, Hutchinson.
8   Rowe and Lambert, op. cit.
9   Walton, R. and Heywood, M. (1971) *The Forgotten Children*, Manchester, University of Manchester; Boss, P. (1971) *Exploration into Child Care*, London, Routledge and Kegan Paul; Parker, R. (1966) *Decision in Child Care*, London, Allen and Unwin.
10   Kellmer Pringle, op. cit.
11   Trasler, G. (1960) *In Place of Parents*, London, Routledge and Kegan Paul; Parker, op. cit.
12   Rutter, op. cit.
13   George, V. (1970) *Foster Care: Theory and Practice*, London, Routledge and Kegan Paul.
14   Righton, P. (1972) 'Parental and other roles in residential care', report of National Children's Bureau conference.

15   Holman, R. (1966) 'The foster child and self knowledge', *Case Conference*, Vol. 12, pp. 295–8.
16   Weinstein, E. (1960) *Self-Image of the Foster Child*, New York, Russell Sage.
17   Thorpe, R. (1974) *The Social and Psychological Situation of the Long-Term Foster Child with Regard to his Natural Parents*, PhD. thesis, University of Nottingham.
18   Rowe, J., Cain, H., Hundleby, M. and Keane, A. (1984) *Long-Term Foster Care*, London, Batsford.
19   Stevenson, O. (1968) 'Reception into care: its meaning for all concerned', in Tod, R. (ed.) *Children in Care*, London, Longman.
20   Berry, J. (1972) *Social Work with Children*, London, Routledge and Kegan Paul.
21   Holtom, C. (1972) *Staff Stress in Residential Work with Adolescents*, lecture to Annual Conference of Association for the Psychiatric Study of Adolescents; Righton, op. cit.; Mason, M. (1968) 'The importance to a child of his family', in Tod, op. cit.; Thorpe, R. (1974) 'Mum and Mrs So and So', *Social Work Today*, Vol. 4, No. 22, pp. 694.
22   Maas and Engler, op. cit.
23   Fanshel, D. and Shinn, E. (1978) *Children in Foster Care*, Columbia, Columbia University Press, p. 487; Fanshell, D. and Shinn, E. (1982) *On the Road to Permanency*, Columbia, Columbia University Press.
24   Stein, T., Gambrill, E. and Witse, K. (1978) *Children in Foster Homes*, New York, Praeger.
25   Lasson, I. (1979) *The Family Links of Children in Residential Care*, M.Sc., University of Nottingham, p. 336.
26   Hall and Stacey, op. cit.
27   Dartington Social Research Unit (forthcoming) *Predicting Children's Length of Stay in Care and the Relevance of Family Links* in Millham, S., Bullock, R. and Hosie, K. *Processes in Child Care*, Aldershot, Gower.
28   Goldstein, Freud and Solnit, op. cit.
29   Jenkins, S. and Norman, E. (1972) *Filial Deprivation and Foster Care*, Columbia, Columbia University Press. Thorpe, op. cit.; Aldgate, J. 'Identification of factors influencing children's length of stay in care', in Triseliotis, J. (ed.) (1980) *New Developments in Foster Care and Adoption*, Routledge and Kegan Paul, pp. 22–40, Rowe, Cain, Hundleby and Keane, op. cit.
30   Rowe, Cain, Hundleby and Keane, op. cit.
31   Parker, R. (1978) *The Future of the Tending Professions*, lecture for the 10th Anniversary of Seebohm, University of Bath.
32   Berridge, D. (1985) *Children's Homes*, Oxford, Blackwell; Rowe, Cain, Hundleby and Keane, op. cit.; Lasson, *Where's My Mum?* op. cit.; Fanshel and Shinn, *Children in Foster Care*, op. cit.
33   Rowe, Cain, Hundleby and Keane, op. cit.

Section II Provision of services

9 Fostering in the eighties and beyond

Jane Rowe

Introduction

During the 1980s, the fostering scene has been exciting but somewhat confusing. Many changes have taken place in foster care services but, although at the start of the decade it seemed as though a major transformation might be achieved, this has not really happened. Development is patchy and what is happening on the ground is often very different from what is being written and talked about. A study of child care placement patterns in six local authorities showed that, in spite of all the emphasis on fostering adolescents, only 15 per cent of all new placements of teenagers were in foster-families (Rowe *et al.*, 1989).

Difficulties continue to arise from confusion over terminology and from lack of definition of the many different types of fostering. These days, the dictionary definition of fostering as 'bringing up someone else's child' is appropriate for only a proportion of foster home placements. Assessment, treatment, relief care and preparation of young people for independent living are all tasks being undertaken by foster-parents who are caring for children of all ages and with a wide range of problems and handicaps. This means that there is an even greater need for clarity about the division of responsibility and who should carry the parental role. This article attempts to provide a descriptive analysis of the current situation.

New Concepts

Permanence

Almost certainly the most important and influential idea to be introduced in recent years is the concept of permanence planning. Concern about 'drift' in foster care was first articulated in the USA but was taken up here following the publication of Rowe and Lambert's *Children Who Wait* (1973). American and British studies showed that often children remain in foster care not from choice but from lack of any clear alternative, that they lose touch with their own family but have no legal security in any other family, and that the longer they stay in care the more likely they are to have a series of moves and many changes of social worker. Writers such as Anna Freud (1955), Kenneth Watson (1968), Marvin Bryce and Roger Ehlert (1971) have stressed the difficulty children have in reaching their full potential when living in 'limbo', uncertain where they will be living next year or who is ultimately responsible for them.

The idea of planning for permanence was first introduced in the UK by

Margaret McKay (1980), working with an area team in the Lothian region. It was developed by Margaret Adcock (1980) who has defined a permanent home as 'one which is intended to last and is given a legal security to make this possible'. McKay, Adcock and others concerned to offer greater security and commitment to children in long-term care have questioned the capacity of any local authority to be a satisfactory parent. They stress that emphasis on achieving a permanent home for every child leads to greater efforts to achieve speedy rehabilitation to the natural family and, if this fails, to consideration of adoption. Since fostering has no legal base, its security is doubtful and its suitability for children needing really long-term care is questioned by those advocating permanence.

The effect of introducing permanence planning in a local authority department has been vividly described by Chris Hussell and Bernard Monaghan (1982) who wrote about their experience in Lambeth. They set out the following objectives:

1   No child should spend the major part of his or her childhood in care. As a target, no child who comes into care under the age of ten shall remain in care for more than two years.
2   Priorities in making plans for children who come into care are:
• rehabilitation with their natural families;
• placement in a permanent substitute family.

Hussell and Monaghan went on to explain:

> Let us be clear, firstly, what the approach is and is not about. Primarily and crucially it is about stopping children slipping into long-term care. It is there-fore as much to do with good-quality imaginative, preventive and rehabili-tation work, as with permanent separation. It is not the operation of an 'adoption mafia' nor is it a management tool for saving money.

Definitions

Interest in preventing drift and insecurity by firmer planning and clearer terminology has led to intensive work on definitions. The BAAF fostering project, which was set up to test possibilities of a fostering 'exchange' through which departments could exchange fostering resources, developed a sixfold classification based on the ultimate plan for the child. Other groups have worked on classifying the various types of substitute family care. This is more difficult than one might expect because several charac-teristics have to be taken into account and they overlap. There is first the too simple but necessary distinction based on length of stay; then the purpose of the placement must be considered as part of the overall plan for the child; and finally the immediate task of the placement needs to be identified. Thus a short-term placement may be part of a long-term plan and either a long- or short-term placement could have as its task the treatment of a specific child-centred problem. The important point is that each fostering placement should have a clearly defined and agreed purpose.

BASW's *Guidelines to Practice in Family Placement* (1982) include a helpful listing of types of placement forming a continuum with relief or holiday fostering at one end and adoption at the other. In between comes a range of foster homes including task-related and medium-term placements. The latter are thought to be the most 'disaster prone'. A BAAF working party developing plans for a comprehensive adoption service for London also worked on a classification of placements which would include length of stay, purpose and plan.

The relationship of adoption to fostering

New thinking about definitions and a realisation that fostering and adoption are both part of a range of substitute family placements has resulted in efforts being made to bring these two services together. Previously they were kept apart artificially as a result of historical developments and different legal bases. Many Social Services Departments now have a combined fostering and adoption service and there are a variety of patterns in the deployment of specialist staff each with advantages and disadvantages.

The BASW *Guidelines* question whether there should be any distinction in the assessment of foster- or adoptive parents and there is much current interest in joint adoption and fostering panels for the approval of applicants and placements. A BAAF Practice Note points out the advantages of joint decision making which allows for greater flexibility, and the new Boarding-Out Regulations (1988) set out in detail the arrangements required for the approval of applications to foster.

The introduction of schemes for payment of adoption allowances removes one of the main differences between adoption and fostering. In combination with S 29 of the Children Act 1975, giving foster parents of five years' standing the right to an adoption hearing, the provision of adoption allowances has made it possible for quite a number of long-term foster-parents to adopt. However, the fact that agencies cannot just decide to pay allowances but must put forward specific schemes for approval and review by the Secretary of State means that there are inevitable anomalies, with allowances available in some parts of the country but not in others. Research by Rowe *et al.* (1984) shows that the need for an allowance is a major factor in decisions about adoption by foster-parents, but by no means all foster-parents who could adopt wish to do so.

New projects

Specialist schemes

In the early and mid-1970s several authorities and voluntary societies launched imaginative new schemes for fostering special groups of children who could not easily be placed by the traditional methods, for example, teenagers, black children or those with special problems or handicaps. Most schemes were explicitly task centred. Instead of being asked to bring up the children as though they were their own, foster-parents in these projects were expected to provide a professional caring service for which they would receive payment over and above the normal boarding-out allowances which are only intended to reimburse costs. The first two schemes were started by Berkshire Social Services Department and the National Children's Home. Both aimed to provide care for children with special needs, problems and handicaps. Next came respite care schemes for short-stay fostering of mentally handicapped children. These were developed in Leeds and Somerset, and a number of other authorities have now taken up the idea with considerable success.

However, much the most influential new development was Kent's special family placement project for difficult and delinquent adolescents. This was based on the Swedish model of community care for adolescents and stressed normalisation, individualisation and participation. It involved some radical changes of attitude and practice. Right from its inception, this scheme 'took off' and caught public and professional attention. This was due in part to the dynamism and enthusiasm of its leader, Nancy Hazel (1981), but also because Social Services Departments were increasingly disenchanted with the low success rate of community homes with education while the proportion of teenagers in care was continuing to rise.

During the past decade many authorities have started specialist schemes. Others, while also seeking to place the same categories of children, have preferred to put their energies and resources into fostering 'across the board'. They object to the potentially divisive system of specialist or professional foster-parents.

The main emphasis of special schemes has been on placing adolescents. A survey by Shaw and Hipgrave (1983) showed that out of 67 local authorities (outside London) which replied to a postal questionnaire, 50 had at least one specialist scheme and of these 42 included delinquent or disturbed teenagers – in fact, about half the projects were limited to teenagers. Most such schemes are small scale, involving not more than ten to twelve foster-parents at any one time and often fewer than this. Workers involved in these placements tend to be enthusiastic about them. Shaw and Hipgrave found that 75 per cent of their respondents considered their success rate high or very high. This is confirmed by Thomas (1982) and in the evaluation by Yelloly (1979) of the first twenty-five placements made by Kent which also showed an encouraging improvement in the young people who had been through the scheme, even if not all the placements had lasted as long as expected.

'Permanent fostering'

The special fostering projects mentioned above all relate to short or medium-length placements. At the other end of the time scale are projects to provide permanent substitute families. These are usually based in special placement units within local authorities or in specialist agencies run by voluntary societies. Among the best known of these are Barnardo's 'New Families Projects', 'Parents for Children', The Children's Society's 'The Child Wants a Home' and the Independent Adoption Service. Most of these projects emphasise adoption as providing the greatest security, but where adoption is impossible or inappropriate some use what they call 'permanent fostering', in which everything possible is done within the limits of a fostering placement to ensure and enhance the feeling of security and mutual commitment of child and family. Though small in scale, these projects have an effect on social work thinking by providing an alternative to traditional, open-ended, long-term fostering placements. The emphasis on permanence sharpens perceptions about what can and should be done to offer security within the framework of fostering as well as through adoption.

Some important current issues

Service to natural parents

Conspicuous by its absence in most discussions of foster care is any adequate consideration of work with natural parents. American research by Fanshel and Shinn (1978) and by Shirley Jenkins and Elaine Norman (1972) revealed a woeful lack of service to the child's family, and similar findings have emerged in this country in reports by Aldgate (1980) and by Rowe *et al.* (1984) and from unpublished work by Thorpe (1974).

One of the benefits of planning for permanence is the urgency and emphasis it brings to providing service to natural parents which will enable them to resume care of their children before the latter put down roots elsewhere and develop bonds with psychological parents. Agencies which work hard to achieve permanence report a significant increase in rehabilitation of children to their natural families. American experience and new approaches to work with natural parents can be studied in collections of papers edited by Anthony Maluccio and Paula Sinanoglu and published by the Child Welfare League of America (1981, 1982).

Access by parents to their children in foster care

Access is an emotive and immensely complex subject, and strongly held views are often based on ambiguous evidence. Studies by Aldgate (1980) and Millham *et al.* (1986) in the UK and by Fanshel and Shinn (1978) in the United States show that the maintenance of close contact with their families is the best indication that children will leave care rapidly. The association between parental visiting and emotional adjustment of children in long-term care is less clear cut. Millham *et al.* found that children and adolescents functioned better psychologically, socially and educationally if they remained in contact with their birth families.

Fanshel and Shinn advocate visiting but their research showed that the day-to-day behaviour of foster-children being visited by their parents was more difficult than the behaviour of those who were not visited. However, the emotional adjustment of the visited children was better. The complexity of the issues is highlighted by Rowe *et al.* in their book *Long-Term Foster Care* (1984).

Almost all research studies on children in care have emphasised the strong risk that children in care for more than a few weeks will lose touch with their parents and relatives. (Only a minority of long-term foster-children ever see their parents.) It is now abundantly clear that parents have faced not only explicit limitations or even prohibitions on visiting (e.g. no visiting in the early weeks to let the child settle), but also implicit restrictions (e.g. distance, lack of encouragement and support in initiating visits, limitations on days and times for visits). In spite of the prevailing belief that visits are beneficial, too little has been done in practice to grapple with the immense practical and psychological problems involved.

Welcome exceptions to this rather gloomy picture are the *Guide for Parents with Children in Care* by Parents Aid in Harlow, Essex, which contains useful practical advice to parents; two training films, *The Visit* and *Its Like a Bereavement*, made by and available from Barnardo's film unit; the BAAF training pack *Working with Parents*; and a booklet by the Family Rights Group, *Promoting Links: Keeping Children and Families in Touch*.

Emphasis on permanence and the need to give first consideration to the child's needs led an increasing number of Social Services Departments to consider ending parental contact when this seemed necessary in order to protect children from distress or disturbance or to make possible a permanent plan for their future. Some sad and well-publicised cases then created concern that access was being terminated insensitively and sometimes unnecessarily. This led in turn to a change in the law and to the publication of a statutory code of practice on access to children in care. This code is essential reading for social workers and child care staff.

Black children

There has been an unfortunate tendency to lump black children together with those who are handicapped and disturbed and to label them all 'hard to place'. Another problem is that foster- and adoptive families for black children have so often been white. As the 1976 'Soul Kids' project showed (ABAFA, 1977), white social workers are handicapped in knowing how best to approach prospective black foster-parents, and black families find the bureaucracy of Social Services Departments particularly difficult and off-putting. In South London, the New Black Families Unit had an all black staff. Hopes that it might be the first of a network of specialist agencies providing services to black children in care have not been realised. However, some fostering units, like those in the London Boroughs of Ealing and Lambeth, have shown that if the right methods are used black families *can* be found even by white staff.

In the black community, concern is growing about the placement of its children in white homes, and quite clearly there are social, political and ethical problems which have to be addressed. There are fears that black children raised in white homes will have difficulties later on, that their identity will be confused, that they will be unable to meet the prejudice which they will encounter, and that if they have no models of black people in their lives they may lack faith in their own potential. Many Social Service Departments and voluntary child care agencies now have a policy of same race placements.

The identity problems of children of mixed racial heritage are as yet largely unexplored, and research into transracial placements is still inconclusive and limited. It has been largely concerned with the adoption of black infants into white families. Few such children are yet adult, but studies such as *Adoption and Race* by Owen Gill and Barbara Jackson (1983) conclude that black children adopted into white families are brought up as white. Even though the children they studied were doing well in their mid-teens, Gill and Jackson urged recruitment of black families wherever possible.

The relationship of residential care and family care

The promotion of fostering is often seen as a denigration of residential care and residential social workers often have reason to feel that the easiest and most rewarding children are removed to foster homes while they have to deal with distress and disturbance following fostering breakdowns and with youngsters who are considered 'too difficult to place'. Part of the problem is that many children in residential care are placed there inappropriately and there has been no adequate study or classification of which children need the specialised services which sound residential care can offer.

There are some encouraging signs that joint efforts to help children to come to terms with their past and to prepare them for life in a new family have begun to break down some traditional barriers between field and residential social workers. Like so many new developments, these seem to be starting mainly in the voluntary agencies. John Fitzgerald, Bill Murcer and Brenda Murcer (1982) have written about their pioneering work at St Luke's run by the Children's Society, and Joan Fratter, Daphne Newton and David Shinegold (1982) have described the philosophy and services provided at Barnardo's Cambridge Cottage. In both agencies residential staff have a key role in direct work with the child.

These initiatives pointed the way and several other 'preparation' establishments have now been set up. But in spite of these steps forward the main task of integrating the two parts of the child care service has scarcely yet begun. If knowledge, skills and resources are to be appropriately used, urgent steps will have to be taken to remedy this situation.

Looking forward

Although there is a great deal to be done before the main body of foster care work approaches the level of the best current practice, there are some encouraging signs as this chapter has already noted. The improvement in *planning* for children is probably the most important step forward, though the development of special placement schemes is also of great significance. More and better work is being done to prepare foster-families and to support them later. The National Foster Care Association's excellent training materials are widely used and are beginning to bear fruit.

Even though more difficult children are being placed, breakdown or 'disruption' rates appear to be somewhat better than in the past, though working out a breakdown rate is complex and potentially misleading and there is wide variation between departments (Berridge and Cleaver, 1987).

Now that foster homes are being used for assessment, for respite care for the handicapped, and for 'bridging' adolescents into independence, foster-parents' special skills are better recognised and used. However, because of dissatisfaction with local authority services, some groups of experienced foster-parents are setting themselves up as independent family placement organisations. This trend may well increase.

The 1988 Boarding-Out Regulations stress the development of a fostering service rather than individual placement decisions which are left to professional judgement supported by Department of Health guidance. The Regulations should have considerable effect on the way foster homes are developed and deployed, and the emphasis on written agreements should be a real impetus toward a more participatory style and improved communication.

In the next decade long-term fostering, which has been the backbone of the traditional foster care service, will feature less prominently. Many of the young people currently in such placement will 'age out' of the system and few young children are now going into long-term foster homes. Considerable numbers of teenagers are found to be in need of family placement, but they need a different style of fostering from the traditional long-term foster-family for young children.

As a cumulative result of these changes, it may well be that the ferment which at present affects only the edges of the service will spread inward and that the solid core of traditional fostering will also be transformed.

Note

This article is based on a pamphlet by Jane Rowe published by BAAF in 1983 and now updated.

References

(1977) *Soul Kids*, a report of the Soul Kids Campaign, London, ABAFA.

ADCOCK, M. (1980) 'The right to permanent placement' *Adoption and Fostering*, Vol. 4, No. 1, pp. 21–24.

ALDGATE, J. (1980) 'Identification of factors influencing children's length of stay in care', in Triseliotis, J. (ed.) *New Developments in Foster Care and Adoption*, London, Routledge and Kegan Paul.

BRITISH ASSOCIATION OF SOCIAL WORKERS (1982) *Guidelines for Practice in Family Placement*, London, BASW.

BERRIDGE, D. and CLEAVER, H. (1987) *Foster Home Breakdown*, Oxford, Blackwell.

BRYCE, M. and EHLERT, R. (1971) '144 foster children', *Child Welfare*, Vol. 5, No. 9, pp. 499–503.

FAMILY RIGHTS GROUP (1986) *Promoting Links: Keeping Children and Families in Touch*, London, FRG.

FANSHEL, D. and SHINN, E. (1978) *Children in Foster Care*, Columbia, University of Columbia Press.

FITZGERALD, J. (1979) 'After disruption', *Adoption and Fostering*, Vol. 3, No. 4, pp. 11–16.

FITZGERALD, J., MURCER, B. and MURCER, B. (1982) *Building New Families through Adoption and Fostering*, Oxford, Blackwell.

FRATTER, J., NEWTON, D. and SHINEGOLD, D. (1982) *Cambridge Cottage Prefostering and Adoption Unit*, Barnardo's Papers, No. 16.

FREUD, A. (1955) *Safeguarding the Emotional Health of our Children*, Child Welfare League of America.

GILL, O. and JACKSON, B. (1983) *Adoption and Race*, London, Batsford/BAAF.

HAZEL, N. A. (1981) *Bridge to Independence*, Oxford, Blackwell.

HUSSELL, C. and MONAGHAN, B. (1982) 'Child care planning in Lambeth', *Adoption and Fostering*, Vol. 6, No. 2, pp. 21–27.

JENKINS, S. and NORMAN, E. (1972) *Filial Deprivation and Foster Care*, Columbia, University of Columbia Press.

JENKINS, S. and NORMAN, E. (1975) *Beyond Placement: Mothers View Foster Care*, Columbia, University of Columbia Press.

MALUCCIO, A. and SINANOGLU, P. (1981) *The Challenge of Partnership Working with Parents of Children in Foster Care*, Child Welfare League of America.

MALUCCIO, A. and SINANOGLU, P. (1982) *Parents of Children in Placement Perspectives and Programs*, Child Welfare League of America.

McKAY, M. (1980) 'Planning for permanent placement', *Adoption and Fostering*, Vol. 4, No. 1, pp. 19–24.

MILLHAM, S., BULLOCK, R. and HOSIE, K. (1986) *Lost in Care*, Aldershot, Gower.

PARENTS AID (1982) *Guide for Parents with Children in Care*, Harlow, Essex.

ROWE, J. and LAMBERT, L. (1973) *Children Who Wait*, London, ABAFA.

ROWE, J., HUNDLEBY, M. and GARNETT, I. (1989) *Child Care Placements: Patterns and Outcomes*, London, BAAF.

ROWE, J., KEANE, A., HUNDLEBY, M. and CAIN, H. (1984) *Long-Term Foster Care*, London, Batsford/BAAF.

SHAW, M. and HIPGRAVE, T. (1983) *Specialist Fostering*, London, Batsford/BAAF.

THOMAS, J. (1982) *Survey of Special Fostering Schemes in London*, London Boroughs Children's Regional Planning Committee.

THORPE, R. (1974) 'The social and psychological situation of the long term foster child with regard to his natural parents', unpublished Ph.D. thesis, University of Nottingham.

WATSON, K. (1968) 'Long-term foster care: default or design?' *Child Welfare*, Vol. 47, No. 6, pp. 331–338.

YELLOLY, M. (1979) *Independent Evaluation of 25 Placements*, Kent Social Services Department.

10 Services for under fives: current provision in context and a glossary of terms

Gillian Pugh

Services for children under five in Britain have never been very high on the national agenda. Despite some interesting initiatives in recent years, levels of provision show considerable variation between one part of the country and another, and are seldom seen as adequate by local families. Day nurseries, family centres, nursery schools and classes, playgroups and childminders are provided by different agencies for different groups of children, and reflect different philosophical and ideological bases. This chapter traces in outline the historical development of these services, considers current levels of provision and looks at the arguments for developing a more co-ordinated approach to the provision of services. A glossary of terms used to describe services is given in Appendix 1. [. . .]

There is no statutory obligation on local authorities to provide pre-school services, and as a result services over the country have developed in a haphazard and unco-ordinated way, and are often in short supply. The fragmented system of pre-school provision, and the philosophies upon which different types of provision are based, have to be seen in a historical context. The evolution and development of the welfare state has been based on an assumption that few families are able to meet all of their own needs. Child health services have adopted an 'open-access' approach for the physical care of all children and families, but there has not been the same level of consensus as to how the state should provide for the social, emotional and intellectual development of young children, nor indeed for the support of their parents.

A brief resumé of the main developments in services reveals four main strands of provision: one concerned with the developmental needs of children and based on principles of free and universally available service; one more interventionist in nature, based on a rigorous selection process, and concerned with the ability of parents to cope with the upbringing of their children; one responding to parents' requirements for day care; and one emanating from the voluntary sector and based on principles of self-help and parent involvement.

The historical perspective

Education

Since the origins of free nursery education in the early years of the twentieth century, successive governments have supported the principle of nursery education, but have seldom found the resources to fund it. Legislation has been permissive rather than mandatory and for many years following the Hadow report (1933) the emphasis was on the physical and moral development of working-class children. The Plowden report (CACE, 1967) accepted for the first time the principle of nursery education on demand, recommending that it should not start until the age of three, and should be part time, on the grounds that a whole day away from home was inadvisable for young children. The 1972 White Paper *Education: A Framework for Expansion* (DES, 1972) accepted the report and recommended the provision of nursery education for 50 per cent of three-year-olds and 90 per cent of four-year-olds. Subsequent cuts in government expenditure meant that this vision was short lived. The 1980 Education Act went further, removing from local authorities any obligation to provide nursery education, and emphasising the discretionary nature of the service. The only statutory requirements upon LEAs for children under five are those imposed by the 1981 Education Act, whereby local authorities have a duty to identify, assess and provide for children under five with special needs, taking into account the views of parents.

Current levels of provision are given in Table 10.1. Apart from an increase in the number of places over all, the two main trends are from full-time to part-time places, and from nursery schools to nursery classes in infant and primary schools. More detailed LEA statistics (DES, 1986) reveal considerable variations between authorities, with nursery education provided for 66 per cent of three- and four-year-olds in Hounslow, whilst in eighteen LEAs fewer than one in ten of children under five gets a place in a nursery class.

Limited resources, mainly provided via the Urban Aid programme, and an emphasis during the 1960s on the role of nursery education in compensating for the perceived inadequacies of some children's homes and families, have resulted in much of the expansion being in inner-city areas. It has not always succeeded in reaching many of those for whom it was intended however (Osborn and Milbank, 1987), not least because it does not attempt to meet the needs of families where both parents work. Osborn's research also reveals that the shortfall in nursery provision has led to local authority institutions (both nursery classes and day nurseries) accommodating disproportionate numbers of children from families experiencing difficulties.

One response by LEAs to the shortfall in nursery education has been to admit children into reception classes during the year in which they become five, so that there are now almost as many children under five in reception classes as in nursery classes (see Tables 10.1 and 10.2). Although children, for many years, have been admitted as 'rising fives' in the term before their fifth birthday, the majority of LEAs have now moved towards a single point of entry – often the beginning of the school year in which the child becomes five (Sharp, 1987). This in effect means that a considerable number of children are now starting full-time school when they are just four. Differences in policies between LEAs also means that there may be up to sixteen months' difference in when a child starts school, depending on where he or she lives.

Playgroups

A second response during the early 1960s was the emergence, through the voluntary sector, of the playgroup movement. Over the last twenty-five years the number of playgroups has grown to the point where they now provide for at least 35 per cent of three- and four-year-olds (see Tables 10.1 and 10.2). The voluntary nature of many of the groups, and their dependence on fund-raising activities and grants (if they can get them) to cover running costs and minimal wages, means that sessional fees have to be charged to parents. This, and the fact that they are predominantly to be found in areas in which there is little nursery education, has tended to give them an exclusively middle-class image which is only slowly changing. Like nursery education, playgroups are also of limited use to working parents. Although currently registered by Social Service Departments, the educational focus of much of their work led the House of Commons Education, Science and Arts Committee Report, *Achievement in Primary Schools* (1986), to recommend that this function should be taken over by LEAs.

Day care

The history of day nurseries also reflects a response to social and economic factors rather than a coherent approach to services for under fives. The national need for women to work in the factories during the Second World War had led to an expansion of day nurseries, under the responsibility of the Ministry of Health. Following the war, however, the publication of a circular, influenced by the views of Bowlby and Winnicott on the importance of the mother–child bond, led to an immediate reversal of this trend:

> The ministers concerned accept the view of medical and other authorities that, in the interest of health and development of the child no less than for the benefit of the mother, the proper place for a child under two is at home with his mother. They are also of the opinion that, under normal peace-time conditions, the right policy to pursue would be positively to discourage mothers of children under two from going out to work; to make provision for children of between two and five by way of nursery schools and nursery classes; and to regard day nurseries and day guardians as supplements to meet special needs. (Ministry of Health, 1945)

Although legislation *requires* local authorities to register private and voluntary child care services (1948 Nurseries and Childminders Regulation Act), and to 'promote the welfare of children by diminishing the need to receive them into care' (1980 Child Care Act), they are only *empowered* (under the 1977 NHS Act) to provide day nurseries or to subsidise childminding or playgroups (1980 Act). Unlike nursery education, they may charge for places. Recent research has shown that shortage of places and subsequent tightening of admission procedures mean that most local authorities 'have moved from a position where day nurseries were seen as a potential pre-school resource for all children, to one where there is a financial, social or medical reason to necessitate admission' (Van der Eyken, 1984). Day care nurseries are often seen as central to an SSD's preventive work with families 'at risk', and as such a stigma tends to attach to those who are offered places. Many day nurseries, in altering the focus of their work, are changing their name to 'family centre'.

As in education, so in day care the short-fall in statutory provision has been met by a response from the voluntary and private sectors: private and community day nurseries, a few work-place nurseries and, principally, childminders. Table 10.1 shows a considerable increase in the number of registered minders over the last ten years (although this may reflect more minders registering rather than an increase in minders *per se*). Whilst childminding was at one time promoted as low-cost day provision (see DHSS/DES, 1976), recent studies have shown that the training and support required by childminders, if they are to provide good quality day care, make it a rather more expensive option to the local authority than was at first envisaged (Ferri and Birchall, 1987; Smith, 1987).

Health services

The health service – the only service which is universally available to this age group – is beset by its own problems of lack of co-ordination, particularly between the 'preventive' and 'curative' aspects of the service. The Court report (Committee on Child Health Services, 1976) reviewed the three main component parts of the child health service – the community health service, provided by health visitors and the school health service, and answerable to health authorities; primary health care, provided by general practitioners and administered by local practitioner committees; and the hospital service – and recommended a service 'increasingly orientated to prevention'. Ten years on from Court, a recent review found that this recommendation was a long way from full implementation and that preventive child health services were delivered differently in each district in the country (National Children's Bureau, 1987). The report recognised the key role of the health visitor in preventive health care, but also noted the continuing reluctance of many GP's to see surveillance as central to their role.

Current levels of service provision

A summary of current levels of provision in day care, playgroups and schools is given in Table 10.1, and the number of places per 100 children (or percentage of children in education statistics) is given in Table 10.2. As can be seen from the notes to the tables, there are considerable difficulties in both collecting and interpreting statistics for pre-school provision and, although the figures are taken from officially published sources, some care should be taken in how they are used. One obvious difficulty is that a child may attend two or even three types of provision, whilst one place (and this is particularly true of playgroups) may be shared by two or more children. Nevertheless, the figures do give an approximate picture of current levels of provision, and of trends over the last ten years.

As indicated earlier, national statistics obscure the very striking differences between local authorities, and these details can be found in the sources given below the tables. It should also be noted that statistical returns have not yet been amended to pick up some of the less clearly defined types of pre-school service, notably family centres and combined nursery centres. Neither are there any reliable figures for community nurseries or work-place nurseries (which are both subsumed within the private day nursery figures), or for parent and toddler groups (which do not have to be registered).

Overall, approximately 85 per cent of children of three and four experience some form of pre-school provision, most of it part time and some of it in primary school classes which may not be staffed and equipped for younger children. Facilities for those under three, and full-day care places for all ages, are in very short supply, catering for less than 6 per cent of children under five. In Britain, the number of women with children under five who work is comparatively low compared to most of our European neighbours and the United States – some 6 per cent working full time, and 28 per cent part time (OPCS, 1986) – and difficulty in finding appropriate day care is seen as a major contributory factor. Bone's survey of 2,500 mothers of pre-school children (Bone, 1977) found that some form of nursery place was wanted for 90 per cent of three- and four-year-olds, as well as 46 per cent of children under three. Other surveys confirm these findings (see Hughes *et al.*, 1980), and a recent survey in all the London boroughs (GLC, 1985) concluded that their provision (which is relatively extensive by comparison to some other parts of the country) would have to be increased by 60 per cent to meet the lowest estimates of unmet demand. The number of full-time places would have to be doubled to meet the needs of mothers currently at work.

From this summary of developments in services for young children and their families, it is possible to see that provision has tended to respond to prevailing political and economic factors rather than to a carefully formulated and sustained policy. Britain lacks a common philosophy about what services should be provided by whom and for whom; and with what overall

Table 10.1 Number of places for children under five in day care and playgroups and number of pupils in schools, 1985 (1975 figures in brackets)[1]

	England	Scotland	Wales	Total[2]
Childminders: places	126,847 (85,616)	7,470 (1,010)	4,506 (1,336)	138,832 (87,962)
LA day nurseries: places	28,904 (25,992)	3,830 (3,500)	230 (62)	32,964 (29,554)
Private registered day nurseries: places	25,242 (25,893)	246 (420)	1,013 (1,183)	26,501 (27,496)
Playgroups: places[3]	409,379 (330,782)	43,860 (46,220)	20,021 (14,742)	473,260 (391,744)
Nursery schools				
Pupils Full time	11,890 (13,740)	2,908 (2,833)	1,387 (1,477)	
Part time	37,723 (29,777)	34,959 (17,629)	2,737 (2,975)	
Total	49,613 (43,517)	37,867 (20,462)	4,124 (4,452)	
Schools with nursery classes[4]				
Pupils Full time	30,473 (23,925)		30,814 (9,776)	
Part time	186,850 (70,476)		15,353 (4,788)	
Total	217,323 (94,401)		46,167 (14,564)	
Total: nursery schools and classes, full time and part time	266,936 (137,918)	37,867 (20,462)	(19,016)	
Reception classes[5]				
Pupils Full time	226,936 (246,717)	11,500 (7,989)	(24,309)	(279,015)
Part time	18,695 (19,251)	—	(184)	(19,435)
Total	245,631 (265,968)	11,500 (7,989)	(24,493)	(298,450)
Independent schools				
Pupils Full time	17,987 (17,463)	1,091 (1,144)	489[6]	19,567 (18,607)
Part time	14,094 (12,603)	—	113[6]	14,207 (12,603)
Total	32,081 (30,066)	1,091 (1,144)	602	33,774 (31,210)

Table 10.2 Places per 100 children under five in day care and playgroups, and percentages of pupils in education, 1985 (1975 figures in brackets)

	England	Scotland	Wales	Total
Childminders				
Places per 100: 0–4 years	4.26 (2.65)	2.30 (0.30)	2.54 (0.70)	4.00 (2.30)
LA day nurseries				
Places per 100: 0–4 years	1.00 (0.80)	1.20 (0.90)	0.13 (0.03)	0.95 (0.78)
Private registered day nurseries				
Places per 100: 0–4 years	0.85 (0.87)	0.08 (0.11)	0.58 (0.60)	0.76 (0.72)
Playgroups				
Places per 100: 3- and 4-year-olds	33.80 (23.30)	33.10 (28.00)	28.50 (17.40)	34.10 (23.60)
Nursery schools and classes				
Pupils as % of 3- and 4-year-olds	22.50 (10.00)	28.50 (12.40)	71.50 (61.90)	
Reception classes				
Pupils as % of 3- and 4-year-olds	20.70 (18.90)	8.70 (4.90)		
Independent schools				
Pupils as % of 3- and 4-year-olds	2.50	0.76	2.50	2.40
Total population aged 0–4 years	2,973,400 (3,227,900)	325,000 (375,700)	177,200 (194,700)	3,475,600 (3,798,300)

Notes:
1. Statistics need to be treated with some caution. Just as there may be children sharing a place (see playgroups), so there are some children who use more than one facility. Figures for schools are for numbers of children; other facilities give figures for numbers of places. Percentages of pupils, or places per 100 children, are given for ages 0–4 years for day care, and for 3- and 4-year-olds for playgroups and schools. There are some 2-year-olds in schools and playgroups.
2. Some figures cannot be added as the statistics from England and Wales are not comparable (see 4 and 5).
3. PPA estimate 1.8 children per place, in which case about 772,920 children attended playgroups in England and Wales, or 61 per cent of 3- and 4-year olds.
4. Figures for Scotland do not distinguish between children in nursery schools and classes.
5. Figures for Wales do not distinguish between children in nursery classes and children under five in reception classes.
6. With England.

Sources: DES (1986) *Statistical Bulletin 10/86: Pupils Under Five Years in Each Local Education Authority in England, January 1985* HMSO: DHSS: DHSS (1987) *Children's Day Facilities 31 March 1985, England*, DHSS; Scottish Education Department, Social Work Services Group (1986) *Statistical Bulletin: Home Care Services, Day Care Establishments and Day Services 1985*, Scottish Education Department; Welsh Office (1986) *Activities of Social Service Departments, Year Ending 1985*, Welsh Office. Office of Population Censuses and Surveys (1986) *OPCS Monitor PPI 86/1*, HMSO: Welsh Office (1986) *Statistics of Education in Wales Vol 11*, Welsh Office.

aims. Despite well-intentioned reports, services remain low status and underresourced, and the different histories and perspectives they embody tend to reinforce the existing divide between education and care. This is reflected not only in the services themselves, but in the different traditions, approaches, training and language of those who work in them.

As far as the needs of children are concerned, there can be few today who would dispute the fact that some form of pre-school experience is likely to be of value to most children. The first long-term British study on the effects of pre-school provision has recently concluded:

> Therefore our assertion is that adequate pre-school provision can improve the quality of life of young children, and their families; this conviction is given further support by the evidence we have presented that pre-school education will in most circumstances aid the child's development, increase his educational potential and in the long run his overall performance. (Osborn and Milbank, 1987)

There is rather less agreement however on whether parents have a right to day care for their children, and on the implications of an equal opportunities employment policy. The Equal Opportunities Commission (Cohen and Clarke, 1986) argues that as long as the care of children is seen as the personal responsibility of mothers, rather than a social responsibility to be shared between both parents, and between parents and others, women will continue to be at a severe disadvantage relative to men. Some call specifically for state-funded provision (see, for example, New and David, 1985), but the fact that such a small proportion of families is currently able to use state-funded or regulated day care services suggests that this view has been translated into neither policy nor practice.

The co-ordination debate

Over the last fifteen years 'co-ordination' has been a recurring theme in most reports and circulars on services for under fives. While some have argued that improving the co-ordination of services is no substitute for increasing provision, there are nevertheless sound arguments for making better use of existing resources, and for providing services that can respond flexibly to the needs of young children and their parents. As services have come to shift their focus from working with the child in isolation to looking at the needs of the child within the family, so there has been a growing recognition that no one agency can respond to all of those needs. Services cannot operate in isolation, and there can be few professionals who have nothing to learn from the skills and expertise of others.

What exactly is meant by co-ordination is rather less clear from some of the earlier publications in which the concept features. The approach of government is a case in point. The fact that pre-school services are provided at the discretion of local authorities creates particular difficulties for central government if it wishes services to develop in particular ways. The

1972 White Paper *Education: A Framework for Expansion* (DES, 1972) illustrated this difficulty when it *advised* that:

> in preparing for the expansion of nursery education, local authorities will need to take account of other facilities for under fives, existing or planned, so as to prepare for a scheme for their area in which nursery classes and schools, voluntary playgroups, day nurseries and other forms of day care all play their part.

Simply encouraging LEAs to 'take account of other facilities' was unlikely to amount to a very substantial increase in joint planning.

The White Paper was followed in 1976 and 1978 by two circulars, published jointly by the DHSS and DES and specifically concerned with the co-ordination of services for children under five. Both were again advisory in tone, the first looking at administrative arrangements for joint planning (though not necessarily joint management) of services, and the second at developments in practice. Neither defined exactly what they meant by co-ordination. The 1976 circular described two of the main aims of the co-ordinating machinery as 'to encourage contact at working level' and 'to create a situation in which the various departments and agencies (statutory and voluntary) concerned with under fives can exchange information, discuss common problems and improve their co-ordination' (DHSS/DES, 1976). The 1978 circular urged local authorities 'through the co-ordination of all available services to make maximum use of existing resources' and stressed a 'continuing need for the co-ordination of development plans' (DHSS/DES, 1978).

A number of working party reports and discussion papers were published at about this time (for example, Tizard *et al.*, 1976; ACC/AMA, 1977; TUC, 1978; CPRS, 1978; Challis, 1980), each with a slightly different perspective on what the main barriers to a co-ordinated service were, and what kind of structure could best remove them. The most detailed study was a two-year research project commissioned by the DES and DHSS into the arrangements and procedures for co-ordination of services. The subsequent report (Bradley, 1982) provides a useful insight into the varied and complex nature of the problem. Bradley looked at structures for planning and managing services, including the introduction of sub-committees and advisory committees with responsibility for under fives; at personnel; at policy issues; and at procedures for co-ordination. He saw co-ordination not as a panacea, but as 'involving a reappraisal of the attitudes of personnel towards one another, seeking jointly to perceive the goals of services in relation to the needs of children and their families while accepting the existence of each type of provision as a separate entity'.

Bradley sought to locate co-ordination on a continuum which goes from dissociation, through separation, domination, liaison, co-operation, coalition, and federation, to unification. Of these, he suggests that 'federation, implying separate sectors working together each accepting the other's goals, and probably focusing upon the needs of the child and the family, comes nearest to the traditional and weakly defined view of co-ordination, and in some respects has to be seen as an ideal'. Federation suggests a planned rather than an *ad hoc* or random approach, in which the budgeting and organisation of services are agreed. Unification, on the other hand, where services have a single administration, is described as 'as much the opposite of co-ordination as is dissociation'.

The characteristics of successful co-ordination procedures are summarised as:

- clarity and simplicity of arrangements and procedures;
- representation for all those involved in service provision;
- the need for communication, consultation, negotiation and collaboration;
- accessibility of senior officers and elected members to practitioners;
- mutual awareness, respect and support between all groups and sectors involved (Bradley, 1982).

Most of the published reports have concentrated on co-ordination between Education and Social Services Departments, with some involvement from the voluntary sector. There appear to be even greater difficulties when attempts are made to include health service personnel in co-ordinated approaches. The only legal obligation to co-ordinate is in fact upon the health authority, although it is difficult to see how it can be enforced. The 1977 NHS Act, for example, refers several times to provisions for co-operation between health authorities, SSDs and LEAs, including the well-meaning words that 'in exercising their respective functions health authorities, family practitioner committees and local authorities shall co-operate with one another in order to secure and advance the health and welfare of the people of England and Wales'. A health authority is also legally obliged under the 1981 Education Act to inform the parent and the LEA if 'in the course of exercising any of its functions in relation to a child who is under the age of five years' it forms the opinion that a child has, or is likely to have, special educational needs. Hereafter heavy reliance is placed again on departmental advice, as in DES Circular 1/83 which emphasises that 'Co-operation between the LEA, SSD, DHA and voluntary bodies will be particularly important in relation to under-fives with special education needs so as to ensure that the best possible provision is made for the child.'

The issue of co-ordination has not been neglected in the last decade, but progress has seemed depressingly slow. Many commentators have pointed to a lack of government policy, inadequate funding, and an absence of leadership. If central government has no machinery for making joint decisions on under fives issues, local authorities ask how they can be expected to take up the challenges. Challis (1980) is not confident that there is an answer and suggests that even a government committee of inquiry would have little power: 'The consumers are, by and large, silent; the practitioners are guarding 'education' and 'care'; and the observers are not personally or institutionally powerful enough to force govern-ment's hand alone.'

There has been no government inquiry, but some progress 'on the ground', within local authorities.

Appendix 1   A glossary of terms

Child health clinics are run by health visitors and doctors as part of the DHA service for families. Health visitors offer routine child health surveillance, programmes of immunisation and general information and advice. Other services may include antenatal groups, creches, parent and toddler groups, or visiting families at home.

Child development centres/assessment centres are for children with de-velopmental difficulties and are funded by DHAs. They can employ, co-opt or consult a range of professional staff, such as paediatricians, thera-pists, psychologists, psychiatrists, teachers, social workers, health visitors, medical officers, nursery nurses. Some centres offer only an assessment service; others also provide therapy and medical treatment.

Childminders look after up to three children under five in their own home, for all or part of the day. Childminding is usually a private arrangement between minder and parent, and fees will be negotiated between them. Childminders should be registered with and supported by the SSD. Some childminders are 'subsidised' or 'salaried' by the SSD, and may be called **day carers** or **day foster-parents**.

Combined nursery centres offer an integrated service to children from a few months to five years, combining day care and nursery education. Many also offer informal support such as parent and toddler groups, toy libraries, drop-in centres. They are usually open from 8 a.m. until 5 p.m. for most weeks of the years. Most are jointly funded and managed by the SSD and LEA

Crèches provide informal short-term group care for children while their parents attend courses or classes, or go shopping.

Day nurseries: SSD day nurseries provide day care on a full- or part-time basis for children from a few months to five years, and sometimes for their parents. As places are very scarce, most are given to children who need specialist help. A means-tested charge is usually made. Most are open from 8 a.m. to 6 p.m. for most of the year. **Private** and **voluntary nurseries** (including **community** and **workplace nurseries**) provide full or sessional care for children of parents who can afford the fees, and who satisfy admission criteria. They may be set up and managed by such as employers, parents, community groups, institutions, hospitals, organis-ations, etc.

Drop-in centres are usually part of a larger scheme or service (such as a family centre, school, clinic, or nursery) offering an informal facility for parents to 'drop in' with their children for a chat and a cup of tea.

Family centres: There is no commonly accepted definition of a family centre, though most offer a range of services to local families. However, five main types seem to be developing:

1   self-help family centres that have evolved from playgroups and other voluntary groups;
2   family centres set up in schools by LEAs;
3   family centres with a community work focus, often established by a voluntary organisation;
4   family centres funded by SSDs, many evolving from day nurseries;
5   therapeutic centres, working intensively with family groups, funded by SSD, DHA or the NSPCC.

Home visiting schemes: Educational home visitors are usually funded by LEAs and can be attached to infant and nursery schools, child guidance centres, special needs teams or adult education institutes. Some community-based home visiting schemes are funded in association with SSDs. In addition to specific schemes, many pre-school workers visit families in their homes. **Homestart** is a national network of voluntary home visiting schemes in which parent-volunteers visit families with young children who are experiencing difficulties. **Portage** projects (named after the American town where it originated) are home-based structured programmes for children with learning difficulties.

Nursery classes are attached to LEA infant or primary schools.

Nursery schools are separate LEA schools only taking under fives. Both have special staffing and facilities for three- to five-year-olds. Children generally attend part time. There are no fees, apart from lunch for full-time attenders.

Parent and toddler groups are small informal groups which offer play opportunities for children (usually under three), and companionship for their parents (who must accompany them). They are often linked to other forms of provision, such as schools, playgroups and clinics. In London some are based in parks and are known as **one o'clock clubs**.

Postnatal/antenatal support groups are similar to parent and toddler groups, but are intended for parents with young babies.

Playgroups offer informal, sessional care for children aged three to five, aiming to provide education through group play. Groups may be set up and run by parents, by staff employed in a local authority, or by a voluntary or private organisation. A small fee is usually charged. Some groups, known as **opportunity groups**, include a higher proportion of children with special needs than are found in other playgroups.

Playbuses are special buses converted to accommodate toys and equipment for a small playgroup, or parent and toddler group. These are often used where there is no permanent service or where outdoor play is restricted.

Reception classes in infant and primary schools: Although children are not obliged to start school until the term after their fifth birthday, many LEAs admit children into the reception class in the year following their fourth birthday. Staffing, equipment and curriculum are usually more appropriate to children over five. There are no fees, apart from lunch.

Toy libraries loan selected toys and equipment. Originally established for parents of children with special needs, many are now more widely available and some have been set up for childminders and playgroups. Some are run by parents; others by professionals as part of a larger service. Many provide an informal setting in which health care and assessment can be carried out.

References

ASSOCIATION OF COUNTY COUNCILS and ASSOCIATION OF METRO-POLITAN AUTHORITIES (1977) *Under Fives: A Local Authority Associations' Study*, Inter-Association Working Party – Provision for Under Fives, ACC/AMA.

BONE, M. (1977) *Pre-school Children and the Need for Day Care*, London, HMSO.

BRADLEY, M. (1982) *The Co-ordination of Services for Children Under Five*, NFER-Nelson.

CENTRAL ADVISORY COUNCIL FOR EDUCATION (1967) *Children and Their Primary Schools* (Plowden report), London, HMSO.

CENTRAL POLICY REVIEW STAFF (1978) *Services for Young Children with Working Mothers: A Report*, London, HMSO.

CHALLIS, L. (1980) *The Great Under Fives Muddle: Options for Day-Care Policy*, University of Bath, School of Humanities and Social Sciences.

COHEN, B. and CLARKE, K. (eds) (1986) *Childcare and Equal Opportunities: Some Policy Perspectives*, London, Equal Opportunities Commission.

COMMITTEE ON CHILD HEALTH SERVICES (1976) *Fit for the Future: Report of the Committee (Chairman: Prof. S. D. M. Court)* Cmnd. 6684, London, HMSO.

DEPARTMENT OF EDUCATION AND SCIENCE (1972) *Education: A Framework for Expansion*, London, HMSO.

DEPARTMENT OF EDUCATION AND SCIENCE (1986) *Statistical Bulletin 10/86: Pupils Under Five Years in Each Local Authority in England, January 1985*, London, HMSO.

DEPARTMENT OF HEALTH AND SOCIAL SECURITY and DEPART-MENT OF EDUCATION AND SCIENCE (1976) *Low Cost Day Provision for Under Fives: Papers from a Conference, Sunningdale Park, 1976*, London, DHSS/DES.

DEPARTMENT OF HEALTH AND SOCIAL SECURITY and DEPART-MENT OF EDUCATION AND SCIENCE (1978) *Co-ordination of Services for Children Under Five*, LASSL (78)1, London, DHSS.

FERRI, E. and BIRCHALL, D. (1987) *Changing Childminders*, Report to the DHSS, NCB.

GREATER LONDON COUNCIL (1985) *Research on Day Provision for the Under Fives: Final Report*, Women's Committee and Ethnic Minorities Committee, London, GLC.

HADOW, W. H. (1933) *Report on infant and nursery schools for the Consultative Committee of the Board of Education*, Board of Education.

HOUSE OF COMMONS (1986) *Achievement in Primary Schools Vol. 1: Report*, Education, Science and Arts Committee, London, HMSO.

HUGHES, M. *et al.* (1980) *Nurseries Now: A Fair Deal for Parents and Children*, Harmondsworth, Penguin.

MINISTRY OF HEALTH and MINISTRY OF EDUCATION (1945) *Nursery Provision for Children Under Five*, Circular 221/45, London, HMSO.

NATIONAL CHILDREN'S BUREAU (1987) *Investing in the Future: Child Health Ten Years after the Court Report*, Policy and Practice Review Group, London, NCB.

NEW, C. and DAVID, M. (1985) *For the Children's Sake: Making Childcare More than Women's Business*, Harmondsworth, Penguin.

OFFICE OF POPULATION CENSUSES AND SURVEYS (1986) *OPCS Monitor PPI 86/1*, London, HMSO.

OSBORN, A. and MILBANK, J. (1987) *The Effects of Early Education: A Report from the Child Health and Education Study*, Oxford, Clarendon Press.

SHARP, C. (1987) 'Local education authority admission policies and practices', in *Four Year Olds in School: Policy and Practice*, National Foundation for Educational Research/School Curriculum Development Committee.

SMITH, C. (compiler and editor) (1987) *Sponsored Childminding: a report of two seminars held in London and Newcastle*. National Childminding Association.

TIZARD, J. *et al.* (1976) *All our Children*, London, Temple Smith.

TRADES UNION CONGRESS (1978) *TUC Charter on Facilities for the Under-Fives*, London, TUC.

VAN DER EYKEN, W. (1984) *Day Nurseries in Action: A National Study of Local Authority Day Nurseries in England, 1975–1983: Final Report*, Department of Child Health Research Unit, University of Bristol.

11   Family centres

Bob Holman

Exploring family centres

Within the last three decades, the Children's Society has changed from a traditional child care voluntary which put most of its resources into residential care to one whose emphasis is on over fifty community-based activities. Their name – community projects and neighbourhood centres are examples – has varied but most are now called family centres and fit into the definition given by De'Ath:

> The phrase 'family centre' is increasingly being used as a generic term for any provision for parents and children where a range of services is offered to families living in a defined area and where the centre acts as a base for carrying out many of the activities. (De'Ath, 1985, pp. 7–8)

I had been the leader of the first centre established by the Children's Society and, after nine years, when a local resident took over as leader, it released me part time to study ten projects. A main objective was to identify the nature of their preventive work but the scope was broad enough to include an investigation of all the activities of the centres. My approach was to spend several days at each centre in order to observe what happened within their premises. More important, using a questionnaire, I recorded interviews with project staff, with users and with 'outsiders' who knew the centres, like local authority social workers and clergy-persons. This method did not constitute sophisticated research in which a representative sample of centres was chosen at random and evaluated by objective techniques of measurement. Rather, it was an attempt to convey, in the words of the participants, an account of what centres aim to do and what means they employ to reach their objectives.

Within the constraints of resources and time, the investigation had to concentrate on the family centres of just one voluntary agency. Obviously, other voluntary societies also run family centres and I have had the opportunity to visit some of them. Again some local authorities also possess family centres and as part of the study I went to ten of these, but the emphasis was on the voluntary sector. However, the voluntary centres cannot be regarded in a vacuum, separate from the world of local authorities, and hence later some comments will be made about the relationship between the two.

So what did the participants say about their family centres? Here there is space to present material from just three of the ten centres. Even within these, selections can be given from only one staff member, one user and one outsider, whereas in the full study interviews were conducted with nearly all staff, several users and two or three outsiders.

Baron's Close Young Family Centre

Located on the edge of a new town, the centre is run by eleven staff who see their activities as providing a 'specialised service to help families cope and stay together and enjoy their children'.

Project leader

Most families are referred to us through the SSD usually while at a crisis or despair point. We start at 9 o'clock in the morning. The children are all under five and are divided into three groups and their activities go on all the time. The parents go to a skills centre on Mondays, have general activities on Wednesdays and a health programme on Fridays. In addition on Tuesday afternoons we have a mums and toddlers group, which is one of the few activities which takes families not referred by the SSD.

The aim of the centre has always been preventive work. One of the hopes is that we will change the parents a little bit by making them into better parents and to help them to understand why their children do things that they do. We are a new town and there isn't mum or a familiar face around the corner. They haven't got anyone to turn to but they find friends here.

Families like this can benefit from the parents' groups here. Films on caring for children are very popular. The police have sometimes brought things like *Don't Talk to Strangers*. We go off on outings. Our best discussions are often in somewhere like the park. They talk about what it is like being with children on your own, what it's like not having any money, how nervous you are going into places and meeting people. People share terrific confidences as when they have beaten their children. They tell about how guilty they felt and couldn't talk to anybody and then somebody else will remember that they have done exactly the same and they can support one another.

I think the centre has helped many families. In one case a very depressed mum was living with a dad who got a four-year prison sentence for attempted manslaughter of the children. When he was inside, the mother found it very difficult to cope. So the children came to us two days a week and mum came on the third day and we kept this up for two years. At first, we had to collect mum to bring her in on the third day but gradually her confidence built up and in the end she was giving us a lot more than we were giving her. You don't get many pats on the back but one of our staff met mum recently at a workshops' meeting where this mum was actually speaking. This mum, whom everybody said was not fit to look after her children, was on the committee of the workshops and she said, 'I would never have coped without the help that the centre gave me', and I know that's true.

There are difficulties in the work. We just haven't got the space. And we went through a phase when some of the parents have said things like 'Oh I'm not going to let my child go there because that's where the battered children go.' Up until a short time ago we did take a mixture of children referred by the SSD and voluntary admissions and that gave a lovely balance. Now they are nearly all referred.

User

Me and my wife separated. She took three of the children and I was having problems looking after the other two. My girl came when she was three and she's just left. It really has got my girl ready for school. It learns them quite a lot like painting, slowly learning things, to speak properly. When I first brought her in she had problems with speech and it's brought her through and now she speaks pretty clear. If I didn't come here I wouldn't know where I was.

SSD area social work assistant manager

We fund so many places at the family centre and fund places not just for children but also for parents. In most cases there is an element of the child being at risk if not of physical abuse then certainly of neglect. Baron's Close is particularly good at work with parents who are not motivated. This is important in an area where there may be inadequate mums who are very young parents themselves but have not got the back-up of friends and relatives. They are also good with mothers who are on the defensive or who are aggressive. They offer a lot of care for the mothers and the children and their way of working is to offer a model which the mothers can follow.

In one case, we were very worried that a mother was not properly looking after a child. She was not accepted in her community and, because of violence in the home, the child was received into care a number of times. Originally the mother went to one of our local authority family centres some miles away but she could not settle. It was the authority thing and the image of local authority places as places for people who batter their kids. So she went to Baron's Close where we wanted the staff to help her cope with a three-year-old who was constantly having temper tantrums. The mother was accepted by the staff and she has accepted what they have to offer. It is still going well and further receptions into care have been averted.

Swansea Family Centre

After operating from previous sites, the present project started in 1985 based on the former co-op shop from which it serves two council estates. Full-time staff number four. An internal document states, 'It is with the aim of breaking a deprived cycle that we are placing a great emphasis on preventative social work.'

Project leader

We try to meet needs by the activities we run in the centre. There is a mothers and toddlers' group which consists of mums who refer themselves. We initiated social drama with the mums. The dramas have covered alcoholism, marital difficulties, sexual difficulties.

Then there are the playgroups which allow mothers to feel that they can leave their child and still feel secure while she goes shopping on her own. Also it gets children orientated to starting school. We do ask mothers to come and help at the playgroup on a rota and for some this prepares them to eventually run the playgroups.

The mother and toddler groups and playgroups prevent mothers reaching the stage or the crises where the family is likely to break up. Certainly we are seeing parents become more confident in the mothering role. Learning to cope with the demands that can sometimes break them. It is being able to mix with other mothers who can say, 'Oh mine was just like that when she was three weeks old.'

After-school clubs and a pre-adolescent group also meet here. They are mainly made up of children who just decide to join but sometimes we get referrals from the school. Some of these children behave negatively and the idea behind the clubs is to get them to come together into groups and so develop something more creative.

We have got fifty volunteers from early morning to the evening although we try to see that none do more than two and a half hours a week. They are nearly all local people and I have found that residents are much more willing to accept their own than they are outsiders. If there is anything I have learnt here it is the tremendous wealth of potential amongst local people. We do provide training which includes first aid, arts and craft, how to run a group, discipline and how to control yourself. We see people's self-esteem improve. Last week I asked a mother whether she would be prepared to be the prime leader in our after school club. And this woman is a single parent – her husband is away 'on holiday' as we say around here – who left school virtually at thirteen and was pregnant at sixteen.

User

I'm widowed with two children. The day my husband died, the vicar brought the project leader and she told me about the family centre. They had the children on the day of the funeral and then my son started going to the after-school club and my daughter to the day care. I've needed help with my son. Like if you mentioned fathers, he'd just go berserk. They know how to handle him at the centre. I think if he didn't come to this place he'd have had to go to a child psychologist he was so disturbed.

I became a volunteer, just doing playgroup first off but I do after-school club as well. When you're cleaning the house there's nobody to say, 'Well done, you've done something.' Here they do, they praise you when you've done a good job.

When I have my off-days I come over here. Everyone's so friendly and if you have got a problem there is always somebody here you can talk to. I have got a social worker although she doesn't come that often now. There's a lot of things I don't say to her. A social worker has their pad and you can't hold a conversation watching everything being jotted down. When you come here, you sit down and have a cup of tea and they listen.

SSD social worker

The staff in the centre are very committed and have a low turnover rate. Many people need to build a personal relationship before they can trust an institution and if there is a high turnover rate this is harmful. I've heard people mention particular names at the centre rather than the centre itself. It is particularly useful for new people going to the centre to have the reassurance from friends that there are people who can be trusted within the centre.

Many of the families because of their low self-image and because of the deprivations are not able to give their children the emotional and physical inputs that they should be getting. What we in the social services lack is that our provision tends to be all or nothing, either bringing children into care or leaving them at home. What we desperately need is intermediate provision so that children can remain at home. The family centre can often stimulate this. It is definitely the case that some children would otherwise be in care but have now been able to remain at home because of the centre.

Millmead Neighbourhood Centre

Opened in 1981, the centre is based in a council house on an estate on the edge of the town. There are two full-time staff members and the objective of the centre is stated as 'to improve the quality of life for children and families on the Millmead Estate'.

Project leader

I'll explain the main groups which use the centre. CHIPS stands for Community Help and Information Project. It is funded by Manpower Services and twice a week holds a surgery here. The local Citizens' Advice Bureau tends to have a very low profile and they are very traditional in outlook. If somebody rings up they give straight advice, say these are your rights, these are your responsibilities and leave it at that. CHIPS is much more relevant to people, is seen to be independent and covers the whole range of DHSS, housing, consumer and other problems. It takes cases up for people and gets results.

First Steps was a response to a small group of mums who wanted a facility for children aged under three. Instead of a standard mothers and toddlers' group they wanted one where they could leave their children but also have the opportunity to talk amongst themselves. So First Steps Playgroup was developed and we found volunteers to run it. Of the dozen mums, some have just joined themselves, some had it suggested by the health visitor and for one or two the social services put on a bit of pressure for them to come.

Centre Link is for three- to five-year-olds with an emphasis on helping families where there is neglect or threat of an injury to a child or very fraught family relationships. It was a response to parents saying we'd like something for the older age group and there were a couple of mums interested in running it.

Twilight Club is an after-school club for the six to twelves. It is run through Manpower Services at the local youth centre and twice a week we bus children there. Volunteers drive and one stays with the children there.

Some time back we drew together people who use the house into the House Group meetings. They give their views on how the house should be run, not only about whether the gate won't work but getting interested in each other's activities and in issues which affect the estate. They also discuss wider issues like the lack of facilities in the area and unemployment. It is not a decision-making body, it is an informal users' group. [The project leader then also described activities with teenagers, keep fit, adult literacy, Open University courses, Gingerbread and an after-school club.]

We have a community development philosophy. We are realistic in that we appreciate you are not going to change the world by encouraging mums to set up playgroups but we can point to the confidence that is built into mums who get involved. Over a period of time, the sorts of activities and involvement which we encourage will make people more aware of their surroundings and more able to cope with them and that is why we have put such a premium on local people volunteering.

I see our work in a pro-active way, in terms of encouraging things to happen rather than in what we are preventing. We are trying to encourage a good quality of life for people, to have more control over their lives, so that they have opportunities and choices. We see the problems of child abuse and neglect not in the traditional social work way of looking at bruises and burns but we look at the overall poor quality of life. We've got to look at indicators of deprivation and unemployment in this area and we want to change that.

We know that a small set-up like this can't magically give people £10,000 a year but we can do something to give them access to and control over more limited resources. So we do not see prevention in the social work sense of concentrating on preventing children going into care although we hope that would happen as more overall improvements occur . . . We are trying to improve people's lifestyles.

The Children's Society sees this as a time-limited project . . . I could concede that the roles of staff may change, possibly fewer staff, but I find it difficult to see how this project would continue if there was not some professional input. It is one of the difficulties of the idea of local control. Yes it is important to give people control over resources, but it is a temptation for the Children's Society to use this as a means of limiting their involvement and saving their money. You can reduce resources and encourage self-help but you will still have to put some in.

Volunteer

My husband was unemployed for six years. We've got four kids so for the majority of their lives he has been out of work. Financially – we're skint now and we only got paid this morning. They all say we're getting this and that on the social but I'd like to see some of these government wallahs live on what we have a week.

When we moved here, one of the kids went to a club at the centre. Then we went to ask something about the dole. Then the project worker started some meetings and got me and some others involved in the play scheme. They made me chairman. I'd never done anything like that before. I found it hard at first, like telephoning people to ask for something. I got the knack in the end. I got a generator, sausages, did letters to companies for donations. We organised a dog show and I went to see people to get sponsorship. Our committee was independent of the centre so that it could raise its own money. Then the play scheme went on for three weeks. Over 170 kids were on the books. It kept them off the streets and gave the parents a break.

It has changed me completely. Made me a different person. I don't sit at home. Before I wouldn't say anything, now I don't keep my gob shut. I'd just sit in the background and listen, but now at the committee meetings I'll have my say.

We have House Group meetings at the centre – for Gingerbread, playgroups and so on. We talked about a community centre there but now it's got a separate committee and so my husband and I are on it. We've visited other community centres to study the layout. Now we're drawing up a plan to put to the council.

Local vicar

If the centre was not there, the estate would be the poorer. It's a beacon of hope. It shows that somebody cares enough to go in there, to be alongside, to encourage. I can think of people who have struggled a lot in their own lives and are now running activities there. The other exciting project, which would not have happened if the centre had not been there, is the pressure on the council to build a bigger community centre. The Millmead Centre has proved that people do want to do something, do want to help the estate.

Three models

The words of the participants give some idea of what goes on in family centres from the perspectives of staff, users and outside professionals. Elsewhere I am using these studies to consider the kind of prevention, its skills and strategies, undertaken at the centres (Holman, 1988). But here I want just to draw upon the material of these and the other seven projects, to identify three models of family centres. Of course, with the total number of family centres now running into hundreds, it would be possible to perceive many more models. From my limited survey, however, I see the three major ones as the client-focused, the neighbourhood and the community development models.

The client-focused model

The Baron's Close Young Family Centre displayed the following characteristics:

i   *Specialised activities*. While not excluding other activities, most resources were devoted to one service and one client category, usually care and training for the under fives, and their parents.
ii *Referred clients*. Access to the service usually depended on a referral from a statutory body, particularly the SSD. To be referred the family, typically, to cite the SSD officer, had to be 'at risk if not of physical abuse then certainly of neglect'.
iii *Restricted neighbourhood outreach*. Local residents were not normally expected to walk in and avail themselves of facilities. Indeed, some of the referred clients were not from the immediate neighbourhood but were bussed in from outlying districts.
iv *Professionalism rather than participation*. The running of such centres rested largely in the hands of qualified staff. Local residents did not occupy leading roles as volunteers, committee members or full-time staff.

The model thus concentrated professional help on a small number of clients referred for severe problems – hence its name of the client-focused approach. It has obvious advantages. The leader of Baron's Close explained that it attracted high-quality staff. The focus on a few families allowed a planned programme for each user using such skills as counselling, play therapy and group work. The gathering together of parents with similar problems enabled them to share in each other's difficulties. Further, the existence of day care resources meant that sometimes the project could respond to a family crisis by providing safe care to avert an immediate breakdown. But the client-focused model also held some disadvantages. The emphasis on referred clients could give the projects a negative image – 'that's where the battered children go'. This, combined with the small span of activities and a 'closed door' policy to those who just walked in, meant that the neighbourhood did not regard the centre as belonging to them. In turn, the closed nature and the domination by professionals tended to exclude the participation of local residents in availing themselves of and running the centre.

The neighbourhood model

Projects like the Swansea Family Centre were located in small areas of high social need and attempted both to serve and to draw upon the life of the neighbourhood. Their characteristics can be itemised as follows:

i   *A broad range of activities*. A variety of groups and activities were on offer. They included advice services, youth clubs, playgroups, tenants' association, mothers and toddlers' groups and sports teams.

ii *An open door*. Staff tried to create a welcoming atmosphere and to establish the practice that callers did not require an appointment or referral but could just drop in.

iii *Neighbourhood identification*. Centres were presented as advocates for and with the neighbourhood. Sometimes festivals were held to boost the image of, or campaigns run to improve services to, the locality. Staff took pains to distance themselves from statutory services so that the projects could in no way be seen as a threat to vulnerable, local families.

iv *Local participation*. The neighbourhoods were regarded as the source of much of the staffing of the projects. Volunteers, numbering up to fifty a week, were recruited not from distant suburbs, but from the immediate vicinity. Sometimes unqualified residents worked their way to become full-time project staff. Usually those involved in running activities were eligible for a users' committee which voiced local opinion.

v   *Flexible staff roles*. Given the wide variety of activities, project staff had to adopt many roles. They acted as service providers who directly ran some clubs; as stimulators who supported self-run groups; and as counsellors who related to individuals with problems. These diverse roles meant that staff tended to see themselves not as professional specialists, but rather as community generalists, while residents looked upon them as resourceful friends.

The neighbourhood model offered distinct advantages in that the projects tended to be extensively used by the local populace, that users were not publicly stigmatised, that staff acquired enormous local knowledge, and that many of the helping capacities of the neighbourhood were utilised. On the other hand, staff admitted that the widespread involvement of local users could lead to conflict between them while the many activities resulted in intense work pressures for staff. Not least, project leaders found that, while SSDs were prepared to give grants on a *per capita* basis to client-focused centres which took referred cases, they were less likely to back financially those neighbourhood projects whose users included many who would not normally be clients of the SSDs.

Community development model

Some project staff commented that the emphasis within the neighbourhood approach on staff directly providing services lessened the responsibilities given to residents. The alternative was what they called the community development model. The project leader at the Millmead Neighbourhood Centre explained it thus:

> We have a community development philosophy. We are trying to enable people to exercise more power over their lives and to enable them to develop facilities and activities which benefit them and their families and actually tend to assist them in having more meaningful and purposeful lives.

Like the neighbourhood approach, the community development model also featured a broad range of activities, an open door, a neighbourhood identification and local participation. Added to these, it had the following characteristics:

i *Indirect work.* The staff deliberately withdrew from running services themselves. They wanted to stimulate residents to organise their own clubs, playschemes, playgroups and so on.

ii *Not social work.* The staff were at pains to disassociate themselves from traditional social work. Not only were they reluctant to take referrals from SSDs but they did not see it as their role to undertake casework with individuals.

iii *Collective action.* The hope was that residents would act collectively to improve the quality of their lives. They wanted to promote movements to improve environments and circumstances and to avoid the kinds of depriving social condition which lowered the quality of life for some families.

iv *Local control.* This was a key term voiced by the advocates of community development. They hoped that eventually users would make the management decisions about how centres should be run. It should be added, though, that progress was slow and in few centres did consumers play a major part in controlling expenditure and staff. And, in discussions, it emerged that some of the advocates considered that the skills of full-time staff provided by the Children's Society would always be necessary to support residents. They believed that deprived localities could not raise large sums of money so that if the Society withdrew its cash then centres would have to cut activities drastically.

The benefits to be gained from the community development model were seen as threefold. Firstly, the concentration on neighbourhood rather than individual needs conveyed no stigma. Secondly, it enabled residents to develop their own skills and confidence in order to have a greater say in shaping their own environments. Thirdly, there was less pressure on full-time staff as they were relieved both of the organisation of services and of intense counselling of individuals.

But staff and consumers were also ready to pinpoint certain drawbacks. One project member admitted that the transferring of the running of activities from full-time staff to local volunteers had led to some lowering in quality as the latter found it difficult to cope with the many demands of organisation and keeping control. Again, some users and volunteers regretted that, as staff changed to a community development role, so their help to individuals would decline. Lastly, project members occasionally wondered if community development was part of a 'political game' used as a 'cover' by which management could justify reducing expenditure on particular centres.

Three models of family centres have now been identified. Of course, models do not reflect exactly what happens in practice. They are just attempts to group together common characteristics in order to distinguish different trends. In reality, the three models overlapped with, for instance, the community development project containing some elements of service provision. Further, the neighbourhood type was in the process of accepting and incorporating community development ideas. Nonetheless, the models do allow some comments to be made about movements within the statutory and voluntary sectors. After visiting ten local authority family centres and reading about many more, my conclusion is that – despite some exceptions – they are predominantly of the client-focused type. SSDs are consistently dealing with a number of families who present severe and worrying difficulties, particularly concerning child abuse and child neglect. Not surprisingly, SSDs which possess family centres draw in, even bus in, the mothers and young children from such families (often called 'statutory cases') from widespread areas. Consequently, they have less if any time and resources to concentrate on residents in the immediate vicinity of the centres.

What of the national child care voluntaries? As chairperson of the Social Work Committee of the National Children's Home, I have had the opportunity to see some of its family centres and to hear reports on others. My assessment is that they are divided between those using the client-focused model (and working in close conjunction with SSDs) and those based on the neighbourhood model. The Children's Society puts far less emphasis on the client-focused approach and its family centres are predominantly of the neighbourhood and community development kinds.

Family centres and stigma

Identifying family centres in terms of different models can enable consideration as to what kind of people they should be reaching and as to whether their characteristics help or hinder them so to do. Crescy Cannan investigated a number of centres run by SSDs and voluntary bodies. While appreciating the extensive services they offered and their commitment to prevention, she perceived one major problem. Some centres gave priority to clients whom they classified as problems. They were of the client-focused type, they bussed people in and they gave particular attention to families with gross child care difficulties such as child abuse. The result, Cannan observed, was a twofold application of stigma. The centre itself could be regarded as only for 'problem people', so alienating itself from the neighbourhood. Simultaneously, the clients had their weaknesses highlighted and perhaps reinforced while their labelling as deviants became part of the 'insidious process' which drew them ever more fully into the net of child protection services (Cannan, 1986).

Cannan rightly pinpoints the conveyance of stigma as one of the major problems of welfare agencies. Stigma is defined by Robert Allen as 'the social disgrace . . . which attaches to different conditions' (Allen, 1983). Noel and Rita Timms explain that it entails being 'publicly marked so that other invidious treatment follows' (Timms and Timms, 1982). Within the welfare state, for all its great achievements, the personal social services have been dogged by the question of how to provide services for a minority of the population without stigmatising them and in so doing undermining their self-confidence and sense of worth. The importance of the neighbourhood and community development type centres is that they appear to have found an approach which draws in some people with marked problems yet which avoids stigmatising them by incorporating them within a plethora of ordinary activities. Why could they do this? The centres I concentrated on belonged to voluntary societies and clearly they lacked the controlling powers associated with statutory bodies. Simultaneously, they could choose not to concentrate almost exclusively on, say, child abuse and neglect. But it was not just their voluntary nature. Rather it was that these models contained features which facilitated the involvement of local residents.

The clubs and groups were not restricted to referred clients. The open-door practice conveyed a welcoming attitude to casual callers. Neighbourhood members could identify with the centres partly because a number participated as volunteers and users and partly because the centres' activities sometimes earned positive publicity for the whole locality. The result was that people entering the buildings did not feel they were being labelled as delinquents or failures. Yet within this atmosphere, those residents who did possess severe problems still felt able to seek help. Indeed, some became volunteers – or even full-time workers – and so benefited from the experience of being givers as well as receivers. At this point, a differ-

ence was noticeable between the neighbourhood and community development type centres. Staff in the former were more prepared to offer close,
personal relationships. In the latter, staff preferred to encourage individuals with marked problems to slot into collective activities.

The future of family centres

Finally, the categorisation of family centres according to three models –
with their attendant advantages and disadvantages – offers some pointers
for the future. Local authority family centres seem most appropriate for
the client-focused model. It is not impossible for them to develop the
other approaches, but the fact that these depend on involving substantial
numbers of residents whose needs do not fit neatly into the brief of SSDs
may give rise to a reluctance to use scarce staff for such purposes. Further,
it is hard to imagine local authorities adopting the community development
wish to hand over the control of resources, including staff, to local neighbourhoods. By contrast, the usual SSD desire to concentrate on its statutory cases does accord with the client-focused model. And this model
possesses several strengths. It entails skilled professional project workers
negotiating contracts and programmes geared to tackle aspects of unacceptable behaviour. It can offer a close relationship not within the traditional confines of the home visit or office interview, but within the group
setting of a family centre. The challenge to SSDs is how to develop this
course while minimising the dangers so well identified by Cannan.

Some local authorities run no family centres whatsoever. Voluntary
agencies may therefore argue that a gap exists there for them to run
centres of the client-focused kind. Generally, however, the experience
and strengths of the voluntary sector gear them towards extending those
based on the neighbourhood and community development models. Their
contribution may well be a valuable one in the context of welfare history
if they continue to demonstrate that the barriers between professionals and
clients, between helpers and the helped, between specialist and generalist
agencies, can be overcome.

References

ALLEN, R. (1983) *Can We De-stigmatise Social Work?* Social Work Today/Uni-
versity of East Anglia.

CANNAN, C. (1986) 'Family centres: sanctuary or stigma?' *Community Care*, 22
May 1986.

DE'ATH, E. (1985) *Self Help and Family Centres*, London, National Children's
Bureau.

HOLMAN, B. (1988) *Putting Families First: Prevention and Child Care*, London,
Macmillan Education.

TIMMS, N. and TIMMS, R. (1982) *Dictionary of Social Welfare*, London, Routledge and Kegan Paul.

12   Residential child care: matching services with needs

Lorraine Waterhouse

Residential care for children and young people is changing. Gone are images of bonny orphans eating cream teas in rural cottages (Bullock, 1987); hopefully too the realities of Dickensian institutions. Out of these historical antecedents, new patterns in the development of residential services are emerging which are almost equally divided between the disquieting and the hopeful.

Recent developments in residential provision

Despite a growing emphasis in child care policy on placing children in families rather than institutions, residential care remains a major option for children and young people in care. Over the last decade, nevertheless, there has been an overall reduction in the number of children in residential care in Scotland, England and Wales, although the pattern of change is uneven. While fewer children are cared for in residential child care establishments, numbers in special boarding schools for maladjusted children have risen (Berridge, 1985; Priestley, 1987), and the number of young people in penal establishments, especially for those aged seventeen and over, is probably growing (Parker, 1988).

This variation across the full range of residential provision is important in that it serves to remind us that residential care is provided by many different organisations, only some of which are local authority Social Services Departments or voluntary and private child welfare services. A considerable and increasing number of disturbed and delinquent adolescents in need of care and accommodation are committed to penal institutions (youth custody, detention centres, prisons) whose primary goals are containment and punishment; similarly, and perhaps beneficially, a growing proportion are now placed in boarding schools. Parker (1988) traces a recent pattern of development that indicates a marked decline in the proportion of severely disturbed and delinquent older adolescents in residential establishments run by Social Services Departments or voluntary organisations. For many of these there is no option but youth custody or prison. Prison disposals cost local authorities nothing, whereas specialist provision within the range of local authority residential services is bound to be expensive (Parker p. 181). How, then, has the scope and nature of residential child care changed over the last decade? What differences can be found between England and Wales and Scotland?

Residential nurseries have virtually disappeared and children's homes, referred to as community homes without a specialist function under the Children and Young Persons Act 1969, have changed dramatically. Only exceptionally do children's homes shelter very young children for whom fostering or adoption is preferred. About 2 per cent of children in children's homes in Scotland (SWSG, 1988a, 1988b) and a slightly smaller percentage in England and Wales (DHSS, 1982) are under five years old (excluding those in homes for the mentally or physically handicapped). Surprisingly, there are only slightly fewer children's homes in Scotland (SWSG, 1988a) and England and Wales (Parker, 1988) compared to a decade ago. The numbers of children sheltered at any one time, however, have been reduced by half, with a larger proportion of children staying in small local authority homes for twelve children or fewer. Children's homes mainly serve adolescents – often when fostering or prospective adoption have been tried and have failed.

The predominance of older adolescents in the residential child care services has stimulated the development of adolescent units or hostels which offer supported but independent or semi-independent accommodation. About one-quarter of general community homes offer such an opportunity in England and Wales (Parker, 1988); no comparable figures are available for Scotland. Yet despite growing need, hostel accommodation for older children in England and Wales has not kept pace with the demand for it (Parker, 1988). A similar trend is evident in Scotland although hostel accommodation there has always been less common than in England and Wales. Over the same period, the number of school leavers in care who are placed in lodgings has been rising.

Many community homes with education (formerly called approved schools in England and Wales) have recently been closed; so too with the former 'List D' schools, their Scottish equivalent. In Scotland, for example, the number of such schools has shrunk by around one-third since 1976, and the bed complement by about one-half. Arrangements for running and financing 'List D' schools in Scotland changed in 1986 and became the responsibility of Departments of Social Work, rather than Education. Nevertheless, the remaining 'List D' schools retain functions similar to those of the English and Welsh community homes with education, and are increasingly referred to by that designation.

Finally, there appears to be a reduction in the number of observation and assessment centres in England and Wales. In Scotland the usage of these establishments remains high. For the year 1984 nearly 40 per cent of all children in residential care in Scotland, compared to 15 per cent in England and Wales, were admitted to observation and assessment centres. This difference may be partly explained by the inclusion of secure units in some Scottish assessment centres – a tradition under revision.

Children and parents find themselves on the receiving end of social and economic policies which seek to recast the range and character of residential services. A diminishing commitment by the voluntary sector to residential care together with the closure of homes by local authorities may alter the degree of choice afforded to both families and professionals.

Consequently, provision may become restricted locally to fostering and adoption with no alternative residential option of comparable purpose, as the following case example illustrates.

Mary was four years old when she was referred for psychiatric opinion following the onset of diabetes. Of small stature with a waif-like appearance, Mary had become unruly at home where she lived with her mother, father and elder brother. Mary's father too suffered from diabetes, frequently failing to maintain his treatment which caused abrupt mood changes culminating in angry and futile encounters with his young daughter. Both parents complained of a sense of growing chaos and helplessness in the house. Mary, according to parental account, refused to cooperate with her treatment regime. She would become fearless, running headlong into the road and only just escaping injury. When seen in the hospital she appeared overly excited and unusually tearful.

Mary's first admission was to a voluntary children's home, pleasant and unpretentious, a short distance outside the city. The home provided round-the-clock care for young and older children suffering from chronic illnesses. The purpose of admission was twofold: first, to offer a moratorium; and second, to teach Mary to manage her injections and accept management of her illness by others when necessary. The latter goal was skilfully tackled by Mary's caregivers; the former proved problematic, for the parents came to prefer the daughter's absence from home to her presence, complaining of her reckless behaviour and tantrums when home at weekends. Matters came to a head when, to the distress of the residential staff, Mary came to ask indiscriminately of them, 'Will you be my Mummy?'

A second admission was arranged to a local authority small family group home near the parents' house. The residential home was run by a married couple and six children of differing ages were sheltered. The small size of the unit allowed intimate care of the children. Its location near the parental home created an opportunity for increased parental involvement. Mary became calmer; a kernel of order in the contact between her and her parents began to take root.

The unit closed as part of the Regional Social Work Department's move to reduce the high numbers of children in residential care (Newman and MacIntosh, 1975). The parents were unable to accept fostering as a fair replacement for the perceived neutrality of the small family group home. Mary was discharged home, which could have been of beneficial consequence. In Mary's case, however, the relationship with her parents deteriorated once again; her medical condition became unstable. Emergency admissions to the children's hospital became all too frequent occurrences.

The role of residential care: some current confusions

The contemporary loss of faith in the ability of public institutions to care adequately for young children, together with tightening fiscal measures, have paved the way for a decline in residential child care services – with detrimental consequences for the value and significance accorded such provision and for the morale of residential workers. Paradoxically, however, recent research by the DHSS and ESRC (DHSS, 1985) has unmasked the central importance of residential care in providing respite care and control for troubled children and adolescents unable to benefit from an orthodoxy which favours placements in families rather than institutions. Recent developments such as the creation of residential prefostering units – albeit few in number – have almost certainly resulted from the questioning of policies that emphasise fostering to the exclusion of any residential alternative, however temporary. For most children loss of family arouses acute anxiety even when this is accompanied by feelings of relief; those who experience further family loss through fostering or adoption breakdown are doubly vulnerable. The specialised use of residential services is now encouraged in some quarters, therefore, to provide planned transitional care as well as preparation for the renewed demands of family life in a fostering or adoptive environment.

When planning admission to residential care for any purpose, it should be possible on the one hand to identify the care needs of adolescents and children, and on the other hand to locate the care contribution of different types of residential establishment within a continuum of residential and other child care services, and to relate the two. Berridge (1985), however, in his study of twenty children's homes in three local authorities, found serious failures in matching the potential care contribution by the residential sector with the needs of children and young people in care or at risk of admission to care. This finding may come as no surprise, given the rapid changes in policy and practice which residential care has seen these past ten years. With the residential sector reduced, the goals and functions of most individual residential establishments have become much more diversified than they formerly were, with all the attendant risks of confusion for children and young people, and of stress and overload for staff. For example, instead of concentrating on the provision of respite from a pathological family situation, *or* preparation for fostering, *or* support following a foster placement breakdown, *or* a regime to cope with disturbed and disruptive teenagers, many establishments are now expected to fulfil all four of these functions – all too often without any preliminary planning, training of workers to undertake these multiple responsibilities, or adequate managerial or supervisory support.

The reverse side of the coin, of course, is the implied recognition that residential care does indeed have a number of valuable functions to perform. In order to clarify the part that residential services can validly play within the total spectrum of child care, a framework is needed to illuminate those factors that are most influential in shaping the purpose, character and style of residential provision.

If we fail to engage in this process of clarification, our planning for children and young people in care is likely to ignore the beneficial experiences with which good residential care is capable of providing them. Residential care may be polarised against family placements as if the former were synonymous with total institutional care and the latter with community care. It is important to remember that families, too, are institutions with problems of their own. There are as many differences in form and style of provision within the available range of residential services as there are between residential care on the one hand and family-based care on the other. The framework we are about to develop in the next section seeks to highlight differences between various forms of residential provision, taking into account the major critical factors on which residential care is based. By testing them against a set of common reference points, comparisons across the entire range of residential services, as well as between individual establishments, can be made more systematically. A word of caution: there is no substitute for first-hand knowledge and observation of particular residential places if we are to assess how sympathetically and effectively different establishments fulfil their purposes. An examination of the underlying structure is only one step towards planning for the better use of residential services.

The role of residential care: an attempted clarification

It needs to be stressed that a disciplined analysis of residential child care is difficult. Three constraints arise. First, residential provision is subject to considerable variation, and differences in scale and type occur between England and Wales on the one hand and Scotland on the other: in England and Wales, for example, intermediate treatment sometimes includes a residential component but in Scotland no comparable provision exists. Secondly, the absence of a shared terminology confounds comparison of residential services between England and Wales and Scotland. Finally, revisions in nomenclature such as occurred under the Children and Young Persons Act 1969, (HMSO, 1969), are not consistently applied. Community homes, for example, are still commonly referred to as children's homes; youth custody establishments as borstals, and community homes with education as approved schools.

It is possible to identify five factors as of particular significance when distinguishing the contribution of different types of residential service. Taken together, these factors constitute a partial framework for understanding the whole range of residential provision; each has the advantage of describing an aspect of the service independently of its geographical or legal context, as well as the disadvantage of separating aspects of service which are highly interrelated. Furthermore, some factors are more likely to remain constant than others: for example, most children's homes are funded by local authority Social Services Departments, while styles of leadership in children's homes vary considerably (Berridge, 1985). The five factors are: the agency administering the service; the primary goals for which residential care is intended; the supportive functions which residential care performs for the wider child care system; the effects of different regimes; and leadership style. I will now say something about each in turn.

Responsible agency

Residential services are managed in one of three ways. The majority are the responsibility of local authority Social Services Departments and rely on public funds. A smaller but no less influential contribution is made by the voluntary sector which maintains charitable status. Some residential services are run jointly by voluntary child care bodies and local authorities – a relatively recent development which may stem in part from growing reliance by the former on central and local government grants. Finally, a small number of private institutions operate independently on a fee-paying basis. They offer some places to local authorities, and are eligible to apply for registration with them.

The primary goals of residential care

Parker (1988) notes five primary goals: care, rehabilitation, education, preservation, and preparation for independence. The first three represent traditional goals of long standing; the latter two break relatively new ground, taking into account young people and children's need to remain in contact with their families and to prepare for future citizenship. Yet new and old have much in common. Rehabilitation, education and preparation for independence represent *instrumental* goals whereby specific outcomes are aimed for according to the likelihood of young people returning permanently to their families, improving their educational attainments or securing a life apart from institutional support. Care and preservation denote *expressive* goals, giving impetus to the creation of a caring environment in which children's physical needs for food, clothing and shelter, as well as their emotional needs for respect, privacy and affirmation, are met in a spirit of mutual partnership between caregivers and the young people themselves.

Should treatment also be a primary goal of residential care? In appropriate circumstances the answer must be yes – although resources will permit only a small minority of disturbed children and young people to take advantage of this opportunity. Historically, residential care has pioneered therapeutic ways of helping children who have been severely damaged emotionally as a result of their early childhood experiences. Such interventions have relied on the residential context as a means for providing a comprehensive environment in which to understand and respond to children's primary physical and psychological needs. To abandon treatment as a goal is to forgo advancement of knowledge about children's and young people's personal or social relations, as well as developments in residential therapeutic intervention. Whilst in the past residential treatment has concentrated mainly on young children, the treatment needs of disturbed adolescents merit special attention.

Fisher *et al* (1986), in their study of adolescents in residential care, found conflicting expectations between parents and residential social workers about the purpose of residential intervention. Parents looked to residential experiences as a mechanism for instilling discipline and winning control over their wayward adolescents; residential social workers expected parents to provide solutions to what the former regarded as family problems. It is only recently that consumer opinion – the views of young people themselves – has begun to feature in shaping residential child care goals.

In practice residential establishments may pursue several goals at the same time; but the need to appreciate which goal is of primary importance for a particular child is highlighted in the following case example based on the practical work of a social work student in training.

Jane, a fifteen-year-old mildly handicapped young person suffering from Down's syndrome, was admitted to a small group home to improve her ability to care for herself. The modern detached house, set in affluent surroundings, was part of a graduated group of residential services imaginatively provided by the voluntary sector for mentally handicapped young people in need of brief or extended stays in residential care. While other establishments in the group of services catered for the care of severely handicapped children, this particular service focused on the development of skills by residents who were expected to remain in regular contact with their family and eventually to return.

The residential staff were concerned by the growing reluctance of Jane's mother to have Jane home at weekends, and were puzzled by the disparity in Jane's behaviour between group and family home. Over time Jane had become moderately confident and competent in food shopping, cooking and personal hygiene; at home by contrast she wandered, threw tantrums in public places and wet the bed at night, causing the mother to insist that she wear nappies. The student was asked to form a relationship with Jane and her mother and sister to explore and hopefully lessen the widening gulf between them. Discussions with Jane's mother gradually revealed that placement for Jane had been accepted in the hope that long-term shelter and care would subsequently be offered. The problems encountered with Jane on weekends at home were real enough as the student soon discovered when she spent a day with the family. From observation the student came to appreciate that Jane, anxious in the face of feared rejection, was unable to sustain her new and tentative attainments and, under pressure to please, her behaviour became disorganised. The mother feared behavioural improvement lest Jane's stay in the home be cut short. She could not be resolute, therefore, in encouraging Jane to practise at home what was attempted in the residential unit.

In Jane's case, identification of this mismatch of expectations about the primary goal of residential intervention helped to clarify future plans, and in so doing pave the way for renewed investment in the purpose of placement.

The functions of residential care for the wider child care system

Berridge (1985), Fisher *et al.* (1986) and Parker (1988) argue that residential care performs important functions that provide essential support to the more favoured child care strategies of adoption and fostering. The relationship of residential care to other parts of the child care system resembles that of servant and master. The former ostensibly serves the latter; but over time the latter comes to depend more and more on the former for his success and high standing. What, then, is the contribution of residential care to the other child care services?

There are at least three contributory functions: assessment, containment and supplementation. None of these functions is the exclusive prerogative of one type of residential establishment. Indeed, the diffusion of all three throughout the range of residential services may lead to the discharge of one function at the cost of another – as is demonstrated in the case of assessment.

Assessment

Short-stay residential establishments are well suited to providing assessment of psychological, social and educational need because an institutional base, unlike fostering or adoption, affords an opportunity for first-hand observation without necessarily demanding loyalty and attachment between residents and caregivers. This function is performed across the range of residential services with observation and assessment centres especially earmarked for the purpose. Two key studies of observation and assessment centres, however (cited in Parker, 1988), suggest that only approximately half of the children who were admitted were actually assessed. This omission appeared to stem from the fact that centres were compelled to perform multiple functions: providing shelter in emergencies, transitional care pending family or other specialist placements, and control of the disruptive. When assessment is 'squeezed' in this way, some children and young people lose out on the very contribution for which the institution is best suited; furthermore, innovative developments that seek to extend the scope of assessment, and to improve its relevance and accuracy, may well be precluded.

Containment

Containment includes both the contribution which residential care makes to sustaining children and young people when other options fail or are unavailable, and also the provision of physical security. With regard to the first of these, recent research (Millham *et al.*, 1986; Packman *et al.*, 1986; Berridge, 1985) has found that residential care is frequently used for children and young people whose foster placements have failed. Berridge (1985), for example, in his study of twenty children's homes, estimated that one-third of all children were admitted or readmitted because of fostering breakdown. Indeed, Bullock (1987) concludes that ordinary children's homes are the main resource for children and young people who depart abruptly from either foster care or adoption. Children's homes, then, have a crucial part to play in supporting children and adolescents under stress until an alternative is found.

Turning now to environments that are to a greater or lesser degree 'secure', disturbed young people who commit delinquent acts may be admitted to observation and assessment centres, youth custody and detention centres as well as to remand centres and prisons; boys and girls over the age of fifteen are eligible for youth custody and boys over the age of fourteen for committal to a detention centre. Detention centres are fully secure, whereas about one-third of youth custody centres are open, having no perimeter fence. Parker (1988) notes that many young people sentenced to custody will already have lived in other types of residential provision earlier in their careers. While some closed institutions attempt little more than the physical containment of young people for whom other types of child care provision are not thought suitable, others try to provide their young residents with something more positive than punitive control – for example, counselling and a range of optional activities. Younger juvenile offenders with serious offences, however, are more likely to be committed to institutions of maximum security.

The exit of older delinquent adolescents from welfare-oriented establishments to tough, custodial provision has happened, as Parker (1988) and others (Millham *et al.*, 1986) argue, too swiftly and too soon. Thus, numbers of young people in need of re-educative or therapeutic experiences (residential or non-residential) within the welfare system find themselves in prison instead. The remedial role which residential care has been expected to take in relation to fostering breakdown may have shifted attention away from disturbed young offenders who are equally needful of containment in the *first* of its two senses (see the first sentence of this subsection).

Supplementation

Residential establishments, as central institutions, are increasingly perform-
ing an important supplementary function by hosting on their premises
a variety of services additional to those which are exclusively residential.
Berridge (1985) found that a small number of large multipurpose children's
homes were offering day-care services as well as weekend and evening
respite care for children of local families under stress. Children's homes,
too, play an important part in preparing children and young people for
fostering and adoption (as well as sustaining them when placements break
down). Berridge and Cleaver (1987) found that short stays of up to a year
in residential care can do much to ensure the success of a subsequent
family placement.

The effects of different regimes

As Quinton (1987) observes, most studies show that about half of all
children in residential institutions display emotional or behavioural problems, as well as behaviour often associated with institutional care – such as
over-friendliness and difficulties in making deep relationships. Residential
regimes, then, must try to respond to groups of children and young people
whose individual members have had a wide variety of unsettling life experiences and display a range of different reactions to residential care. That
any one regime will suit all residents equally well is improbable: instead,
a pattern of gains and losses for individuals is a more likely outcome
(Whittaker *et al.*, 1984). Parker (1988), however, reminds us that good
daily care and nurture are essential ingredients in any residential approach
if children are to grow, to develop self-respect, and to learn. Furthermore,
as Whittaker *et al.* (1984) conclude, all children in residential care may
need help in coping with day-to-day life in the home or in understanding
their past and current experiences.

Millham (1987), reviewing the effects on residents of institutional
regimes, emphasised the considerable variation between establishments,
not only in providing the satisfactory physical care which deprived and
damaged children need, but also in the nature of relationships and quality
of interaction between caregivers and children. Warm child-centred
relationships were found to reduce problems of absconding and violence
(Millham *et al.*, 1978); overtly punitive regimes, indifferent to the needs
of individual children, were ineffective whatever the children's backgrounds. The long-term benefits of different regimes, however, are much
less easy to estimate, because improvements in children's personal and
social development during their time in residence tend to be overshadowed
upon discharge by the same problems (for example, of childhood background, and family and social deprivation) that they were facing before
admission.

It is tempting to describe regimes along single dimensions – for example, punitive or permissive. Research (Millham, 1987; Colton, 1988) suggests instead that the ethos of a residential community is made up of multiple components. When particular indicators of success, such as reduced reconviction rates or improved levels of academic attainment, were set against the nature of the regime, six factors emerged as associated with favourable outcomes: young people feel cared for; young people see an improvement in their skills; leadership is clear and consistent; there is some consensus amongst residents and caregivers about goals and means for their achievement; they are in small group living environments which foster resident responsibility; and they are in accommodation which respects privacy.

Regimes that cater for highly disturbed children and young people draw, for the most part, on one of two broad traditions: either a psychodynamic orientation which emphasises the importance of understanding intra- and interpersonal conflict for emotional development; or alternatively behavioural psychology, which stresses the importance of the environment in shaping new behavioural patterns. The former, for example, gave rise to the development of therapeutic communities which generated treatment regimes based on the principles of democratisation, permissiveness, communalism and psychological honesty (Barr, 1987); and to 'milieu therapy' which focused on the creation of a total living environment responsive to severely emotionally impoverished children for whom primary affectional experiences were either missing or damaging. Behavioural approaches, on the other hand, are linked to 'token economy' systems in residential settings, where desired behaviour by residents is rewarded with extra privileges and undesirable behaviour either ignored or punished. There is a risk of misuse if such controls are employed to engineer conformity by residents to institutional norms, rather than to develop their capacity to make responsible decisions for themselves. The case of David helps to illustrate the potential impact of different regimes.

David, aged eight years, was admitted urgently to a children's hospital because of arm and leg injuries following an aggressive outburst by his mother. He was a big, handsome, friendly lad yet there was an aloofness about his manner. At three years of age his father (no longer living with the family) was purported to have struck him on the head, causing him to be permanently partially sighted. Following admission, the mother, although fond of David, complained that she had never felt close to him and refused to consider his returning home lest she injure him further. David was transferred to a large multipurpose children's home with a view to assessing the likelihood of reintegration into his family.

The children's home was a large stone building, as shabby on the inside as grand on the outside. Children slept in dormitories and were expected to remain only briefly. The atmosphere was friendly, busy and noisy, but impersonal. The logistics of providing good practical care, running case conferences as well as liaising with field social workers, dominated the overstretched work schedules of residential staff. The meaning of daily activities, and their significance for a philosophy of residential care, were sadly ignored – with the result that caregivers and children were frustrated by a sense of futility in daily encounters with each other.

A further move occurred when David was transferred to a community home where special educational provision was included. The home was very different: it was smaller, in a rural setting and better equipped. Children were encouraged to participate in the running of the home; they were made to feel they belonged. Children and staff met in small groups to review weekly events, good and bad, or to plan ahead. Children's behaviour was interpreted as a form of communication: staff, and to some extent other children, were encouraged to explore its meaning.

David made more progress in the second home than in the first. The differences in regime were, however, partly the outcome of contrasting purposes. The first sought to provide a neutral transitional environment which contributed to assessment and planning; the second sought to integrate personal, social and educational care over time. While the community home with education seemed the more sympathetic milieu of the two, both it and the ordinary children's home went some way to achieving their respective goals.

Leadership style

Sinclair (1975), in a study of probation hostels for young people, found that the attitudes of wardens towards control and regulation were closely related to the rate of absconding. Wardens who adopted a patriarchal style, were strict with residents but nonetheless warm towards them, did better at holding on to residents as well as keeping them out of trouble than those who were, for example, relatively cold and punitive.

Leadership style also has important implications for the quality of residential care practice, both by residential social workers and domestic helpers. Berry (1975) evaluated the quality of daily care in forty-four residential establishments, to find clear differences amongst homes in such daily routines as putting children to bed, waking them and spending time with them. Good-quality care was associated with leadership which either directly supported staff or created opportunities for staff support and development. Similarly, Berridge (1985) discovered a relationship between size of establishment and style of leadership. Heads of small homes (sheltering between six and ten children) were more likely to be involved in daily child care and to assume major responsibility for running the home; domestic work was often allocated to other carers who tended to be discouraged from involvement with the children. This matriarchal style of leadership caused heads of homes to be highly influential, for better or worse, in setting the ethos and standards for group living. Contact with other services, as well as with local communities, was often tenuous. In contrast, heads of large multipurpose homes (accommodating upwards of twenty children) operated a bureaucratic style of leadership in which daily regulation of the home and responsibility for contact with residents was delegated. Consequently, hierarchical accountability was expected, perhaps suggesting to young people that adult authority rested only partially with their immediate caregivers. Links with other child care services, as well as with local community interest groups, were achieved mainly through heads of homes, who were not tied to daily child care commitments.

The extent to which heads of small homes can adapt their professional and personal style to suit the needs of individual staff and children is questionable. Research which has sought to observe the interviewing practices of field social workers suggests that professional interviewing style tends to remain remarkably consistent within one individual worker, despite the considerable differences between the recipients of his or her services (Leishman, 1985). While large establishments run the risk of providing less intimate care than smaller ones, there may be compensating advantages if the diffusion of caring functions amongst many caregivers allows children and young people the freedom to seek out special relationships of their own choice.

Looking to the future

Residential services will continue to need to adapt to changing circumstances. Short-stay adolescents, now the largest group of residents in children's homes, will require a style of provision which balances their need for shelter, care, education and personal support. To this end, three characteristics of residential regimes are likely to warrant special consideration (Willcocks et al., 1987): first, residents' freedom to determine residential lifestyle (e.g. getting up, going to school or work, bedtimes); secondly, residents' privacy as individuals or in their contacts with other residents, friends or family; and thirdly, residents' participation in decisions which affect the organisation of home or centre.

Research (Millham et al., 1986), emphasises the importance for children's well-being of maintaining links with their families. This process might be easier if the structure of the child care services was designed to support flexible movement of young people and their families in and out of residential care. Accommodation might, for example, cater for the admission of families as well as individual young people – a practice developed in a small number of hospital in-patient psychiatric units for children and adolescents.

Closer collaboration between day and residential services is likely to be an important future development. Some community homes are beginning to offer day-care provision as well as accommodation. Combined services may help to increase the range of available child care options, especially in times of crisis. Some children who might otherwise be forced to move between residential care and fostering if one or the other should fail could instead move between linked day and residential care. This would improve continuity of care for children and their parents. Furthermore, some young people could benefit from linked day care when they are preparing to leave residential care, whether to return home or to take up another placement.

Disturbed and delinquent young people, however, present a major challenge for the future. That so many young people in need of care of high quality end up in prison or other comparable regimes simply compounds the adversity that afflicted them in the first place. Aggressive or seriously disruptive adolescents are not likely to be eligible for fostering or adoption. Residential child care services, then, have a vital contribution to make in providing young people with consistency, security and opportunities to learn. By taking delinquent youth back into residential child care, at the very least a protective interlude (Parker, 1988) might be offered which has proved no less (if no more) effective than prison sentences in the preventive of reoffending. Reappraisal of the commitment by residential child care services to delinquent boys and girls is urgently needed.

Traditionally, residential care has contributed to the whole field of child welfare a diversity of services which has yet to be equalled by other forms of provision. This tradition of diversity remains resolute in the face of the changing patterns of need displayed by troubled children and young people. Increasingly, brief transitional admissions are sought for the purpose of assessment, respite or preparation for other child care alternatives. Yet there remains a place for residential services which are responsive to the interests of children and young people who might benefit from longer stays, or for whom the residential experience assumes primary importance for therapeutic, educational or protective purposes. Residential care is more than a means to an end: it provides a vital link in matching child care services with child care needs.

Acknowledgements

Most of the examples given are drawn from my own practice but I would like to thank my student, Kathryn Whitehurst, for allowing me to use an example from her practice and the children whom I have had the privilege of knowing.

References

BARR, H. (1987) *Perspectives on Training for Residential Work*, London, Central Council for Education and Training in Social Work.

BERRIDGE, D. (1985) *Children's Homes*, Oxford, Blackwell.

BERRIDGE, D. and CLEAVER, H. (1987) *Foster Home Breakdown*, Oxford, Blackwell.

BERRY, J. (1975) *Daily Experiences in Residential Life: A Study of Children and Their Caregivers*, London, Routledge and Kegan Paul.

BULLOCK, R. (1987) 'Children's homes: some recent research findings', *Maladjustment and Therapeutic Education*, Vol. 5, No. 2, pp. 12–17.

COLTON, M. (1988) 'Substitute care practice', *Adoption and Fostering*, Vol. 12, No. 1, pp. 30–4.

DHSS (1982) *Children in Care in England and Wales*, London, HMSO.

DHSS (1985) *Social Work Decisions in Child Care: Recent Research Findings and Their Implications*, London, HMSO.

FISHER, M., MARSH, P., PHILLIPS, D. and SAINSBURY, E. (1986) *In and Out of Care*, London, Batsford.

HMSO (1969) *Children and Young Persons Act 1969*, London, HMSO.

LEISHMAN, J. (1985) *An Analysis of Social Work Interviews Using Videotapes: Behaviour Effectiveness and Self-Fulfilling Prophecies*, Ph.D. thesis, Aberdeen University.

MILLHAM, S. (1987) 'Residential schools: issues and developments', *Maladjustment and Therapeutic Education*, Vol. 5, No. 2, pp. 4–12.

MILLHAM, S., BULLOCK, R. and HOSIE, K. (1978) *Locking Up Children*, Farnborough, Saxon House.

MILLHAM, S., BULLOCK, R., HOSIE, K. and HAAK, M. (1986) *Lost in Care: The Family Contact of Children in Care*, Aldershot, Gower.

NEWMAN, N. and MacINTOSH, H. (1975) *A Roof Over Their Heads? Regional Provisions for Children in South East Scotland*, Edinburgh, University of Edinburgh.

PACKMAN, J., RANDALL, J. and JACQUES, N. (1986) *Who Needs Care? Social Work Decisions About Children*, Oxford, Blackwell.

PARKER, R. (1988) 'Residential care for children', in NISW *Residential Care: The Research Reviewed; Literature surveys commissioned by the independent review of residential care*, London, HMSO.

PRIESTLEY, P. (1987) 'The future of residential schools for the maladjusted', *Maladjustment and Therapeutic Education*, Vol. 5, No. 2, pp. 30–8.

QUINTON, D. (1987) 'The consequences of care: adult outcomes from institutional rearing', *Maladjustment and Therapeutic Education*, Vol. 5, No. 2, pp. 18–29.

SINCLAIR, I. (1975) 'The influence of wardens and matrons on probation hostels', in Tizard, J., Sinclair, I. and Clarke, R. (eds) *Varieties of Residential Experience*, London, Routledge and Kegan Paul.

SOCIAL WORK SERVICES GROUP (1988a) *Statistical Bulletin: Residential Accommodation 1987*, Edinburgh, Scottish Education Department.

SOCIAL WORK SERVICES GROUP (1988b) *Statistical Bulletin: Home Care Services, Day Care Establishments and Day Services 1987*, Edinburgh, Scottish Education Department.

WHITTAKER, D., COOK, J., DUNNE, C. and LUNN-ROCKLIFFE, S. (1984) *The Experience of Residential Care from the Perspectives of Children, Parents and Caregivers*, York, University of York.

WILLCOCKS, D., PEACE, S. and KELLAHER, L. (1987) *Private Lives in Public Places: A Research-Based Critique of Residential Life in Local Authority Old People's Homes*, London, Tavistock.

13   The case for residential special education

Ted Cole

A century ago attempts were being made in parts of America, Europe and Britain to avoid the need to send children with special needs to boarding schools. Community care and integration were called by different names but they were topical issues then as now. However these sometimes longlasting attempts foundered in London, Glasgow and elsewhere. As the practical difficulties of organising semi-integrated special classes in day schools came to appear more and more intractable, so the popularity of the residential school increased until it reached its heyday in the third quarter of this century, with boarding schools being opened for children from each of the eleven categories of handicap defined by the 1944 Education Act (Cole, 1989).[1]

In the 1960s Jenny was a timid blind girl with no additional social or educational difficulties, who lived in a comfortable house with her stable parents in a small rural town. During this period integrated educational provision was extremely scarce, so she was sent to a special boarding school 90 miles from home. A decade later, Cathy was a four-year-old with very little hearing at a special pre-school unit. Her teacher reported an increasingly silent and lethargic child, who was frequently short of sleep, seemed physically neglected and showed no signs of becoming toilet trained. While disputing the alleged inadequate caring, her parents agreed reluctantly that she should go to a residential school for the hearing impaired at the age of five. Angie has cerebral palsy and spends most of her waking hours in a wheelchair. As an adult, she looks back with displeasure at the residential school she entered at the age of six. In those days, boarding placement seemed the natural response to her special needs. Early in the 1980s Janet was a frail nine-year-old when admitted to a mixed junior boarding school for the maladjusted. At home, her sometimes bizarre behaviour had included killing her pet rabbit and defecating in her bedroom. At day school she had made little progress in reading and numbers, and had been unhappy, fretful and listless. In class, she was quietly disruptive and destructive. If reprimanded she would react violently and would pick continuously at scabs on her wrist, or occasionally cut herself with a knife. Baffled by her behaviour, parents and day school staff were pleased for her to receive help at a boarding school.

Darren's father had a drink problem and had served prison sentences for repeated minor offences. His mother could not cope with her son's naughty behaviour, and his day school found him disruptive. His parents then parted. His social worker and educational psychologist agreed that boarding for the ten-year-old would help tackle his learning difficulties and would 'prop up' the family situation. Alex had caring parents who could not believe it was their son's fault when he was suspended from comprehensive school at the age of fourteen for aggressive and defiant behaviour towards staff and other pupils. They were similarly stunned by his delinquency around the neighbourhood. His parents were happy that he should be given a fresh start at a residential school for children with emotional and behavioural difficulties. Paul was a withdrawn eleven-year old who suffered from epilepsy, although this was controlled by drugs. His well-to-do parents knew they were overprotective and did not want him to attend the local day school for children with moderate learning difficulties or the authority's own boarding school for epileptics. They pressed for him to go to an independent school. Eventually the LEA agreed to fund this.

These brief sketches illustrate the wide variety of children attending residential special schools and their differing family circumstances. Further contrasting examples could have been given – for example, the mentally handicapped child with severe behavioural problems in a residential school who would otherwise have lived in a subnormality hospital; or the disturbed and suicidal teenager of high intelligence studying in boarding school for university entrance. But whatever the differences in their case histories, boarders in special schools can be divided into two categories.

First, there is a numerically small and shrinking group of children of which Jenny and Angie were members. These usually have physical or sensory impairments. No suitable local day special provision is available and both LEA officials and parents accept that these youngsters' educational needs cannot be met in ordinary day schools. These boys and girls are likely to attend well-resourced regional centres of expertise generously staffed and specially adapted to the needs of the particular clientele they serve. For these pupils, the residential side of boarding school life is a necessary but definitely subservient feature. They attend the school primarily for *educational* and, in the case of some physically impaired children, *medical* reasons. Whenever possible pupils sleep on site only on Monday to Thursday night and they do this because it is too far for them to travel home each night to their families. Their physical or sensory impairments are not compounded by the serious behavioural, family or other social difficulties which characterise the second, much larger, group of children at present receiving residential special education. (Some of these attend the same special boarding school as the first group.)

For the majority of boarders, providing a suitable education is not the primary reason for their placement. The proliferation of day special schools and classes since the mid-1950s for the children labelled, until 1983, educationally subnormal (ESN), has brought special provision within easy reach of nearly all such pupils' homes. Gone are the days when the slow-learning child, like the sensory impaired, *had to board to receive suitable teaching*. Nowadays, for a child with moderate learning difficulties to be in boarding school, he or she is likely to have posed severe 'acting out' or withdrawn and neurotic behaviour in day school. In addition, there are likely to be severe problems in the boarder's home situation. For example, a single parent might find it hard to cope with her son's behaviour, as in the case of Darren. Where a child lives away from his or her natural family, foster-parents or children's home staff may be overtaxed if a disturbed child in their care attends day school and lives with them throughout the year, but they may be able to cope with him or her during holidays from boarding school. Sometimes the roots of the boarder's difficulties lie in the parents' lifestyle. Occasionally, the difficulties presented by siblings – perhaps the severe handicap of a sister – may cause a child to board.

Increasingly the same applies to children with physical or sensory impairments. As integration programmes have proceeded or special day provision has been expanded – for example, the rapid expansion of day units for the partially hearing – so the need to board has lessened, *except* where children with these impairments also exhibit behaviour problems at school and/or come from stressful or inadequate home circumstances (as in the case of five-year-old Cathy).

Similarly, if a child has emotional and behavioural difficulties (the term now used by the DES to describe children who until 1983 were called 'maladjusted'), that child will usually only board if he or she presents problems at home and school. To be 'maladjusted' at school but not at home might justify alternative day provision, but not boarding education except in rare circumstances. If parents are asked to support residential placement for their child and he or she does not pose severe problems in the family home, the parents might fairly ask whether the child is to board for his or her own benefit, or merely to rid an ordinary secondary school of a member deemed disruptive.

Such parents' right of veto will not be available to the families of children in care who have been in court. Until the 1969 Children and Young Persons Act, placement in residential approved schools' run by the Home Office, and after that Act, their successors the CHEs (community homes with education provided on the premises) run by local Social Service Departments, was almost a standard response. But concern grew at leavers' high reoffending rates and the enormous costs, and community-based responses such as 'intermediate treatment' became more common. Children in CHEs are now far outnumbered by those in special boarding schools.

DES statistics for 1986 showed that about 19,000 children were boarders in English and Welsh maintained, non-maintained and independent special schools (nearly 18 per cent of the total special school population). However this is an underestimate. It does not include boarders who still did not have 'statements of special educational needs', special boarders aged over sixteen, boarders in Scotland and Northern Ireland, and inmates of CHEs or residential hospital schools. If these are included, Anderson and Morgan (1987) calculated, from their careful and wide-ranging survey in 1986–7, that there were 27,600 children in some 700 special residential establishments.

Over two-thirds are boys. There is a mixture of co-educational and single-sex establishments. According to DES statistics, only one-third of the children experience a curriculum which closely resembles that provided in mainstream day schools. There is a definite preponderance in special boarding schools of children with learning difficulties *in addition* to other handicaps. Further, boarders often span two or more of the pre-1983 categories. In that year approximately one-third of boarders' primary handicap was maladjustment, a little under one-third learning difficulties and one-third physical or sensory disability – with the rest split between children with epilepsy, speech defects, mental handicap or autism. Dyslexia was not recognised as a category.

For most groups in the 1970s there was movement away from the residential approach. The number of boarders in maintained and non-maintained English and Welsh schools declined between 1973 and 1983 as follows: ESN(M) by about 44 per cent; physically handicapped and delicate by 50 per cent; deaf and partially hearing by 38 per cent; blind and partially sighted by 35 per cent. These figures are in part explained by declining numbers in the school population as a whole, but also reflect the growth of day alternatives. There has also been a greater willingness to provide daily transport to schools as far as 50 miles from the child's home, which motorway developments have helped to make possible. To a lesser extent the patchy advance of integration may also be a contributory factor. In contrast, over the same decade, the numbers of 'maladjusted' pupils in residential education expanded by about 30 per cent. There was also an increase, although numerically very small, in the numbers of boarding pupils with speech defects and severe learning difficulties.

Although precise statistics do not exist, it seems certain that in late 1988 well over 20,000 children with a wide variety of special needs continued to attend boarding schools. It is also worth noting Anderson and Morgan's finding that 38 per cent of special boarding schools were experiencing increased demand for places and that 28 per cent reported no fall in the number of referrals, although headteachers were perhaps likely to paint a rosier picture than actually existed.

These children are attending schools of various shapes and sizes – small town houses, large country houses, old vicarages, Victorian 'cottage' style buildings, red-brick monoliths, flat-roofed concrete modular units. Many are run by LEAs, but some (generally the non-maintained schools) by charities and about a hundred by independent owners whose schools are inspected and approved by the DES. LEAs must seek special permission to use the few surviving independents not on the approved lists – for example, some establishments guided by the philosophy of Rudolf Steiner and a handful of very expensive therapeutic communities. The differences in the way these schools are run can be equally marked. A few of them concentrate exclusively on a behaviourist of psychodynamic approach. The vast majority, however, are eclectic in style, stressing close relationships between children and staff, offering a wide range of educational and social activities, and pursuing widely recognised social and educational objectives.

In a better world all children with special needs would come from stable family backgrounds in communities where they had friends of their own age, sympathetic neighbours able to give consistent support, and social and health services with sufficient resources to provide necessary financial, practical and physical help to the families in their own homes. Likewise, all children with special needs would go to mainstream schools which found it possible to satisfy the formal, academic and competitive aspirations of the majority of parents and children (now more openly encouraged by government in the form of the National Curriculum), yet still manage to create the tolerant, non-competitive atmosphere usually considered necessary for effective integration. Even the disturbed teenager without a family would slip happily into a warm substitute family provided by foster-parents. Unfortunately, achievement of this on a national scale is likely to remain an impossible dream, so for many children with special educational needs (and often difficulties at home) it is necessary to weigh up the pros and cons of non-ideal alternatives and choose the best feasible option. Historically throughout the world, boarding has certainly proved to have enduring worth whatever its past and present faults. The Warnock report in 1978 and the ILEA's Fish report in 1985, as well as many commentators described in the last chapter of a previous book (Cole, 1986), saw the residential approach as the best choice for some children. The wide-ranging Schools Council survey in the late 1970s found pupils enjoying boarding life and not ashamed of their schools, suggesting that the stigma supposedly attached to boarding can be much exaggerated. Significantly, major voluntary organisations such as the National Children's Home, Barnardo's and the Spastics Society, while moving in the direction of preventive, community-based work, continue to maintain popular boarding schools. While some disabled people have campaigned for greater childhood integration, other groups such as the British Deaf Association have fought vigorously for the retention of special residential education. Meanwhile, parents have also opposed local authority plans to close various boarding schools, and in one case bought and reopened a school for delicate children. Therefore, not surprisingly, many special boarding schools are alive and well, some increasing their usefulness by staying open through traditional school holidays.

Many people apparently appreciate the lack of substance in most of the allegations commonly made against boarding schools. It is misleading to suggest that the child who has been isolated and largely rejected in the mainstream school and local neighbourhood is suddenly cut off from his or her roots when placed in a boarding school. If one believes in an ecological approach to residential work, whereby change in one part of a child's 'system' has a knock-on and often beneficial effect on other parts, the boarding experience can effect change in a child's self-concept and behaviour while the stress level in the family situation is dramatically reduced; and such changes can sow the seed for a more normal and satisfying relationship between the child and his or her family and community. During regular weekends and holidays at home this seed often grows healthily. Bonds can be strengthened rather than weakened. The child failing hopelessly in the mainstream class, who has become the butt of peers and who reacts with disruptive behaviour, which in turn leads to negative labelling by teachers, is helped to escape from this downward spiral and is given a fresh start in a contrasting school environment, receiving more individualised teaching and experiencing a wider range of social activities.

For some physically, sensory or intellectually handicapped children, used to a lonely and perhaps overprotected existence in their family homes, boarding life can provide friendship and social opportunities while developing their ability to fend for themselves and to gain self-confidence to go out into the community. In London, boarding schools for the hearing and visually impaired were created in the early years of this century as the most effective practical means of preparing teenagers for an integrated, self-supporting lifestyle. While it is true that some residential schools have failed and continue to fail in this aim, plodding comfortably along as inward-looking, overprotected regimes where children are insufficiently challenged, there are some which succeed admirably, and which now provide further education opportunities which are not matched in much mainstream provision.

It is likewise false to suggest that all special schools provide a narrower curriculum than mainstream schools and thus deny life-chances to the child with special needs. This has undoubtedly occurred, as was exemplified earlier in the case of Angie. However, for many children with learning difficulties it is highly unlikely that they would have been able to take advantage of the wide curriculum supposedly available in the large mainstream school. They would commonly have been withdrawn from many activities to receive remedial help in '3R' work, or been placed in a special unit with contact with only one or two teachers. They would certainly not have left their day schools with a clutch of GCSEs. Sally Tomlinson (1982) and other recent critics of special schools also need reminding that parents sometimes fight the local authority to have their children placed in special schools because of their academic excellence. Many special schools, often residential, are doing what they were created to do – opening the door to self-supporting, integrated adulthood for the handicapped child.

Poor child care has often taken place in boarding schools. I look back in horror at my own experience some years ago, when with two colleagues I had to control, entertain and care for seventy-five sometimes difficult, backward children every third evening and weekend, in addition to teaching a full timetable – a situation judged quite satisfactory by the standards of the time. Since then staffing levels and conditions of service for carers have improved considerably, and in good schools the quality of life for the boarder has become much richer and staff are more able to meet individual needs in homely environments which avoid institutionalised approaches. Staff are able to control the physical and emotional environment to prevent the formation of damaging subcultures and to provide positive role-models for the children. They have minibuses to take the boarders out into the community regularly, and a wide range of recreational equipment with which to keep the children stimulated and challenged.

Providing good boarding schools is not cheap; but it is becoming more widely realised that providing effective integrated education linked to community care is not only expensive but also extremely difficult to achieve.

When one looks at the beneficial effect of boarding on many children it often appears to be a worthwhile investment. I gave a self-image test to the highly disturbed Janet, mentioned earlier. After eight months in her new school she saw herself as less quarrelsome, more reliable, polite and popular. Her class teacher believed she was happier, kinder and more honest. Janet appreciated the relationship she had developed with her teachers and with her carers. She was proud of the progress she had made in swimming and learning to play table tennis, but more importantly, after her very unhappy day school experience, she valued making more friends in boarding school (Cole, 1981).

Of the other young people mentioned earlier, Darren enjoyed his boarding school career, made steady if unspectacular educational progress and was able to leave local authority care. Likewise Paul flourished, gaining in confidence and in educational and social skills. His parents fought against the local authority's wish for him to return to day school. Alex, despite one serious relapse, when in the holidays he shot and wounded a neighbour with an air rifle, was accepted into the army soon after leaving. In his last year at school he had changed from a sullen, resentful and defiant youth into a responsible and helpful young man.

In the present imperfect world the special boarding school system, now leaner and hopefully fitter after the closures of the last decade, continues to have an important role to play for some children with complex educational, social or physical difficulties.

Note

1   Some sections of this article are reproduced by permission of the Open University Press from Cole, T. (1986) *Residential Special Education*, Milton Keynes, Open University Press.

References

ANDERSON, E. W. and MORGAN, A. L. (1987) *Provision for Children in Need of Boarding/Residential Education*, London, Boarding Schools Association.

COLE, B. E. (1981) *The Use of Residential Education to Improve Pupils' Self-Image*, unpublished dissertation, University of Newcastle upon Tyne.

COLE, T. (1986) *Residential Special Education*, Milton Keynes, Open University Press.

COLE, T. (1989) *Apart or A Part? Integration and the Growth of British Special Education*, Milton Keynes, Open University Press.

COMMITTEE ON EDUCATION OF HANDICAPPED CHILDREN AND YOUNG PEOPLE (1978) *Special Educational Needs* (Warnock report), Cmnd. 7212, London, HMSO.

COMMITTEE ON PROVISION TO MEET SPECIAL EDUCATIONAL NEEDS (1985) *Educational Opportunities for All* (Fish report), London, Inner London Education Authority.

DEPARTMENT OF EDUCATION AND SCIENCE (1987) *Statistics of Education (Schools)*, London, HMSO.

TOMLINSON, S. (1982) *A Sociology of Special Education*, London, Routledge and Kegan Paul.

Section III Practice

14 Communicating with children

Clare Winnicott[1]

I think we would agree that communication between people takes place on different levels of existence or experience. There is the ordinary everyday exchange between people which may take place on a somewhat superficial level, but which nevertheless serves to keep communication channels open and has an important binding and socialising effect. It keeps civilisation going, and the world ticking for us all, because it reduces suspicion and the latent paranoia in us all.

Then there is the communication [. . .] which takes place between certain people and in which the feelings and needs of each are recognised and reciprocated. The true self of each meets and responds to the true self of the other.

The third kind of communication is that which concerns the exchange of ideas either in words or in art forms of all kinds. This is, at its best, a sophisticated elaboration and extension of the true self communication; at its worst it can be an attempt to hide the true self, and even to become a substitute for it. Strictly speaking when this happens communication is not taking place, although it may seem to be. What is said or painted on to canvas is then the private concern of one person – and the world guesses.

We know that when we are in communication with other people not only does it take place on different levels, but different ways will be used to convey meaning. What the voice *says* will only be part of the story, and sometimes the least important part. The rest will be in terms of attitude, posture, tone, gesture, look or touch – or the non-verbal signs and sounds we all make when what we feel will not go into words.

Then, too, often the things not said speak more loudly than the words said. For example, a woman patient in a hospital said to the almoner, 'This has been a good year for roses, I wonder what they will be like next year.'[2] The real communication here was not about roses, but concerned the patient's knowledge that she would not live to see them next year. It was this knowledge that she wanted to communicate. Or another example would be that of a child being moved from one home to another who said to the child care officer, 'Did David cry when he went away?' The real communication here was not about David, it was quite simply: 'I want to cry *now*.'

For those who would be in communication with others simply everything counts, and all our faculties are needed if we are to receive and interpret with approximate accuracy what others are expressing in what they are, or what they do and say. Fortunately experience increases our awareness of what people communicate and how they do it, but nevertheless we find that each case presents a new task in understanding simply because each individual is unique.

In order to reduce this fascinating but vast subject of communication with children to manageable proportions, I shall confine what I have to say to three aspects of it. The first is to try to put briefly into words what we are *aiming* at in communicating with children. Then, secondly, to raise questions concerning how we communicate, and thirdly to spend some time in discussing five kinds of case which present special problems in communication.

With regard to the question of what we are aiming to achieve in communicating with children, I would say first of all that we are not *aiming* to collect information or to take a case history, although of course we do all the time incidentally collect information about the children and gradually piece together their life story as seen by themselves. This is important to us, and to the children, because it helps us in our assessment of their problems, and it helps them to become aware of continuity. But behind this, our real aim is to keep children alive, and to help them to establish a sense of their own identity and worth in relation to other people. By keeping children alive I am of course referring to maintaining their capacity to feel. If there are no feelings there is no life, there is merely existence. All children who come our way have been through painful experiences of one kind or another, and this has led many of them to clamp down on feelings and others of them to feel angry and hostile, because this is more tolerable than to feel loss and isolation. Our work, therefore, is not easy because it will lead us to seek contact with the suffering part of each child, because locked up in the suffering is each one's potential for living and for feeling love as well as feeling hate and anger. To feel a sense of loss implies that something of value, something loved, is lost, otherwise there would be no loss. Awareness of loss therefore restores the value of that which is lost, and can lead in time to a reinstatement of the lost person and loving feelings in the inner life of the child. When this happens, real memories, as opposed to fantasies, of good past experiences can come flooding back and can be used to counteract the disappointments and frustrations which are also part of the past. In this way the past can become meaningful again. So many of the children we meet have no sense of the past and therefore they have no sense of the present and of the future. The child who has reached his or her own loving potential is then in a position to discover new loving relationships in the present and the future. If we attempt to reassure children and to jog them out of their despair we can deprive them of the chance to reach their own potential, that is, to reach the love they were capable of before they suffered loss.

I now want to turn to the question of *how we set about* trying to get into touch with a child's real feelings. We find that usually it is no good if we set about this task in a deliberate way by trying to delve into the child's inner world because we shall be resisted if we do. The question and answer method simply does not work, and, moreover, we recognise that children have a right to their privacy, and only as we gain experience in implicitly recognising this can we hope to gain their confidence. We know that we must relax, and see first that we adequately fulfil our role in relation to the children. Our role will be broadly determined by the nature of the responsibilities we carry on behalf of our agency. This will need to be made clear so that the child gradually comes to know what he or she may expect of us, and who we are and why we are there anyway.

Then within our role there is the question of what we ourselves are like as people. Do we talk to the grown-ups and ignore the child, or do we ignore the grown-ups and make an immediate fuss of the child in an attempt to evoke a response at all costs? Do we give time to the child and do we also give our undivided attention? Are we reliable? Do we keep promises, or do we forget? Are we the cheerful type, or the quiet type, and are we the same every time? There is a great deal about us as people that children need to establish, and they, even more than grown-ups, are quick to find us out, but this they must do if they are to know how to use us.

As I suggested earlier, real communication which involves direct giving and taking between people does not go on all the time. It happens at certain moments and with certain people and on the whole we select very carefully the people with whom we communicate in the deepest sense which involves our real feelings. Communication involves giving away a bit of ourselves and we are careful to whom we give it. Usually the people with whom we communicate are those whom we have come to trust and with whom we have something in common. In our work with children we therefore find that we spend a good deal of time creating the conditions which make communication possible. We try to establish between ourselves and the children a neutral area in which communication is indirect. In other words we participate in shared experiences, about which both we and the children feel something *about something else*, a third thing, which unites us, but which at the same time keeps us safely apart because it does not involve direct exchange between us. Shared experiences are perhaps the only non-threatening form of communication which exists. They can concern almost anything in which we both participate – walks, car rides, playing, drawing, listening to something, looking at something or talking about something. A child care officer found that the only way that she could feel in touch with an unhappy four-year-old was to sit quietly beside him watching his favourite TV programme. This was not a waste of time because the programme brought them together and united them in a way which was tolerable for the child. When this had happened a few times the child was able to sit nearer to the child care officer so that she could quite naturally put her arm round him. Thus was achieved non-verbal communication. If the child care officer had tried to put her arm round the child to begin with, he would have felt threatened and would have resisted.

Shared experiences form invisible links between people which become strengthened as they begin to have a history. Gradually experiences will be referred to and talked over and relived in retrospect, and we shall find that there evolves between us and the child a language for talking in, which is quite special to each child because it contains his or her own words and way of remembering, and imagery, which we take the trouble to learn and to use. If we first take care to learn a child's words and his or her special meaning for things then in time the child will incorporate and use our words and meanings as his or her own.

Once indirect communication has been established by means of shared experiences then there exists an area of life within which direct communication, direct giving and taking, is possible. In fact anything is now possible; the floodgates could be opened or the sparks could fly. Both these events would be signs of life and evidence that real relationships between people, which involve giving and taking, loving and hating, were being established. For instance, the end of the story of the child care officer and the four-year-old boy watching television together was that, once having established communication by means of her arm round him, he then on a later occasion was able to throw himself into her arms and cry for his mother who was in hospital. The intensity of his love and longing for his mother was felt in these moments, and this in a sense restored her again for him, and made the mother more real. He could not have reached this point alone. After this event he was noticeably less depressed and unhappy, and began to eat more. On later visits this little boy did not want to cry again, nor did he want the child care officer to put her arm round him again. He wanted to go back to the indirect communication of shared experiences. He brought her his books and his toys and she read and played with him. He certainly looked forward to the child care officer's visits and needed them because he knew that at any time communication of his real feelings to her was possible. And so it is that indirect communication involving a third thing – the shared experience – takes the strain out of life, because it enables people to meet, and at the same time to maintain their separateness, because they feel about something else, not about each other. Within this neutral area no demands are made either way, although at any minute they always *could* be made.

When we have created the conditions for communication between ourselves and the children it is important that we recognise it when it happens, and when they speak to us in the language of feeling we must answer in the same language and not in the language of facts. Feelings are illogical, and it is no good our being logical about them; this simply shows the child that we are not on his wavelength after all. To illustrate what I mean there was the case of a twelve-year-old boy in a remand home[4] being visited by a child care officer who had known him before. Towards the end of the interview the boy's father was mentioned and suddenly his eyes filled with tears. The child care officer said, 'Are you worried about your father?' The boy said, 'Yes, I worry about him a lot because his health isn't good and he often seems ill.' The boy looked very distressed and there were more tears. The child care officer said, 'Perhaps you sometimes even feel that your father might die?' The boy said, 'Yes, I do think that, often, and I hate it when he goes out on his bicycle because I always think that he will be brought home dead.' At this point the child care officer lost her nerve and said, 'Well, when I saw your father last week he didn't look at all ill, in fact he was looking very well.' This statement is in the language of facts, and it simply does not reach feeling, and moreover it creates a gulf between the adult and the child. In this case the child care officer might have said something like this: 'I know you are very fond of your father, but perhaps sometimes you feel very angry with him too.' Actually this boy had a great deal about which to be angry with his father, because the father had left the boy's mother, taking the boy away too, and was now living with another woman. At this point the boy started stealing.

So the question of language is an important one, and means that we have to be constantly aware of which language the children are speaking in and to answer them in the same terms, otherwise we shall block communication and leave them frustrated and even more hopeless than ever of being understood.

I now come to the third aspect of my subject and this is to consider why it is that some children present special problems in communication. This matter is of course related to the subject of the social diagnosis in each case. This involves an assessment of the developmental problem with which each child is struggling and the ways in which he is dealing with it. This kind of assessment, which is part of our professional responsibility, is in fact an extension of something which we do automatically in ordinary life. When we meet a child we quite naturally wonder what sort of a child he or she is and what sort of an approach on our part is most likely to meet with a response. In our work, however, we do all this more deliberately and with conscious effort and care because more depends on the success or failure of our efforts and, moreover, if we cannot get on to the wavelength of the individual child we ourselves, as I have suggested, can become the block to communication.

In each case the reason for the difficulty in communication will be a complex one and a highly individual one. The reason will not be an actively deliberate one but will be related to unconscious processes and the drive for self-preservation which is behind all symptoms. The word 'reason', therefore, is a misnomer because it implies conscious thought and choice.

I should like to discuss five kinds of case in which the ability to communicate is seriously impaired or virtually non-existent because the will or drive to communicate is no longer present. These cases will be familiar to all social workers. They are: *the suspicious; the hostile; the withdrawn; the restless extrovert; the depressed.*

1   First, then, there are the children who keep themselves to themselves because they are *suspicious* of anyone or anything outside themselves. The world outside is a bad place and the only way to ensure self-preservation is to have no dealings with the world. A certain amount of suspicion is of course normal and is part of the natural tendency for self-preservation which is present in us all. Usually, however, we do not remain suspicious

– we take the next step, which is to test out the situation or the person to prove if our suspicion is realistic or unfounded, and then we act accordingly. This is happening all the time without our thinking about it. Children are less experienced than adults and therefore have the right to be that much more suspicious. But some people, for a variety of reasons, have lost the courage to test out the situation because they have a deep conviction that their worst fears will come true and they will find that people in the world are as punishing and vindictive as they are feared to be. So they never try to find out, and this at least keeps disaster at bay, although the cost of doing so is high in terms of all that they miss. In many cases suspicion of the world is not a total thing. It becomes fixed on to one thing, for example, food, or certain places or people or certain activities. This can be difficult to handle but, so long as the suspicions are respected, it does at least give elbow room for development in other directions.

The establishing of communication with a child who is unduly suspicious will obviously take time and patience, because any attempt on our part to break in will only increase suspicion. These children need the opportunity to see us in action so that they can weigh us up and assess our attitudes towards other people and towards themselves, and then one day they may have the courage to test us out in some way or other, when they are ready to do so. I remember seeing a boy of nine, who was a deeply suspicious person, come up to his house-father saying that there was something in his eye. Fortunately the house-father took this very seriously because it was the first time this boy had asked for any personal attention, and, although there was actually nothing in his eye, it was bathed and treated with great respect. This was the beginning of a gradual lessening of suspicion. The child communicated, and the communication was received as such. Another example is that of a child care officer who, over a period of many months, had spent much time in the playroom of a children's home with a suspicious little girl of four years. As soon as the child care officer came into the room this child never took her eyes off her and surreptitiously watched every movement and every contact the child care officer had with any other child, but strongly resisted any move made towards herself. After months of this seemingly futile attempt, the child care officer was one day sitting on the floor talking to another child, when the child in question rolled a ball very slowly across the floor until it touched the child care officer. The child care officer then rolled the ball equally slowly back to the child. The rolling game continued at each visit for a long time and by means of it tension was lessened and communication was gradually expanded.

In the kind of case in which suspicion dominates the scene we know that what is happening can be stated in theoretical terms as the projection by the child of all his or her hostile feelings on to the outside world in an attempt to preserve the goodness within him- or herself.

2   The next kind of case I want to discuss presents the opposite picture. The child himself feels so *angry and hostile* that he fears that he will

destroy everyone and everything in sight. Therefore, in order to preserve the outside world, which somehow he at the same time values, he hangs on to his anger and attempts to keep it inside and under control. Such a child will be unable to communicate his real feelings because he fears their destructive potential. When we attempt to get near to him he seems indifferent, passive and uncooperative. These children are often easier to help than the suspicious ones, because deep down they do believe in goodness and are capable of love. First of all, however, we have to meet and survive the hostility and aggression such children truly feel but dare not communicate. We have ample evidence of its existence. Usually it shows on their faces and in their attitude of calculated indifference. Before we can get anywhere this needs facing and putting into words. I am reminded of a probation case in which a twelve-year-old boy remained actively passive for many weeks and obviously found great difficulty in making the slightest response to the probation officer. One day the probation officer went to collect the boy from the waiting room and on the way out of the room the boy suddenly punched another boy in an angry way. The probation officer took him away quickly before a fight started up and said to him, 'You must be pretty mad with someone to hit out like that, and I don't think it's with that boy in the waiting room. I guess you're pretty mad about having to come here at all and with me for insisting that you do.' The boy admitted that he was angry at having to come and thought it was all a waste of time, etc. As this boy's hostility was met, and recognised, it became possible at last for the two people to meet on a realistic basis. Obviously the boy intended the probation officer to see his anger and it was then possible for the probation officer to deal with it. But he could not have done so earlier.

3   A third kind of case in which communication in the real sense of the word is very difficult to establish is that of the child whose effective personality is *withdrawn* into him- or herself as a protective measure against dependence and the frustrations and disappointments that go with it. Inadequate personal care and loving attention or the sudden withdrawal of it, or the actual loss of the person depended on, can result in this state of affairs. The child withdraws and so to speak 'looks after' him- or herself. These children do not seem to suffer actively, nor are they overtly hostile or suspicious, because they have put themselves beyond the reach of the ordinary feelings that are part and parcel of all relationships.

Outwardly they comply just enough to maintain their existence with the least effort. We must expect to fail to communicate with many of these children, but that does not mean that we should give up trying and write them off. Perhaps they need our presence in their lives as *the person with whom they do not communicate* and from whom they have withdrawn. This may involve us in silent sessions or in some activity, such as reading a story, which makes no demands on them. If we can accept this role of the person with whom they do not communicate, without seeking to force our way in, then one day the situation could alter, but if we do not put ourselves in this position and contract out, there is little hope that it will alter. I remember trying to help a young woman in her twenties. She had been a very withdrawn child, actually spending most of her time in a large cupboard under the stairs. In here she kept her toys and her possessions, including her radio for listening to *Children's Hour*, which she never missed. She only really felt secure when she was in this place. She actually slept in it as well, and as far as possible she kept everyone else, especially her mother, out of it. Many times when I saw her I had to say, because I felt it was true, 'Today you are in your cupboard with all your possessions, and I know that I must not come into it.' Some months later she had a dream that she was in an underground cave – it was warm and cosy – 'rather like her cupboard', she said, and there was plenty of food, and I was there and we were going to cook a meal. So there had been an alteration in the situation, and for once I was allowed into the cupboard. But I am sure that this would not have happened if I had not accepted the role of the person who was *there*, but who was kept outside. In this rather negative way eventually something positive could happen, but what a pity it could not have happened years before.

For some of these withdrawn children maybe only a regression to dependence on the person who is actually living with them and caring for them will bring them through to the place where a real relationship based on the meeting of dependence needs is possible. In other words, the place which enables them to give up 'looking after themselves' and be dependent on someone who can then take them forward in the natural way until they can be truly independent within the setting. If this is to happen the person caring for the child will need much support from the child care officer. I have known people who can take children through this kind of experience, but they do not do it easily and need constant reassurance.

4   By contrast with the children who withdraw from the problems of everyday life there are others who may deal with their problems by the opposite kind of reaction which we call a 'flight to reality'. We may regard them as *extrovert*, and find them full of activity, talkative and co-operative. We can easily be misled by these children partly because they are such a relief from the more unresponsive children on our caseload. But in time we notice that their activities change too frequently and they lack sustaining power. They talk too much, and too easily, about anything that comes to mind for comment. What they are doing is clutching at anything that is available outside themselves to prevent themselves from feeling, because feeling would lead to despair and hopelessness. In working with these children we have to beware that we ourselves do not get caught up in their endless merry-go-round that leads nowhere. Here again we have to play a waiting game, establishing ourselves in their lives as someone who can be trusted and with whom they might eventually share their hopelessness. But they have to make quite sure first that we are not taken in by their excitability. If they could reach with us a moment of true feeling this might enable them to reconstruct their lives on a sounder

basis. In other words if they can *feel*, even if it is only to feel the pain of loss and despair, then the way is open for other feelings to come to life again. Many children will not be able to reach this point because it is altogether too painful, and they will construct their lives on an artificial basis. Some may achieve much and be the life and soul of many a party, but they will be inwardly dissatisfied because they are incapable of any real relationship.

5 The last group of children I want to mention as presenting to us problems in communication are those who are obviously in *a depressed state*. They are difficult to reach because they are preoccupied with their own anxieties which may concern their health and bodily functions or their lack of achievements or relationships. Life feels futile because they feel dead inside. We know from experience that any effort we make to encourage these children out of their depression or to distract them or cheer them up, although it may seem to work temporarily, is, in the long run, of no avail, because it simply does not reach them. Children in this state cannot believe that anything is good because they doubt their own goodness. They may say, 'Mother is not good' or 'My parents are bad', but even if this is true it is only another way of saying that they themselves are no good. It seems to me that the only way to reach these children is that we ourselves should believe in and acknowledge their feelings of badness and deadness, because they are *real*. We may know that this is not the total truth about them, but at the moment it is. To attempt to cheer them up or get them to snap out of their depression is like a rejection of them, and as such it confirms their feelings about themselves, and removes them still further from us.

If we can 'hold' them as they are in their despair, and understanding is a kind of holding, then there is some chance that they might come to life again. Of course we may find that we do actually hold them physically at times when it seems appropriate. The point is that we cannot bring them to life again in any artificial way by trying to inject them with our belief in their goodness and that life is worth living. Only their own belief will enable them to find it so.

When we fully acknowledge the hopelessness and despair that many children we meet carry around with them, not only is this evidence to them that we are in touch with them, but it means that their feelings are now a stated fact and, as such, are objectified and put outside themselves. This can bring relief and the possibility of an alternative way of living. But if nobody acknowledges the existence of the despairing self the children themselves have to keep it going. It is here that people tend to say that the child is wallowing in despair, but what else can he do with it except to lose touch with feelings?

I have spent some time describing various kinds of case in which we find communication difficult to establish. I am aware that I could add to this list and that I have for instance not mentioned the children who are overtly hostile, but it seems to me that in practice they are not so difficult to communicate with as the cases I have mentioned.

When we feel we are failing to make contact with a particular child, it is only fair to ourselves, let alone to the child concerned, that we should give careful attention to this question of diagnosis, because this affects not only what we do but how much we can reasonably expect to do. We all too easily blame ourselves when we fail to establish communication and feel that our techniques are inadequate (and then we blame those who taught us, or did not teach us) but I suggest that, more often than not, it is our assessment that is not adequate.

To sum up I would say that if we believe in the reality of children's feelings we shall not find it difficult to communicate. If, on the other hand, we do not have this belief, we cannot get round the difficulty by learning techniques. It is better then to leave alone the subject of communicating with children.

Notes

1   Readers will note that, while Clare Winnicott writes from an exclusively psychodynamic perspective, this is not (as would now be common) explicitly stated in the article. At the time of its publication courses in psychology for social workers were based predominantly on the teachings of Sigmund Freud and his followers.
2   Helen M. Lambrick (1962) 'Communication with the patient', *The Almoner*, Vol. 15, No. 7, October.
3   The term 'child care officer' ceased to be used after 1971; the equivalent category of worker is now a social worker who works primarily with children.
4   The term 'remand home' is no longer used. Currently the nearest equivalent is an observation and assessment centre.

15   Assessing children's needs

Margaret Adcock with Roger Lake and Andrew Small

A framework for assessment

Children on social workers' caseloads have often had traumatic experiences of abuse, loss, separation and discontinuity. The social worker's task is firstly to protect these children from further risk, and secondly, to try and create a favourable environment for their recovery and future growth. The most important objective for social workers is to offer children a permanent family who can provide them with secure attachments, opportunities for enjoyment, and increased self-esteem, as well as activities to facilitate growth, development and the mastery of new skills. The role of the social worker is to help parents, or those who are to care for the child, to understand the way in which earlier developmental needs have not been met, and to help them provide good enough parenting in the future. It may also involve helping children to identify any feelings they may have about past events, and aiding them in making sense of any confusion they might have about these.

Studies of children coming into care suggest that the key factors which seem to put them most at risk are:

- a number of changes of placement;
- the instability of the home and the rejection of those caring for the child;
- the child's perception of the impermanence of his or her present home.

Children themselves, however, can precipitate family breakdown by their behaviour, and by their misinterpretations of situations. There is a continuous process of interaction between children and the significant people in their social world. For example, the separation of children from adults to whom they have been very attached may, in consequence, cause them to behave in ways that other adults find intolerable. As a result, these adults become unwilling or unable to provide the continuity of care which the child longs for. Wolkind (1984) described a study he undertook of children in residential care, where a considerable continuity of disorder was found over a five-year period. He concluded that the children's original disorder influenced the care system in such a way as actually to create conditions which then *increased* the disorder.

To plan a permanent family life for a child, therefore, social workers must recognise not only the importance of providing continuity of care, but also the importance of assessing children's difficulties in the context of their history, their home circumstances, their school situation and the effect of past decisions made by professionals about them. As Herbert (1985) points out, the term 'problem child' is an oversimplification: it makes it sound as though the problem belongs to the child alone, whereas it may be the 'problem situation' which needs attention. A treatment plan should be based on assessment of the child, his or her environment and the interaction between the two. The case study of 'Clifford' in this chapter demonstrates how the worker paid constant attention to this interaction.

To make an assessment it is necessary to acquire factual information from files and records, and to observe and talk with children, parents, professionals workers and others concerned with the children's welfare. Assessing children means getting to know them and creating an atmosphere of trust in which they feel free to communicate both verbally and non-verbally. To this end, play is likely to be one important medium of communication.

Preparation and assessment

Workers need to prepare themselves for working with a child. There are two steps which must always be taken. The first is to clarify the presenting problem and ask why an assessment is required at this time. The presenting problem may be:

- Concern that the child's current living situation is not 'good enough'. The child may be experiencing rejection, neglect and physical, sexual or emotional abuse. An assessment of both the child and his/her situation is necessary to ascertain whether parenting is 'good enough'.
- The child's behaviour, which is causing concern and which may lead to a request for removal from his/her family or placement and may prevent return.
- The child may have had a traumatic experience, accompanied by loss or separation. An assessment is necessary as a basis for plans to provide the child with opportunities for recovery and 'good enough' care in the future.
- The child may be in an impermanent placement. An assessment is necessary in order to plan a placement which can be permanent.

The second step is to prepare oneself. Andrew Small writes:

> It is a basic casework principle and is part of the way one sees a client as a unique individual. If the worker has not prepared, 'cleared the decks', then he/she is not going to be able truly to engage that client as there will be too much psychological clutter getting in the way. In my work with Michael, I did this by:
>
> (a) Giving myself enough time and space to do the work. This meant negotiating with management for the 'space' on my caseload as well as preparing the real space, the working playroom.

(b)   Booking the sessions, so that they were regular and consistent.
(c)   Communicating with residential social work colleagues to make sure they had some understanding of the work and were in agreement with it.
(d)   Using supervision to think through the range of activities that might be useful in helping Michael.
(e)   Practising the techniques in role play before the sessions.
(f)   Going to the workroom and familiarising myself with the materials, that is, clay and paint. I would use this time to play and get in touch with some of the things I was feeling just before a session.
(g)   Using techniques of relaxation/breathing exercises, both on myself prior to sessions and with Michael in the session.

Clarity about the presenting problem and the purpose of an assessment will make it easier both to engage children and adults in the process and to help everyone make sense of the information that is collected. I once took a little girl and her brother to lunch in a solicitor's office. We explained to them what would happen in court, what the judge needed to know and what decisions he would have to make. Angela, the little girl, then put on the black gown hanging on the door and said she was going to be the judge making a decision. For the next half an hour she involved us all in enacting the court situation. Through this we learnt a great deal about Angela and her perceptions of her situation, which helped us in our assessment. She had an opportunity to express her fears and worries in a situation which she could control, and therefore begin to understand.

History-taking

To begin an assessment, we firstly need to know the history of the child in some detail. How many moves and changes of carers has the child had? What was happening to the adults at these times? What was the effect of change on the child and the adults? How did they respond? What sort of behaviour did the child show? The answers to these questions can help workers, children and those caring for them to understand more fully the problems and difficulties that the child has encountered. Roger Lake's case study of Clifford, aged five, illustrates the use of history-taking:

Clifford, aged 5½ years, is an attractive boy of black Afro-Caribbean origin. He currently lives with his mother, Yvonne, aged twenty-five years, and sister, Michelle, aged two years. By the time he was five, Clifford had been in care three times under Section 2 of the 1980 Child Care Act for relatively short periods and for a variety of reasons.

Clifford's behaviour had been deteriorating over several months, according to his mother, social worker and health visitor. His mother found his frequent temper tantrums, disruptive behaviour and attention-seeking activities extremely difficult to tolerate. He was particularly difficult to control at meal and bedtimes, becoming aggressive and abusive towards his mother and sister. On such occasions, Yvonne had expressed the wish that he had been adopted.

The health visitor and the social worker saw the problem from a different point of view – their concern was with Yvonne's parenting. They had been worried about her difficulty in providing him with basic stimulation at home – his lack of toys and play materials, and her lack of involvement in his play. One consequence of this was a serious speech delay for which, when he was three, he had been referred for speech therapy. All these problems were a reflection of his mother's general feelings of depression and of her isolation, insecurity and lack of a permanent residence.

A previous social worker had described her as being 'sharp and impatient' with Clifford. On one occasion two years ago, a burn-mark on Clifford's arm had been reported and it was strongly felt that he was frequently hit. He was certainly a witness of extreme violence between his mother and father, a relationship which was turbulent and unhappy. His father (Leroy) spent several periods in prison for criminal offences including crimes of violence. Eventually, when Clifford was one, their relationship broke down, with Yvonne and Clifford fleeing to a Women's Aid hostel. The subsequent moves she made were ostensibly to avoid Clifford's father for fear of further violence. She had several transient relationships with men and after one such affair Michelle, her second child, was born.

Clifford's first period in care came during Yvonne's confinement with Michelle. He went home after two weeks but came back into care for a short period about a month later because Yvonne was feeling depressed and exhausted. When Clifford was five, both children were in care for a further week when Yvonne went to hospital for a termination. According to social work records, these relatively short periods in care had always been marked by Yvonne's depression, her sense of isolation, her inability to cope with the demands of the children and her ambivalent feelings towards Clifford. In addition, she appeared to have a very poor self-image and was unsupported by relatives or friends.

I started working with the family shortly after Clifford's last period in care. My own contact with the family added the following information. The family were rehoused by the Council to their present address towards the end of the year prior to my beginning work with them. To her credit, Yvonne had made great efforts to use social work help to improve the quality of home life for herself and her children. Her finances and budgeting were better managed and she made use of a number of community supports – a day nursery, a mother and toddler group and the health visitor. In addition she referred herself for psychotherapy. Clifford had started school in September and reports suggested he had settled in well, his language having improved during a spell at day nursery. But throughout these improvements, his mother continued to express negative feelings towards him and complained about his behaviour.

Initial plan for action: the need for further information

The history-taking made me realise I still had a lot to learn about Clifford before I could formulate any specific treatment goals. But Yvonne and I did agree at this point that the main identified problem was the management of Clifford's behaviour. With Yvonne's agreement, therefore, it was decided that I should make a developmental assessment of Clifford. This had not been done previously and I felt it important to ascertain how far he was behind the developmental norms for his age (Sheridan, 1986). I also wanted to investigate the quality of his attachment to his mother, and his interaction with significant adults, siblings and peers (Fahlberg, 1981a). In discussion with my supervisor, we anticipated that this would take three sessions. I suggested to Yvonne that, when this work was completed and we had discussed it together, I might then embark on a series of direct work sessions with Clifford and, concurrently with her, help them improve the quality of their relationship.

Born 10.1.80 in Hospital, London. Lived with Mummy at Granny's house for two days. Moved to Flat. Went to Hospital for two weeks. Tummy problem.

Daddy goes into prison. Move with Mummy to two other houses in London. Daddy hurts Mummy sometimes and they cannot live together because it makes them unhappy.

Moved to Southwark. Go into Hospital for two weeks for some tests. Start at Nursery. Move to another house a long way away at the seaside because Daddy hurt Mummy.

Move to flat in Wandsworth, go to new Nursery and meet new friends. Michelle is born. Go to 1st Foster home (Aunty Julie's). Go to 2nd Foster home (Aunty Eileen) for 1 week. Mummy not well.

Go to 3rd Foster home (A. Alison's) with Michelle for a 'holiday' because Mummy is not well. Start at Poplar Av. School. Move to new house.

Understanding Clifford's development: flow charts and growth charts

My starting point was the use of a flow chart to plot the significant changes, moves and separations which had taken place in Clifford's life (for guidance on construction of flow charts see Batty, 1984). Batty believes flow charts have two distinct purposes in child care practice:

First, they make an excellent recording aid. A blank flow chart at the front of a file can be filled in quickly and easily as events happen, or can be 'made-up' at a time of movement or crisis more readily and for easier reference than a written report. The other purpose is less obvious and perhaps more significant. Flow charts are valuable aids to evoke feelings. An adult constructing his or her own flow chart will find him or herself experiencing again some of the feelings of joy and pain that accompanied the original events. These feelings are sometimes modified when perceived in sequence with other events on the chart as it is constructed, but as a result of the exercise, the subject's awareness of the feelings evoked in childhood is heightened. (Batty, 1984, p. 50)

Yvonne sat Clifford on her knee whilst we compiled the chart. He showed little interest and was constantly distracted. He soon became bored so I changed the format we were using to an 'orange segment' as I felt he might find this easier to understand (see Figure above).

Despite saying he couldn't remember early events, he spoke with excitement about his foster placements as 'holidays'. In watching this, Yvonne came to feel that he had been less affected by his brief periods in care than by witnessing the violence between herself and his father which had led to a move to the Women's Aid refuge.

In completing the 'orange', I was immediately struck by the number of moves and separations that had taken place in Clifford's life. Yvonne's presence had also helped us to clarify together the tenuous and transitory relationships Yvonne established with people.

Having established details of significant events in Clifford's life, the next task was to make some assessment of Clifford's physical, cognitive and emotional development. Research from abused and neglected children suggests that this is an important initial area of investigation (Beezley *et al.*, 1976). There is also a need for continuing comprehensive developmental assessments, and for social workers to be aware that many medical, behavioural and emotional problems may continue after the original abuse (Hensey *et al.*, 1983, Lynch and Roberts, 1982). Significantly, Lynch and Roberts found that social workers were not always aware of the importance of medical and developmental follow-ups. They describe a case where a social worker spent considerable time talking to a mother about her relationship with her child, without seeing very much of the child, who was found by the authors to have a severe visual defect, learning difficulties and severe behaviour problems when with her peers. A similar point was made in the Beckford inquiry (Blom-Cooper, 1985), which reprimanded social workers for their lack of detailed observation of children's development.

Paediatricians stress the importance of looking at children's growth and monitoring this by regular use of weight and height charts. Social workers can also make use of these tools to identify basic developmental milestones. Cooper (1986) believes that charts should be kept for all young children where there is concern about the adequacy of care. The growth curve is much more important than any single measurement. Weight, height and head circumference should be checked every 2–4 weeks during the child's first year of life and every 6–12 weeks in the second and third year. Even in older children the growth curve may demonstrate periods of severe stress due to a variety of adverse environmental conditions. Social workers will always need to collaborate with medical colleagues in obtaining these details but may also find it helpful to use Sheridan's charts (1986) as indicators of normal development or delay. These illustrate the developmental progress of infants and young children up to five years old in terms of posture and large movements, vision and fine movements, hearing and speech, social behaviour and play. If there are serious areas of concern, these should be discussed with a paediatrician.

Emotional development: assessing attachment and interactions between children and adults

Emotional development is of primary concern to social workers. All children need secure attachments if they are to flourish and develop their potential, and it is important to get to know the details of the current and past attachment figures in a child's life. In doing so, the considerable diversity in acceptable patterns of attachment should be remembered. Quoting the work of Kennell *et al.* (1976), Fahlberg describes attachment as 'an affectionate bond between two individuals that endures through time and space and serves to join them emotionally' (Fahlberg, 1981a, p. 7). It is widely agreed that, for the majority of children in our culture, the family provides an excellent context in which attachments may develop.

Attachment helps the child:

- attain full intellectual potential
- sort out what is perceived
- think logically
- develop a conscience
- become self-reliant
- cope with stress and frustration
- handle fear and worry
- develop future relationships
- reduce jealousy. (Fahlberg, 1981a, p. 7)

In assessing attachment, social workers should make detailed observations of children and their interaction with the adults responsible for their care. It should be remembered that the function of attachment is protection. The primary carers provide a secure base from which children can explore, and to which they can return, especially should they become tired or frightened. Their behaviour complements children's attachment behaviour (Bowlby, 1986) and it is important to look at the sensitivity of parents or carers to a child's overtures, their awareness of children as individuals, their interactions with their children and how they set limits and discipline them.

Many children who come into care may have experienced their parents as unpredictable, inconsistent, unresponsive, insensitive or rejecting (Bretherton and Waters, 1985). This may create a pattern of attachment behaviour in the children which then makes it difficult for adult carers to respond to their needs. The issue of whether early attachments irrevocably influence a child's later capacity to make affectionate bonds is contentious. There is, however, no doubt that childhood experiences can influence many factors in adulthood, particularly the pattern and stability of relationships (Rutter, 1981, 1985; Rutter and Quinton, 1984). Recent evidence also indicates that changes in attachment patterns can occur through emotionally corrective experiences in relationships. These changes can be a result of:

1   a change in the pattern of the early relationships through time;
2   through repeated experiences in other relationships that break the pattern of earlier experiences;
3   through an especially strong emotional experience within a single relationship that breaks the pattern of earlier experiences.

It is clearly an important task for social workers both to assess the nature and quality of a child's attachments and then to seek to provide the kinds of experience that help to facilitate change.

Children's personalities and their reactions to their experiences

Attachment is only one aspect of children's emotional development. We also need to find out how children have reacted to other important experiences (Beezley *et al.*, 1976). We must understand the nature of their peer relationships, their relationships with other significant adults such as teachers, their schooling, their interests and their cultural and racial experiences.

In a follow-up study of fifty abused children, Martin and Beezley (1977) found that over half had poor self-images, were sorrowful children and acted in a manner which was upsetting to their parents, teachers and peers. Some were withdrawn, others were difficult and defiant. Certain characteristics could be noted with disturbing frequency:

• impaired ability for enjoyment
• behavioural adjustment symptoms
• low self-esteem
• withdrawal
• opposition
• hyper-vigilance
• compulsivity
• pseudo-adult behaviour.

Throughout all of what has been said above, it is important to remember that children's development is the result of the interactions between them, their family and their environment. Problems in any one of these areas can interrupt the normal process of growth and change.

Roger Lake used the developmental charts in conjunction with checklists of attachments in three sessions with Clifford and his mother. They helped to emphasise the relationship between Clifford's development and the quality of his attachment to his mother. In the first two sessions, Roger asked Clifford to complete simple tasks such as copying a triangle and a square and identifying colours, and in so doing Roger was able to observe Clifford's vision and fine movements. Similarly, using Sheridan's guidance on large movements, he asked Clifford to run, jump and dance to music. These activities were performed willingly and with enthusiasm, particularly the dancing (information which Roger was to use later in his direct work sessions). Clifford's speech was studied and his memory tested. He knew his name but found it difficult to remember his address, which was perhaps not surprising as they had recently moved. He understood times of day but, like many five-year-olds, had difficulty with clock time. Overall, it was clear that Clifford was easily able to accomplish the majority of tasks set.

Roger Lake also involved Clifford's mother in the process, by affirming her value as an information giver:

> In relation to his social behaviour and play, Yvonne had informed me, and I had already observed, that he is usually well able to use a knife and fork, cannot wash his own face but can dress or undress himself, although he often gets muddled with buttons. Yvonne also said that she thought his behaviour had been getting generally worse, particularly at meal times and bedtimes.

Out of these sessions Roger was struck by two significant factors. Firstly, Yvonne's lack of encouragement for Clifford during the tasks; she found some of his efforts amusing, appearing to laugh at him in a mocking way; and secondly, the tentative way in which Clifford approached the tasks. Roger felt Clifford was going to need regular encouragement and praise at appropriate times during any play sessions.

Roger comments:

> For the next session, I wanted to make my own observations of Clifford's behaviour and his relationship with his mother, so I deliberately did a home visit at a meal time, identified by Yvonne as being 'difficult'. Not for the first time, the house was full of Yvonne's friends. Despite the chaotic atmosphere, we managed to spend time with Clifford in the kitchen, before and after his supper. Clifford was in a tetchy mood, unable to settle at the table, hurling cutlery around, and shouting that he wanted to watch TV. Despite his remonstrations, he eventually ate his food with little fuss.
>
> Using Fahlberg's checklist on attachment (1981a), I noted several problems in Clifford's behaviour. He made defiant responses to his mother's requests, characterised by 'No, I won't' or 'Do it yourself'. He seemed most preoccupied by television, often displayed inappropriate reactions in the presence of adults and appeared 'too familiar' and sophisticated in their presence. He expressed frustration by shouting, being physically aggressive or excessively moody. He did respond well to physical affection from his mother when sitting on her knee or when given a cuddle, but the overtures were not particularly spontaneous.
>
> I observed that the measures to discipline Clifford were inconsistent and dependent on his mother's moods. 'Bedroom' was a punishment, as was 'smacking'. A positive fact was that Yvonne was able to show some interest in his development, commenting on his rate of growth and how his speech had improved since starting school. Although there did appear to be signs of a genuine affectionate relationship between them (she often spoke of how she loved him, and there were cuddles), Yvonne spoke of how Clifford's

physical appearance and behaviour had reminded her so much of his father that she sometimes had nightmares that he was 'mad, just like his father'.

Finally, I checked out details of Clifford's functioning with his school teacher, since he spent a significant part of his day at school. Here, he was described as 'a rather isolated and independent little boy who had difficulty in making friends, often having fights'. (This was in contrast to Clifford's own version, which was that he had 'lots of friends at school'.)

Putting the assessment together

From being with Clifford and talking to his mother, observing them together and constructing flow charts and developmental charts, Roger had learned a good deal about Clifford's functioning, his interaction with his mother, his physical and emotional development and the impact of his past separations and moves. Roger's assessment was as follows:

1 Clifford's mother had difficulty in relating his behaviour to his past experiences or her mixed feelings towards him. Sadly, she did not have the parenting skills to understand his need to explore his own world through his imagination or play, and had not been able to enjoy him as a child.
2 These feelings, coupled with the numerous separations in his early life, had contributed to his shaky sense of trust in his mother, and had blunted his confidence.
3 There had been a deterioration in Clifford's behaviour both at home and at school and a worsening of the relationship between Clifford and his mother so that their interaction was in danger of becoming a downward spiral leading to family breakdown. The more Clifford behaved badly, the more his mother was likely to reject him.
4 Weighing the pros and cons of Clifford's development and his relationship with his mother, there were pointers to potential for change, such as warmth between them and concern from Yvonne about his progress. A critical factor was that any positive responses from Clifford would be dependent upon his mother initiating positive interaction with him, thus promoting his self-worth and self-esteem.

Formulating goals

This assessment led Roger Lake to formulate goals and a treatment plan which would take approximately three to four months. The overall goal, within the context of permanency planning, was to prevent family breakdown. To achieve this, Roger proposed a treatment plan on two levels. Firstly, there would be six direct work sessions with Clifford, aimed at helping him to sort out his confusion about the past and to build up his sense of self-worth by learning to play as a five-year-old. Secondly, these sessions would be followed by work with Yvonne to increase her under-standing of Clifford's behavioural problems and to help her change her own behaviour towards him. This might be achieved by direct one-to-one work, family therapy and linking her to community supports such as a family centre, or providing her with a family aid.

In involving both Clifford and his mother in the programme, Roger Lake recognised the danger that workers can become so involved in direct work with children that adults caring for them feel jealous and excluded and children's permanent relationships may be placed in jeopardy. The worker's task is not to become a substitute parent. Fahlberg's three publi-cations (1981a, 1981b and 1982) provide a helpful discussion of these issues.

Outcome

Assessment and treatment go hand in hand. Space precludes a detailed discussion of the treatment plan for Clifford and his mother. Roger Lake had to prepare for his direct sessions with Clifford, working out the techniques and materials which he would use. During the sessions he learned more about Clifford's problems and potential. He recognised that assessment was ongoing throughout his intervention. Sometimes, infor-mation about the child's problems can be discovered only when a child feels confident enough to trust an adult. You can only assess the potential for resolving problems by providing a context in which progress can be made. So it was with Clifford. By giving him the time, space and oppor-tunities for therapeutic play, Clifford's behaviour began to improve, which, in turn, provoked a more positive response from the adults around him. This was only a beginning, but enough change had occurred in Clifford's behaviour to confirm that the original assessment had been correct in predicting potential for change. The direct work sessions revealed that more work would have to be done with Clifford and his family to consolidate his progress.

Roger Lake was about to begin his planned work with Clifford's mother when another crisis occurred: 'Yvonne rang me to say she had left her home and was in a Women's Aid hostel with the children. Leroy was pursuing her – and she had fled in fear. I realised there was still much work to be done'. A new phase of assessment and treatment was about to begin.

References

BATTY, D. (1984) 'The use of flow charts', *In Touch with Children: A Training Pack*, London, BAAF.

BEEZLEY, P., MARTIN, H. and ALEXANDER, H. (1976) 'Comprehensive family orientated therapy' in Heffer, R. E. and Kempe, C. H. (eds) *Child Abuse and Neglect: The Family and the Community*, Cambridge, MA, Ballinger.

BLOM-COOPER, L. (1985) *A Child in Trust*, London, London Borough of Brent.

BOWLBY, J. (1986) 'The making and breaking of affectional bonds', in *Working with Children*, BAAF.

BRETHERTON, I. and WATERS, E. (eds) (1985) *Growing Points of Attachment Theory and Research*, Monograph of the Society for Research in Child Development, Vol. 50, Nos. 1–2.

COOPER, C. (1986) 'The growing child' in *Working with Children*, BAAF.

FAHLBERG, V. (1981a) *Attachment and Separation*, BAAF.

FAHLBERG, V. (1981b) *Helping Children When They Must Move*, BAAF.

FAHLBERG, V. (1982) *Child Development*, BAAF.

HENSEY, O. J., WILLIAMS, J. K. and ROSENBLOOM, L. (1983) 'Intervention in child abuse: experience in Liverpool', *Developmental Medicine and Child Neurology*.

HERBERT, M. (1985) *Caring for your Children*, Oxford, Blackwell.

KENNELL, J., VOOS, D. and KLAUS, M. (1976) 'Parent-Infant Bonding' in Helfer, R. and Kempe, C. H. (eds) *Child abuse and neglect*, Cambridge, Mass: Ballinger Publishing Co.

LYNCH, M. and ROBERTS, J. (1982) *Consequences of Child Abuse*, London, Academic Press.

MARTIN, H. and BEEZLEY, P. (1977) 'Behavioural observations of abused children', *Developmental Medicine and Child Neurology*, No. 19.

RUTTER, M. (1981) 'Stress, coping and development: some issues and some questions', *Journal of Child Psychology and Psychiatry*, Vol. 22, No. 4.

RUTTER, M. (1985) 'Resilience in the face of adversity', *British Journal of Psychiatry*, Vol. 147, pp. 598–611.

RUTTER, M. and QUINTON, D. (1984) 'Long-term follow-up of women institutionalized in childhood: factors promoting good functioning in adult life', *British Journal of Developmental Psychology*, Vol. 18.

SHERIDAN, M. (1986) 'Chart illustrating the developmental progress of infants and young children', in *Working with Children*, BAAF.

WOLKIND, S. N. (1984) 'A child psychiatrist in court: using the contributions of developmental psychology' in *Taking a Stand*, BAAF.

16 Children in care: the racial dimension in social work assessment

Shama Ahmed

I will start with an attitude in child care work which is anathema to me, and that is the belief that the needs of black and white children are identical. One often hears field and residential workers say 'children are children', or that they 'serve children not black children'. Some go further and maintain that the best interest of a black child is served by giving him or her an opportunity to acquire a 'white identity' as this would facilitate integration. Sometimes, examples are quoted where black children in care have refused black foster homes and expressed a preference for white substitute families and white professionals, such as teachers, social workers, doctors, etc. This identification with core culture is interpreted as positive indication of cultural assimilation. The reason why black children show a strong preference for the dominant white majority group and express a tendency to devalue their own group is insufficiently understood, because British social work has not yet developed the race relations dimension in teaching and practice. Some superficial interpretations could be avoided if there was more awareness of the process of internalising the white ego ideal.

In a recent court case in Wolverhampton, concerning a West Indian mother's appeal against the assumption of parental rights by the local authority, evidence emerged which showed that the children, aged seven and five, were already showing disturbing symptoms of self-rejection. The five-year-old was trying to bleach herself with powder, and had in many ways expressed her desire to be white. The foster-mother admitted that the children considered black as dirty. She was a loving foster-mother, but had not been sensitised to the children's racial problems. Clearly, in such cases love is not enough. In giving independent testimony on the identity problems of a black child in a white home, I emphasised the need for the children to see themselves as black with pride, but this stand was considered racial and unhelpful by many.

In no way was this case or the foster-parent's evidence unusual. These are the usual experiences of children in care. At times the problems for Asian children seem even greater than for children of Afro-Caribbean origins. Asian children in care have been deeply confused and disturbed because their parents dress differently; 'dad' may wear a turban; they speak a different language; they often leave instructions concerning forbidden foods. Even the gifts they bring can be different, for example Asian sweets rather than chocolates; in a recent case, the relatives of a Bangladeshi child gave the foster-mother's own children a pound each. The foster-mother was annoyed; she said that a gift would have been quite acceptable. There was a need to explain that, in a non-industrial society, money rather than consumer goods is often given as a gift.

Youngsters of eleven and twelve make comparisons of lifestyles, parents' mannerisms, material possessions, styles of furnishing a house, etc. and feel unhappy and ashamed because their parents' lifestyle is so different.

Many residential staff and foster-parents, who care deeply for the Asian child in their care, seem to become suspicious and ill at ease with the children's parents. The linguistic and cultural differences enhance tensions: for instance, the way in which friends and relatives often present as brothers, sisters or aunts – a cultural trait – quickly arouses suspicions of the Asian's deceit and deviousness. This tension and the negative evaluation of the family and their ways does not fail to communicate itself to a culturally, racially and emotionally insecure child. Very often the youngsters react by refusing to see their parents; this can be an expression of a desire to avoid embarrassment and conflict. Sometimes, they develop a pattern of misbehaving after the visits and one can find the residential staff suggesting a reduction in contact with the family. In such situations the planned rehabilitation work, which always requires the support and tolerance of many people, suffers.

The consequences for the young person, who severs contact with the family and identifies totally with the dominant group, may on an overt level be a reduction of conflict for a short period. However, the internal stress is usually too great and problems manifest themselves in other ways later. The usually intense early socialisation experiences of the Asian child mean that family values continue to dominate the individual internally, although outwardly the tie may be disrupted.

While most black children in white society are in danger of growing up with a devalued self-image, I consider children in care separated from their parents *and* their community to be at special risk. The psychological well-being of these children is particularly threatened, because a white child separated from its parents can hope to experience love and care from other white adults; black children separated from their families rarely have the opportunity to experience close and loving relationships with black adults. They interpret it thus: 'my black mum rejected me and my white mum loved me'; Asian and Afro-Caribbean children tend to generalise what they experience as rejection by their parents, and tend to develop negative attitudes towards the entire black community. The media and the school books do not help much either. In these circumstances it becomes extremely difficult for a black child to separate being black from being bad. Child care workers need to develop their role in helping the child to differentiate between being black and being bad, because ultimately, for a black child, it is not only a question of holding a poor stereotype of another group in his or her mental mirror, but a question of the child's own image and identity.

My experience is that workers rarely talk to the youngsters about race. Yet, when one listens to children and young people it is quickly apparent that colour and cultural differences are a constant issue for them and not something peripheral. When black people living in England experience constant attacks on their self-esteem, it is unwise for social workers, probation officers and teachers to assume that no positive intervention is needed to assist black children with their self-concept. Many social workers may acknowledge that the language of the playground is racially very abusive, but they often argue that it does not mean anything at all. I suggest that this attitude merely reflects that social workers have yet to try and develop an understanding of what it is like to be black in a white society.

One consequence of the racial prejudice that persists and accumulates in our society is what amounts to a *psychic* assault on black people. Aggression towards others takes many forms, and is by no means confined to, say, shouting racial abuse and spitting. A recent study of five West Midlands newspapers carried out for UNESCO by Birmingham University researchers concluded that local newspapers tend to portray black people as primarily involved in crime, or as being the cause of some social problem like overcrowding, or strain on the social services. These negative images, the report says, result in a massive failure by the press to communicate any sense of what it is like to be black and British.

How do Asian children cope with constant attacks on their self-esteem and self-regard?

Coping strategies vary. As Milner (*Children and Race*, Penguin, 1975) and others have shown, children find it difficult to identify with a socially rejected group. In the doll tests a significant proportion of the Asian children and 50 per cent of the West Indian children denied their own identity, and they also chose the white doll as the nice one. The attempt to pass as white and the denial of their colour is a coping mechanism. Calling oneself 'tanned' rather than Asian, black or brown, as one twelve-year-old does, is another. This child, when taken to an office where there were some black staff and visitors, said that she did not like being there and added, 'There are too many dirty Pakis here.'

Another case that I would outline briefly is of an Asian girl, who now at the age of thirteen is experiencing a tremendous identity problem. The rest of the children at the children's home call her 'black bastard', 'dirty Paki' and other such names. She is now trying to pass as a Fijian; she feels that she will then be accepted since one of her white teachers is married to a Fijian woman.

Overcompensation – being extremely good and totally conforming with the residential staff's expectations within the hostel situation – can be another coping strategy. This mask is often maintained at tremendous emotional cost, and usually ends in the individual escaping from the situation by running away or making a suicide attempt.

Aggression is another form of coping with racism and although, as yet, there are no stereotypes of violent Asian children, some Asian girls of twelve and thirteen do present aggressive behaviour, often to counteract the image of the 'timid' Asian girl.

Increasingly, young people of both Afro-Caribbean and Asian origins, who may have shown assimilationist tendencies, reverse when they reach the age of sixteen or seventeen. At this stage young people become progressively more aware of the low esteem in which most English people hold them, and the hostility which they encounter in finding good jobs; also the unlikelihood of their being fully accepted by English people, even if they should attempt total cultural assimilation. As young Asians come to see the realities of their situation, assimilationist tendencies tend to be halted, and sometimes they are reversed. Faced with rejection many ask 'Who am I?' and try to identify with authentic roots.

I do not wish to suggest that young people in care overcome their differences with parents – they often continue to defy parents – but they attempt to assert their differences with white society in a more confident way. On the whole, social workers become alarmed by assertions of 'black power' or Rastafaria or resurgence of turbans. This would seem to be a failure to appreciate that consciousness of self is not a closing of a door to communication with others but a necessary step for its achievement.

I would like to conclude by linking up the main strands of this chapter with some recommendations for work with young Asians in care.

First, very often the professionals show a resistance against accepting problems of racial prejudice in this society. It has not always been accepted that Asians and West Indians are a specially disadvantaged group, with special needs which require different approaches. What social work accepts is that cultural practices differ and that cultures can vary in the kinds of stress they produce. In fact, as stated earlier, 'culture conflict' as a diagnostic label is overemployed. Frequently, in utilising this concept there is a tendency to see negative aspects of other cultures and to make broad generalisations about entire culture groups based only on a knowledge and experience of client groups. This is particularly so for residential staff who may rarely see any other Asians except the parents of children in care.

Second, from the point of view of black people, culture conflict has to be seen in the context of racial prejudice and hostility. This means that a rejection of parental culture does not necessarily indicate total identification with existing core culture (as frequently assumed by social workers) but a desire to forge a new black consciousness. It is the lack of a race relations dimension in social work assessment which perpetuates these erroneous assumptions. The need is for not only a knowledge of cultural backgrounds, but an understanding of the *political position* of black people in white society, the historical linkages with Britain which explain black people's presence here, and the effects on children of living in a racially prejudiced society during the most formative years of their lives.

Third, child care workers should recognise that in the present unsatisfactory race relations situation, non-white children who grow up isolated from their racial group risk psychological damage. I believe that the principle of maintaining positive cultural and racial identity and the psychological value of this in terms of good mental health and emotional

well-being should be established as firmly in child care work as the principle of maintaining religious identity was at one time. It would seem
more caring to acknowledge that black children in care are different from
others but to communicate an acceptance to them and help them to take
pride in their racial identity. This means conveying positive regard for
other races. To promote this each home should have adult Asians and
West Indians in its support group. For black children this scheme helps
to provide positive role models; it can also help to alter perceptions of
white children and staff. The same service could be given to white foster-
parents who take black children. Reading material could be selected with
sensitivity for the black child's feelings; it is only in the ethnic press that
black adults are portrayed in positive roles.

Fourth, staff can develop their awareness of race issues and talk to
children about race. The evidence is that race awareness in children starts
early. In the last few years the media coverage of race has also increased
and is generally negative. The reports of Malawi Asians living off social
security, or the massacres in Zaire, or the return of white people from
Zimbabwe, do not show the imperialist roles of the whites. Black people
have been deeply disturbed by media reports in the last year. White social
workers with responsibility for young Asians should surely try and find
out how the children isolated from their racial group are coping with
attacks on their self-regard.

Fifth, in their assessment reports to courts and case conferences, social
workers could and should incorporate the racial dimension in social work.
The training of social workers is tied to the psychodynamic model and
interpretation of behaviour is made on that basis. Social reports contain
information on black children's early separation experiences (often caused
by migration), adjustment problems, cultural conflict and rejection by
parents, but the racial dimension is usually missing. The fact that an
individual's sense of identity depends not only on how the child's parents
valued him or her, but also on how the parents were valued by society,
is not acknowledged. Invariably, the demoralising effects of rejection by
society remain unwritten.

Sixth, some specialisation may be necessary for social workers involved
in child care work among racial minorities. Not only do they need theoretical information on cultural and race dynamics; they also need an opportunity to develop contacts with members of the minority community other
than the client group. Without helpful contacts even racially aware social
workers could feel helpless when clients were victims of discrimination:
for example, recently a social worker felt strongly that a child on whom
she was preparing a court report had been a victim of police hostility but
she did not mention this in her court report. Another colleague found
that, of three girls involved in starting a school fire, an Asian and a West
Indian girl were charged with arson, whilst their white friend was only
cautioned. Some of us wonder if there is a bias in cautioning procedures
and in the use of non-custodial sentences for ethnic minority offenders in
juvenile and adult courts.

I believe that social workers have a role in influencing social policy. They are in a position to identify the deficiencies and stresses of the system; but how workers choose to use their skills and energies will depend on the dissatisfaction they feel with current patterns of service. Teachers have formed an association for multiracial education; social workers also need to take account of the stresses on black people in white society.

17   Working with girls

Val Carpenter[1]

I come from a working-class background, East End of London. When I left school having failed all my O levels, I had no particular qualifications. I took a whole host of jobs – typing, temps, that sort of thing – but I wanted to do something more creative, like nursing or teaching. At that time I had no idea that there were other jobs around women could do.

Then when I was twenty-three I bumped into the youth worker of the club I used to go to when I was fifteen. He asked me to go and do some work there. At first I thought, 'I won't be any good with adolescents', but I found I had a flair for it, and thought I'd become a teacher. So then I kept registering to do A levels – and kept jacking it in, thinking that by twenty-five I could go to college as a mature student: you don't always need A levels then! I didn't even know you could do full-time training to be a youth worker. Anyway, at my interview for a teacher training course, I soon realised I didn't want to do that. Then I saw an advertisement for a youth work course in the *Morning Star*, and wrote off.

When I qualified, in 1975, after the two-year course, I had thirteen job interviews. It was the time when they were beginning to make education cuts, and there were lots of teacher-trained people looking for jobs in youth work. Interviewing panels were more impressed by them, taking on men in preference to women, teacher-graduates rather than youth-trained workers, even though our training was, of course, much more relevant. I lost one job to a bloke who'd just done a degree in engineering! Well, finally I did get a job in East London, and stayed there for three years.

Youth work means working and building relationships with young people, either in particular clubs or premises like schools, church halls, etc, or in places where young people go, like pubs, street corners, or wherever they happen to be. The problem is that not only do girls stay away from youth clubs, they also don't hang around street corners, so they are almost invisible in the youth service. In addition, it is relatively difficult for women workers to be out and about because of street violence and the like – so, as always, it is mainly boys benefiting both from workers' energies and from existing facilities.

In the spring of 1976, I went to the twice-yearly workers' conference and joined the new workers' group. Just coincidentally there was a large proportion of women in it, and three of us were already feminists. It just came alive for us: we spent the whole weekend looking at the specific problems women workers have – violence against us, child care, promotion. And for the first time we began to recognise the extent to which girls were being neglected. We realised, too, that there must be lots more women needing, like us, to set up women workers' groups. When I got back to London, I helped set one up.

This London group went on meeting for several years, and came to include all sorts of women youth workers. And from it came a lot of the ideas which have later developed into girls' projects, girls' nights, and girls' centres. Just as important, we learnt to share our problems, and give each other support.

For example, obviously you come up against a lot of violence amongst and from the boys. It's often been found in youth work that women are able to diffuse fights and are 'better' with boys in some ways – because women don't pose any threat to them. But once you become a committed feminist, boys start to react to you more aggressively. If you show them your attitude towards their sexism, their knowledge of your feminism can increase the violence you want to dispel. Also, of course, there is always the danger of individual attacks by boys and young men – one woman came home to find a boy she'd been supportive to waiting for her, and he raped her. These are the sorts of situation women need to discuss together. At first we blamed ourselves, or our professional capabilities, or just put it down to 'lack of confidence and experience'. But gradually we realised it wasn't any of those, but that the boys and male workers found our ideas very threatening. We learnt that the more energy we put into girls, the more the boys and men would feel threatened. It is still difficult to work out how to deal with all this. At that time, though, we were operating on the level of, 'If if feels right, do it.' Whereas now we have a conscious awareness of the very real risks to us, in the whole context of male assertiveness and violence, and that has helped us to make better judgements, and stop feeling personally inadequate.

Besides discussing these sorts of problem, we also got down to looking at the ways we were treating the girls. We began to develop an awareness together of how we were neglecting them: when I'd go back from our meetings to the club, I'd be horrified at what I was doing. All my close relationships were with the boys, all my energy and time went to them. With the girls it was just, 'Hallo, how's tricks?' and that's all – nothing. So I made a commitment to get closer to them. At first they just weren't interested, but what I didn't realise was that I wasn't picking up the right signals, or I was ignoring them.

But one night there was a big disco, and I was very busy, whizzing about ensuring that things were running smoothly, and I just put my head around the door of the girls' toilets. My response would usually be 'What do you want to hang around there for, there's lots of nicer places to be', and to try to encourage them out. So crazy: it never occurred to me it was the only place they could be on their own without boys. Anyway, this time one of the girls said, 'Come on, ask her, she'll tell you.' I replied, 'Come on, quick, what?' 'Go on, ask her.' 'No, you.' And they all started laughing, till one of them said, 'Tell us, have we got three holes down there, or two?' I suddenly realised that this was important, and that this sort of thing happened to me countless times, and that I'd been too busy to pick it up. We've been encouraged all our life to put down women's talk – and I'd fallen right into that trap.

Anyway, we had this most amazing talk together. We stayed in there the whole evening, didn't go to the disco at all, talking about so many things. It caused a terrible scene because all the boys were outside wanting to come in – why were there no girls dancing? In the end the caretaker threw us out. It was a school-based club that closed at 10.30, but we were still outside at a quarter to twelve. The girls were avid for information, and wanting to share their experiences. They asked me how I knew so much, and I told them about the women's health book *Our Bodies Ourselves*. They asked me to bring it in – the American edition was like gold dust, so easy to look at and flick through. So that was how girls' work in my club really got started.

Then I began to notice other things, too, like the girls wanting to use the billiards table. At first, when they told me the boys wouldn't let them, I said, 'Well, make sure you've booked it', but it was clear that not only the boys, but also the two male youth workers were actually taking the girls bookings away from them. Most of the boys belonged to the club because of the table, a full-sized one, and they treated it as their right to use it all the time. One boy actually beat his girlfriend up because she was trying to play billiards. So I would go and stand by the table to ensure they'd get a turn, but the boys, who were generally older and bigger, would stand around intimidating them. One of the girls kept asking me to have a go, so one night I finally did and, as luck would have it, I potted the ball in just one shot, and then another. The blokes looked outraged. Then I potted another one, three in a row. I couldn't believe it – but I just acted dead cool, as if it were an everyday occurrence, and finally the boys said, 'Well, Val, you never told us you were shit hot at billiards.' It ended up with the boys teaching the girls to play, a real sharing attitude, instead of believing males are born with the ability to play the game. After that, there was a lot less trouble in booking the darts and table tennis, too. But I really had to work hard on the male workers to show them how unfair it was for the girls not to have access to all those games.

I began to realise that girls really do want to be energetic, having a good run around – but they don't want to do it in front of boys. I could see how it was important to have events just for girls, where they weren't overlooked by boys. Once I took some girls ice skating at the sports centre. By mistake I got there too early, but we were let in after I explained that this particular group of girls had to be home on time. As soon as the girls got on the ice I noticed something I hadn't realised before – instead of standing about with their arms crossed they were skating around perfectly. After having the rink to themselves for a while, other people started to arrive – amazed to see all these girls skating. Immediately the girls started to fall over – couldn't skate because they were falling off balance trying to cover their breasts and so on. It had been my own experience in adolescence too – and I'd forgotten it. Sometimes other workers say that what we should really be aiming for is mixed-sex situations. Then I remember all my own experiences as a girl, and with working with girls recently in single-sex situations, and think, 'Hmm, mixed sex provision? That's just pie in the sky for the time being, if we really want girls to have a fair share.'

So these were the sorts of realisation we went on discussing in our support group, with each of us beginning to try out new ways to work with girls. Most of us tried out 'girls' nights' – evenings at the club, on a regular basis, for girls only. This meant getting other women in to help, not necessarily youth workers, but feminists. My youth officer (in charge of the area) totally opposed me. He wouldn't pay for part-time helpers, either. I had to fiddle the pay, and do the nights all in my own time. And there were endless hassles at the door – boys trying to get in, and my car tyres slashed. The girls went through hell, being called slags and lessies. They didn't want to be perceived as lesbians, but at the same time they realised that the boys were trying to undermine them, and the women workers, as well as the girls-only nature of the activity. Finally the girls got extremely angry, and gained strength both as a group and individually. Gradually more and more girls started to come along. In the end we asked the male workers to go on the door and deal with the hassles, so we could put our energy into the girls. This placed the male workers and the boys in a situation where they could no longer duck out of discussions about masculinity and sexuality. Male workers are mainly into sport and horse-play with the boys – they invariably back out of any kind of relationships. They organise ace football teams – but rarely look at the politics of competition.

Once our women workers' group held a special girls' bop, with a women's band who let the girls play their instruments. Some of the girls brought along their mums and grans. It was nice for us, and nice for the girls who came and stayed. But again, I think we'd forgotten how we'd at first felt unsure and unconfident about being in an all-female situation, particularly a bop . . . how we'd once felt ourselves: 'How can you enjoy something like this without men being here?' It's part of how we fall into the trap of assuming girls are different from us, or from how we were, and of course, they're not. A lot of the girls saw their first real live lesbians and were freaked out when they saw two women kissing. That new experience opened a whole new area of discussion for them. I'm not suggesting we should consciously set up situations where we 'expose' girls to 'experiences', but I certainly don't think we should be 'protecting' them from the real world, or censoring it. We've learnt that it's really important to do a lot of basic groundwork with girls before presenting them with an all-girls bop (unless they suggest it themselves) because it takes such a leap to understand you can relax and enjoy being at an all-women's event. After all, there are still many grown-up feminists who still haven't made that leap, which shows just how powerful men's control is over the things we are 'allowed' to do together without them there to supervise or enhance the proceedings.

By this time, early 1977, things were also starting to happen on a more national scale. A group of women working within the National Association of Youth Clubs started organising some all-girl conference weekends.

called 'Boys Rule Not OK'. These gave girls the opportunity to do things they don't normally have a chance to do – motorbikes, canoeing, assault courses, karate, electronics, and discussions. NAYC had to add more weekends to the programme, as they were all oversubscribed. Following the success of these, they put on a training conference for workers – a mixed one – at which people came to understand why provision for girls, particularly single-sexed, was so important and exciting. Around this time I was thinking of leaving the job I'd been in all this time – and saw the post of Girls Work Officer at NAYC advertised. Under the circumstances, it seemed like a really challenging job. I applied, and to my surprise I got it.

It was a completely new post. The appointment of a Girls Work Officer at NAYC was in itself a very significant event in the history of youth work in this country. It isn't widely known that there *was* once quite widespread provision for girls in girls-only clubs, but that gradually it all got whittled away – whereas provision for boys-only has gone from strength to strength and has always been comparatively generously funded. For example, if you think about the YMCA, everyone has heard of it, knows it owns property and where the 'Y' is in any town or city. But obviously the YWCA has much less property, and is far less conspicuous, a much poorer organisation. Traditionally people have thought it much more worthwhile to fund boys' organisations and projects. Firstly, they are the next gener-ation of breadwinners, so need special attention and training (whereas girls will just be home-makers and mothers, skills they are supposed to be born with). Secondly, boys on the loose might get into trouble, so need clubs and projects to occupy them (whereas girls are just invisible). Sport and so on – all the traditional male pursuits – seem worth funding, because they have tangible outcomes, whereas a girls' discussion group isn't seen as at all worthwhile. Even today, funding still goes to predominantly all-boy or mixed projects.

Originally NAYC was the National Girls' Club Association! Then it was completely staffed by women. Then it became the National Association of Girls and Mixed Clubs . . . then Mixed and Girls . . . and then Youth Clubs. Once again, it shows how, once you let men into the organisation, they take over. Of course, most of the senior youth officer appointments are nowadays men.

It's all very well seeing 'mixed' provision as more progressive than single-sexed provision, but what we have had in practice is a steady decrease in facilities for girls, instead of a growth of equal provision. So it seems that for the time being, to protect girls' interests, we have to go on claiming the right for girls-only provision – that's why the appointment of the new post at NAYC, extending and co-ordinating girls' work and projects nationally, was a crucial one.

One of the exciting things about youth work with girls is that, unlike, say, teaching, any feminist who wants to, who has an interest and a commitment to it, can get involved – you don't necessarily have to train to be able to work in informal ways with girls.

Also, unlike schools, the girls are there because they all want to be, and there's a much more relaxed atmosphere. You can discuss with them what *they* want to do, you don't work under the severe restraints which most teachers have to put up with. There is at the moment a reasonable amount of 'official' interest in girls' projects. In London, a group of women recently conducted a survey on provision for girls in the boroughs of Camden and Islington which they presented to the Youth Committees in their areas with a list of demands. This list included the appointment of a woman worker specifically to work with girls in each area, and the setting up of girls' centres. The research group had only really expected to get these issues raised in discussion, but it was phenomenal! All the demands were agreed to, and there is now a girls' centre in Camden, and a permanent girls' project in Islington, with hopes for a properly housed centre eventually. And all over the country there have been girls' nights, girls' weeks, videos, plays, and sharing of resources between feminist teachers and youth workers.

It would be good if more and more feminists were involved in working with girls. After all, we are the ones who have tried to build a conscious understanding of sisterhood, and to extend the range of choices in front of us – we are the ones who can remember our earlier experiences in the light of our feminist experience and can extend that support of sisterhood to younger women whose choices are still so restricted. And we are the ones who understand girls-only provision in the light of our own hard-won fight for autonomy, and who are not put off by cries of 'Sexism!' every time men and boys think they are missing out on something!

Note

1   This account by the author of how she came into youth work with girls is taken from taped conversations between Val Carpenter and Susan Hemmings and is edited by them both.

18   Observing and recording children's behaviour: A framework for the child care worker

James K. Whittaker

It is the purpose of this chapter to explain in detail the four different forms of recording: *critical incident recording, individual recording, group recording,* and *behaviour rating scales.* Careful attention will be paid to the question, 'What should be recorded?' as well as to how the material should be organised. A final section will be devoted to exploring some pitfalls to accurate recording.

The case examples derive directly from the recording system at the Walker Home, which uses with varying emphasis all four forms of recording: individual, group, critical incident, and behaviour rating scales. We present the following examples not as a recording model to be duplicated exactly by all child caring facilities, but rather as concrete illustrations of the four different forms of recording.

Critical incident recording

The data is kept in a separate notebook and contains the following kinds of information.

1   Unsettled or unclear problems or 'issues'

Illustration: To morning staff: Dick and Arnie had a scuffle at bedtime last night over the ownership of a fishing reel. Dick claims that he sold it to Arnie last week, but then bought it back with Arnie's approval. Arnie disputes this and says Dick merely 'took it back'. Staff put reel in the office and told both boys that this would be dealt with in the morning. My hunch is that Dick's story is probably correct, but that Arnie feels somehow 'gypped' or 'conned' into selling the reel back. Suggest that someone get to this early, as I'm sure that Arnie and Dick will wake up, rarin' to go!

E.B.W., 10–7–65

2   Noteworthy incidents or interviews involving one or more children

Illustration: Re: Harold   Evidently, last evening Harold took both sets of Caroline's keys and had hidden them behind the desk. Ostensibly, he took them because he was angry at Caroline for shutting him out of the cooking activity when he became unmanageable (fighting with Doug). Harold retrieved the keys and then proceeded to 'beg' to go outside. I told him that I wanted to do some talking with him about the keys, since they were kind of a signal to him (and to us) that he was pretty worried about something. I asked specifically about home and he responded in a pretty gloomy manner:

'Momma has laryngitis, Dad has headaches, is out of work', and the family was planning to move. I asked Harold what things were like at home when Dad was out of work before. 'You just don't have money to buy all of the things that you want to buy, and you have to live in a place that is not so nice.' . . . Back on the 'key' issue, I just reiterated the events of the last few days for Harold:

He calls home and Mom has laryngitis, can't talk and has to be interpreted by Dad . . .

Rosemary (counsellor) 'locks' Harold out of school and he breaks down part of the door to get in . . .

Monday evening there is trouble in the kitchen and Caroline tells him he must leave . . .

Harold takes Caroline's keys and hides them behind the desk . . .

I said that it seemed to me that he was getting shut out of a lot of places – home, school, activities, etc. – and had this ever happened before, i.e., had he ever been 'locked out' at other places.

'Sometimes, when I came home, my mother would have left and she would leave a note for me telling me where the key was.'

'That must have been pretty surprising, even frightening, when you came home and found that your mother was gone!'

Comments: Two things were significant here:

1   Harold was able to relate a past feeling state (being locked out of home) with the current situation at W.H. In other words, he was acknowledging in so many words that his behaviour had a purpose and was not simply random activity. He also was able to recall some of his old feelings (loneliness, confusion) and agree that this was the way he felt last night.

2   Harold was able to see (at least somewhat) that his choice of behaviour was really a signal that he was getting to feel left out: the keys, the car locks, etc.

J.K.W., 7–3–66

3   Other pertinent data: notes on phone calls, home visits and interview summaries

Often telephone calls to home provide material to talk over with the child at a later date.

Illustration: Harold called home after dinner this evening; earlier in the day he had appeared quite agitated when he learned that his family was planning to move again. His sister answered the telephone and told Harold that mother had gone to 'some hotel' and that she was all alone. Later, it turned out that father was home and he did speak briefly with Harold. Bulk of conversation was spent in Harold telling sister about recent activities at W.H. Later, staff talked with Harold about problem of moving, his feeling left out of picture, etc., promised to see social worker tomorrow to set up visit. (See individual notes.)

J.B., 5–9–66

All critical incident entries are dated and initialled; space is provided in the margin for staff comment. This type of recording is most helpful in providing day-to-day information on children. It is most often the entry that is read first when new staff are coming on duty.

4 Additional critical incident criteria

Critical incident, of course, does not necessarily mean noisy, obviously disturbed, or disturbing behaviour. A casually given new piece of *personal history* (e.g., 'I remember the day my dog got killed.') can often be a critical sign of readiness to move in a new direction. An *interesting fantasy* or softly muttered *fear* should also be considered critical incidents. One other kind of incident also has 'critical' value. It is one that goes on in the adult rather than in the child's head. You might call it the *suddenly seen pattern*: for example, 'I never noticed before, but I believe Billy usually gets upset every Sunday morning or every time another boy mentions dogs, etc.' Personal history, fantasies, fears and suddenly seen patterns should all be considered critical incidents worthy of note.

> *Illustration:* Re: Toby: Toby woke up in a grumpy mood today and engaged in two fights with his roommates before breakfast. This has become a regular problem for him during the last week, and I talked with him after breakfast to see if I could determine the source of the difficulty. At first, he would give me no hint as to what was bothering him except to say that he had a 'problem' but wasn't going to talk about it. I commented to him that he looked tired and that perhaps if he could tell me about it he would be able to get more rest at night. At this, he shouted, 'Well, you'd be tired too if that goddamn Alice [night staff] was waking you up every night.' (Earlier that month, Toby had been wetting the bed and had asked staff to wake him during the night so that he would wake up dry in the morning.) 'Do you mean you have a hard time getting back to sleep after this?' 'Yeah, and besides it doesn't work anyway, 'cause I wet the bed again this morning.' Toby then opened up with a long conversation about what it was like to lie there awake when everybody else in the room was sleeping. It turned out that this was one of the reasons that he was having troubles in the early morning: i.e., just as he was getting to sleep, the others would be waking up and would wake Toby in the process. This would anger him and it would usually end up in a fight. Toby also expressed a good deal of concern over a forthcoming visit home. I went over past situations where he had become worried about something and bedwetting had become more of a problem for him. I told him that I was more concerned with his getting to sleep and that for now, we would not bother about the bedwetting and let him sleep undisturbed. Toby agreed to this and felt that, for the time being, he would not mind waking up in a wet bed.
>
> J.B. 17–6–66

Individual recording

In individual recording we attempt to look at each child through the matrix of five major categories: *the individual child*; *relationships with peers*; *relationships with adults*; *response to change and managements*; and *handling suggestions*.

Illustration:

Date: 6–3–65	Child:	Patrick	
	A.M.	P.M.	X
	Staff:	J.K.W.	

I   The individual child
Pat appeared quite happy when I came on duty today; he told me that today was the day he was going to buy a new baseball glove that he had been saving up for. It seems like only a few months ago when he was afraid to get in a game with the other boys. Pat spent an active afternoon and evening and fell asleep easily at 8.45.

II   Relationships with peers
Pat used his new glove quite appropriately with the other boys, though he had some difficulty in not being 'first' at bat. He and Gerry were vying for power in trying to decide who should be first, but Pat settled this by letting Gerry use his glove in return for letting Pat be the first one at bat. There was some mild horseplay with Danny at bedtime with Pat doing most of the initiating.

III   Relationships with adults
Pat stuck pretty closely to male staff during most of the shift today with one notable exception. Shortly after lights out, he bellowed for a counsellor, and when I went into his room, he said that only Mary would do. Mary went in shortly and Pat showed her a fairly large blister that had developed on the sole of his foot. It is not unusual for Pat to seek out female staff when he has some somatic complaint, particularly when they occur around bedtime. I've noticed that Pat is joining more and more into activities with the other boys, he is spending less time seeking out one to one relationships with staff.

IV   Response to change and management efforts
I had to limit Pat tonight at bedtime when he began to try to make loud noises during the story. He tried for a while to get Danny involved in this when it was fairly obvious that Danny was trying to get to sleep. I found that direct appeal served to quiet him down, saying both that Danny was tired and wanted to go to sleep and that his making noises made it very difficult for the other boys to listen to the story.

V   Handling suggestions
I think it would be wise to think of some parallel activities for Pat and Gerry, since neither one of them seems to be able to handle direct and open competition. Perhaps staff can suggest to Pat some other activities besides baseball (perhaps woodworking?). I think the novelty of this game will begin to wear thin after a while, particularly if he is competing with Gerry who is so much better than he is.

Obviously, if individual recording is done over longer periods of time, it will include a more detailed picture of the child's growth and changes in his or her development. At Walker Home, individual cases are usually summarised twice yearly using the daily recordings as the primary data.

Group recording

Typically, group recordings consist of a very brief tonal picture of a group for a given shift. Each group recording contains at least the following information: major group activities, significant group events (runaways, group projects, etc.), changes in group structure (power structure, leadership structure, activity structure), and significant group processes (ranking, scapegoating). These daily group recordings are supplemented periodically by a more detailed analysis of group structure and processes. This latter type of recording might be done simply with the idea of getting a picture of the group over periods of time, or it might be carried out with a specific problem focus: e.g., an analysis of the realignment of the power structure after a new boy's arrival. The basic purpose of the daily group recordings is to provide us with a concise picture of what the group is like for a particular time period. Counsellors read the daily group notes almost like a barometer, before they go on duty.

> *Example:* Total group engaged in some cohesive activity around skating, but when the others were ready to leave, Tim refused to get off the ice. Mike, Al, and Pete began calling names at him and threatening him with harm if he didn't hurry up. Back at Walker, boys were rather lethargically watching television and Tim sank into the television oblivion which took the heat off him somewhat. Before lunch today, little subgroups were going especially strong. Jeff and H's subgroup deteriorated when H. lost interest in J.'s new cabinet. Children seem to be drifting from group to group without too much thought as to the pertinence of the subgroup. There were no major group upsets, though there may well be if Tim continues to set himself up against the total group.
>
> R.A.S., 14–1–67 p.m.

Behaviour rating scale

This last form of recording is used to indicate the presence or absence of a particular behaviour. It is the most predetermined form, in the sense that what is sought is specified before it actually happens. Simple behaviour rating scales may be completed simply by checking off the appropriate category. For example:

(1)	Frequently seen	Seldom seen	Absent
Nail biting	X		
Eye tic		X	
Facial grimace		X	
Hand wringing			X
Eye rolling			X
Head banging			X

(2)	Fighting	Fire setting	Destroying Property
Joe	X		
Tim	X		
Arny	X		
Howard		X	X
Alan	X		
Sam	X		

Other scales may seek to obtain data on a particularly problematic situation: for example, the following scale was used to learn more about the counsellor's response to a particularly troublesome behaviour, and the child's reaction to the management technique.

> *Illustration:*
> (a) *Presenting behaviour.* Joe told Sam to go fuck himself this morning, as soon as he came in for breakfast.
> (b) *Counsellor response:* I told Joe to cut it out, or he would have to leave the room.
> (c) *Child's reaction:* Joe laughed and said he was only 'fooling': I told him that nobody liked to be greeted that way.

Using a simple scale like the above one, it is possible to analyse the various management techniques pertaining to a particular 'issue' and the degree of success they achieved.

One of the obvious problems in working with a checklist system is to define the categories in such a way that the observers are all agreed upon what constitutes the specific behaviour to be charted. For example, if recording the frequency of a 'temper tantrum', the observer had better be quite clear as to exactly what behaviour constitutes a 'temper tantrum'. The greater the number of observers, the greater the problem becomes.

What to record

The whole question of what to record is often one that throws the new worker into a state of mild panic. 'How can I ever remember everything that happened?' is usually the first question asked by the novice child care worker. The answer, of course, is that no one can 'remember' everything that happened, and, indeed, to attempt to write such a complete daily chart on each child would make a cumbersome report to read. Finally, good observing and recording skills must develop over time; the process of developing insight into what is significant behaviour must develop in the same way as the management skills of the counsellor.

The following material is based on the recording outline developed by David Wineman for the University of Michigan Fresh Air Camp. This outline has been supplemented in certain sections by some of the questions found to be useful by the Walker Home staff.

Individual recording form

1   The individual child

(a) Physical description of the child including general appearance, grooming, manner of dress and habits of cleanliness.
(b) 'Atmospheric' elements, such as facial expressions, mood-peculiar mannerisms, gait, manner of speech, intelligence, etc.

(c)   How does he seem to view himself? Does he think he is lucky? Unlucky? Does he see himself as good? Bad? Is he fatalistic in regard to his behaviour? His future?

(d)   What does his value system appear to be? Is he identified with 'middle-class' values, delinquent values or others? How are these value positions expressed? How deeply imbedded are his values? Are there conflicts between them? Does he show guilt? At what times and in what way?

(e)   What is his ability to tolerate frustration? What types of frustration are more difficult or less difficult for him? How does he react to frustration?

(f)   Indicate insights into his fantasy life, day dreams, future goals, and ambitions. What kinds of stories and comics is he attracted to? What fantasy roles does he like to play?

(g)   Does he have any particular fears? Unusually strong interest in some particular activity or stereotyped avoidance? Are there any striking habits that appear peculiar or out of the ordinary?

(h)   How much control does he seem to have over his behaviour? Do controls break down under certain conditions? What are they?

(i)   What kind of a self-image does he have? What does he think his assets and liabilities are? What does he see as his biggest problem? What does he think is the best thing about him? The worst?

(j)   How does he deal with hurt, anger, sadness, and joy?

(k)   What is the character of his anger? For example, is it chronic annoyance, or emotional flare-ups?

(l)   What have been the changes between the beginning of treatment and now?

2 Response to activities

(a)   What is his general response to activities – enthusiastic, bored, excited, etc.?

(b)   What activities is he attracted to: those entailing infantile gratifications, adult-like activities, activities with high fantasy content, dangerous activities? Which does he avoid? Is there a preference for activities that are more individual or that require considerable interaction with peers?

(c)   What is his general skill level? Is he especially adept at any particular craft or activity?

(d)   Are there activities he characteristically turns to when he is sad or lonely?

3 Relationships with peers

(a)   What kinds of response does he seek from peers? What does he do to get them? How successful is he and how does he react when he obtains the response he seeks? How does he react when that response is denied? Does he seek power? Affection? Submission?

(b)   What types of children does he seem closer to? Which does he avoid? How friendly is he with other children? How is the friendliness expressed? What types of children does he come into conflict with and how is the conflict expressed?

(c)   What seems to be his perception of other children? Is he accurate in judging the motives of other children? When is he inaccurate?

(d)   Does he seem to need other children? Is he content to be alone? How often and under what conditions?

(e)   How do the other children react to him? View him? Is he popular? Respected? Feared? Ignored? Is there a general consensus among the children in their attitudes toward him?

(f)   Does he seem to show any sexual interest in his peers? How strongly is this interest shown and how frequently?

(g)   Is he attracted to any particular subgroups? What are their characteristics?

(h)   What are his skills in approaching other children? In avoiding them? In influencing them? In being influenced by them?

(i)   Does he have difficulties functioning in large groups? What kinds of difficulties?

(j)   What changes have you seen between the beginning of treatment and now?

4   Relationship to adults

(a)   Much of what was outlined under 'Relationship with peers' applies here as well.

(b)   How comfortable is he in seeking help, encouragement, affection from adults? What form does it take? Does he have favourites among counsellors? What seems to be the basis of choice (male, female, older, younger, etc.)?

(c)   Is he generally obedient or defiant? What is the quality of his obedience or defiance? How does he show it? Are there differences in whom he will listen to? How does he express aggression and how frequently is he aggressive? Are there certain times or conditions during which he becomes more aggressive or defiant? How does he behave afterwards? Sulky? Worried? Hostile? Friendly?

(d)   How does he seem to make you and the other counsellors feel toward him? How does he try to make you act? Does he succeed?

(e)   How accurate is his perception of adult movies and actions toward him. Under what conditions are the perceptions more or less accurate?

(f)   Has he expressed any sexual interest toward the counsellors? Toward the males? Females? How strong does this interest appear and what form does it usually take?

(g) What is his characteristic manner of showing affection for adults? Hostility?

(h) What changes have you seen between the beginning of treatment and now?

5 Response to change and management efforts

(a) What management techniques seem to work best to get him to comply? Which ones seem to reduce defiance?

(b) Does he appear interested in cultivating insight into his problems?

(c) What is his reaction to threats?

(d) Does the use of activities or peer group pressures appear to be influential in limiting his behaviour? We refer here to the short-term management of his behaviour.

(e) What is his reaction to limits? Does it make a difference who is setting them? Does it make a difference whether they are being applied to the group, or to him alone?

(f) In general, how does he handle the structure of the day: the rules, the routines, the activities? Are there particular rules, routines, or activities which give him special difficulty (e.g., bedtime, meal time, etc.)?

The more specific the counsellor can become in his or her recording, the more benefit it will have for the reader: for example, the statement that 'Joe reacted very negatively today to limit setting and engaged in several aggressive outbursts' leaves the reader with many unanswered questions: What kind of limits were being set? How were they presented? By whom? What was Joe's position in the group at the time? What does 'aggressive outburst' mean?

One final note about individual recording: a good record should raise as many questions as it answers. The child care worker should not feel responsible for giving the 'definitive' answer to any of the questions in the preceding outline.

Group recording

The following model has been found to be useful in organising daily group records.

1 Major group activities

The chief function of this category is simply to reduce the chances of 'loading' the system with too many of the same kinds of activity. It will also tell us something of the group's ability to handle certain kinds of activity.

2 Group structure

The first question to be answered here is: 'Who did what with whom?' This is often the first place where we begin to notice the formation of certain subgroups within the larger culture. Certain 'structures' will be watched more closely at different times in the life of the group: for example, a discharge of two high-status members would mean an almost certain realignment of the power structure. Some other questions to be answered under this heading are: 'What is the group's ability to handle issues and problems?' 'What kinds of control are the children to exercise on each other?' 'What particular affectional bonds seem to be developing between pairs or subgroups of children?' and 'Who are the group's current leaders, scapegoats, low-status members?'

3 Group processes

In what manner is the group dealing with disappointments and changes in the routine? What is the nature and frequency of 'ranking', cursing and scapegoating? To whom is this behaviour usually directed?

4 Mood of the group

What has the group been like to work with today? Have they been overly demanding, industrious, defiant, bothersome, 'groupy', separated, provocative or lethargic? An accurate picture of the 'group atmosphere' can save the incoming child care staff immense amounts of time and trouble if they can plan for it in advvance.

Some pitfalls to good recording

As in any form of recording, there is always some discrepancy between the event as it actually happened and the manner in which it is transcribed. The following suggestions are offered in the hope that they might help to improve the accuracy of the recording without limiting its style. I am indebted to Dr Marvin Silverman whose thoughts about recording formed the basis for many of the following suggestions. Some of these may be looked upon as 'pitfalls' to be studiously avoided, others as helpful hints to be incorporated into one's observing and recording skills.

1   Turning the daily log into a 'gripe sheet' is an easy trap to fall into; individual supervisory conferences and staff meetings are perhaps more appropriate contexts for airing our grievances with each other and with the children. One is reminded of Erving Goffman's description of the 'paper shadow' which follows the mental patient through-out his entire institutional life. We should, of course, exercise discretion in putting down our feelings about a child; this kind of

information is valuable, but remember that you have a responsibility to state the child's 'case' as well as your own.

Tim had a totally bad morning; he was into trouble all over the place and just wasn't quiet for a minute. He was just obnoxious and kept asking for things in that real whiny way of his.

2   Overgeneralising or being overly specific is another trap that the child care worker might fall into. For example, nobody 'constantly' fights or 'always' gets into trouble. Similarly, the observer can dwell too long on the minutiae in the situation.

3   A merely chronological account of what a child did for an entire day simply does not tell us very much. It might be better to pick the most salient, or critical, feature in a child's day and record that alone.

4   As a general rule, it is better to avoid cumbersome phraseology and the use of clinical language and simply state what the child did or said: for example, instead of 'made a demonstration of positive feeling toward the counsellor', you could say, 'put her arm around the counsellor'.

5   Use behavioural illustrations carefully. They are most appropriate when a more general statement somehow fails to capture the essence of what you are trying to say.

Billy almost seemed to be setting himself up as the scapegoat tonight; during dinner he began to dribble food on the table and make vulgar noises until finally Tommy and Winslow began to kick him under the table and had to be physically restrained from attacking him.

6   The recording of 'hunches', or hypotheses, or offering behavioural interpretations is a valuable adjunct to recording. These remarks should be set off from the process material in such a way that the reader is able to easily discern what is factual and what is conjecture.

Toby woke up quite angry this morning and got into a fight with Tim before breakfast. (I think this might have had something to do with the fact that Toby had wet the bed the night before and was feeling pretty upset about it.)

7   Recording is a developed skill that takes time to perfect and master. It is not necessary that the counsellor 'remember' everything that happened, as he or she will spend more time 'remembering' than serving the children. Also, it is good to develop a sense of selectivity about what one records, as all behaviour does not carry the same significance. We must stress the confidential nature of the records with children and make it clear that they are not 'bad lists' to be shared with parents or family.

8   Unless you are making a direct quotation, avoid use of slang, such as 'kids' or 'the child "took off" '.

9   Particularly with records that might leave the agency, we should be careful about assuming that the relationship *we* had with a child was

representative of the relationships he or she had with *all* the adults in the setting.

10   There is nothing wrong about being puzzled about the meaning of a child's behaviour. You are not expected to know everything.

Carl burst into tears tonight after supper and was comforted by staff; he couldn't give any reasons for the behaviour except to say that 'the kids are buggin' me.' Can someone shed some light on this?

11   Give consideration to the space that you allot to each point in recording. Long rambling reports are not read as carefully as short concise ones.

12   Above all, respect the confidential nature of any report. This is not casual material to be discussed with friends or anyone else who is not directly connected with the child. The ultimate success, or failure, of the child's total treatment is in large measure dependent upon the quality of the reports that accompany him or her along the way.

References

REDL, F. (1972) 'Just what am I supposed to observe?' in *When We Deal with Children: selected writings*, New York, Free Press.

REDL, F. and WINEMAN, D. (1957) *The Aggressive Child*, Glencoe, Ill., Free Press.

19 Daily experience in residential care for children and their caregivers

Juliet Berry

The discussion below focuses explicitly on residential child care (community homes, observation and assessment centres, special boarding schools, hostels, etc.), but the ideas are also applicable to foster care, hospital care and even to children at day school and at risk in their own homes; similarly, to dependent adults (physically or mentally ill, handicapped, delinquent, elderly) living either in institutions or at home. A generic theme is relevant to people of all ages, in a wide range of situations, who depend upon other human beings meeting their daily needs for physical, mental, social and emotional care.

Having been variously involved with residential work throughout a long working-life, I know from personal experience that there is often a gap between theory and practice, between our aspirations and actions. I am bedevilled by that gap as much as anybody else; although possessing some certainties and a lifeline bridging the gulf, I am equally liable to slip off my tightrope when it actually comes to doing the job, so am in no position to exhort any residential social worker to do better. In any case, exhortations tend to be indigestible (causing heartburn or constipation) to those whose ears are bigger than their stomach. What I hope to convey is how we might better *care for the caregivers* in their difficult task, because this caring (or lack of it) passes all the way down the hierarchy (or pecking order) and directly affects the quality of care which caregivers in turn are able to offer the children.

When writing earlier about communication with children,[1] I was thinking largely in terms of a special one-to-one relationship, in which the worker tries to create a safe climate where the child is free to explore some of his or her thoughts and feelings, and to express them directly or indirectly (that is, in words accurately or obliquely phrased, or in play and behaviour) while the worker tries to tune in and respond helpfully. It can bring great relief for a child to risk being in touch with his or her feelings, which lose some of their negative influence once they reach the light of day, when they are expressed and contained without any terrible repercussions. So the child who is given opportunities to communicate tends to gain more control over his or her own behaviour and to feel less at the mercy of haphazard events. He or she is less isolated; life begins to have more coherence, pattern and meaning.

Sadness, frustration and uncertainty will still exist in many children's lives, but they no longer become a nightmare when at least one grown-up is prepared to join in facing them. Indeed, the above applies not only to children. It also applies to adults under pressure, perhaps especially to caregivers of all kinds, who may have just the same need for a skilled listener – for someone who helps them to put their experience into words, in order to digest it and live with it, rather than feel at the mercy of 'horrible imaginings', with things happening in chaos or in a meaningless vacuum. But I will return to this idea later.

I still think this verbal and non-verbal communication with children is vitally important, but visualise it nowadays in a much broader context. Here I am not thinking so much of setting aside a special time to be with a child, whether for a formal hour per week or a few minutes' conversation snatched during the day, but rather of the whole pattern of the child's daily life experience being the most powerful medium for communication that exists. There are 168 hours in a week so, whether a child is in his or her own home, or at day school, or in foster care or in any other residential setting, there is bound to be some pattern of ongoing daily experience, some caregiver at least in the background (unless the child is literally on the run) and surely the ordinary patterns of routine events carry more significance, for better or worse, than odd snippets of conversation. This is both a comforting thought (for example, when we have just exchanged a few cross words but can see this in a wider perspective of continuity of care) and a sobering thought, when we consider the conditions under which some children exist for lengthy periods. [. . .]

The gist so far is so simple that people cannot always grasp it. If I speak of 'an experiential approach', they may imagine it refers to some high-flown esoteric form of group therapy external to daily life. Whereas the message is simply that the care itself is a communication; that people learn most convincingly from their own daily experience (for good or ill); that the proof of the pudding is in the eating rather than in the recipe book, and that the main opportunity for residential *treatment* is inherent within the actual experience of living together.

Clare Winnicott[2] summarised the idea thus: 'Children need from the residential worker something direct and real, and treatment surely lies in the worker's ability to provide for them real experiences of good care, comfort and control.' She went on to explain that we can often make important gestures of caring for individuals en masse in token form: 'The token can be used because behind it is both the *recognition* of the need and the *will* to meet it.' To me, this rings true. Children are acutely aware of their grown-ups' attitudes underlying tiny gestures; they tend to be easily satisfied with little tokens when these feel right for both parties. In fact children are less greedy and demanding than we sometimes fear – they only clamour for attention and 'fair play' when desperately near emotional starvation. They do not usually demand the top brick off the chimney if they are basically fairly confident of emotional warmth rising from the fireplace below.

In mentioning tokens, I do not merely refer to special gestures representing concern for the peculiar needs or whims of each individual; I include all the daily events which adults tend to take for granted. Imagine a single meal time: a child will have learnt something from it; it will have been a more or less nourishing experience, physically and emotionally, according to whether he or she enjoyed the food and company, or whether the experience was stressful because adults were largely concerned with table manners and may have punished the child if he or she dared to criticise their good food or failed to leave a clean plate. One meal time is perhaps neither here nor there; however, three meals a day over a period of weeks, months or years, plus a dozen other routine aspects (all of which provide endless opportunities for demonstrating positive or negative attitudes in the caregiver) are surely very cumulative in their effect.

Most material aspects of daily life carry emotional symbolism, social significance. Most people, even if unwittingly, perceive food in terms of affection, of satisfaction given or withheld, generous or grudging attitudes, freedom to choose or coercion. Similarly, clothing is related to a sense of identity, pocket money to self-worth, sleep to personal safety. . . . Choosing to harness the facts of routine experience (rather than to regard the residential task as mere maintenance of a group of bodies) immediately gives rich scope for milieu therapy, inbuilt, right on tap ready for use. Perhaps the strongest argument is that residential work necessitates the provision of material things such as food, clothes, beds; so while we are inevitably saddled with such mundane details we may as well realise the therapeutic possibilities in the situation which is thrust upon us.

Moreover, these are usually the very aspects in which children have lost out in the past, and also the medium through which they test out current caregivers. When things go wrong, it is not usually in abstract ways but in concrete practical ways – for example, residents being reluctant to rise from bed or to settle down at night, bed-wetting, refusing or messing their food, tearing or losing their clothes, misspending their pocket money plus dozens of other possible problems. It takes two parties to create a behaviour problem: the irritant and the irritated. Therefore daily events offer endless scope either for a destructive battleground or for constructive learning. What matters to residents of any age is whether they are living in an environment which on balance is basically friendly or hostile. They know well enough which it is over a period of time, and respond accordingly.

Milieu therapy can be designed both for ordinary group living and for particular individual needs. For instance, bed may be regarded by some children as a refuge for relaxed privacy and by others as a place where one is banished for punishment, a place of fear, discomfort and resentment (cold and perhaps wet). It means different things to different people as well as similar things, so these meanings can be recognised both generally and specifically. Generally speaking, caregivers should regard all children's beds with respect as warm places of safety in the hope that all will learn to experience them as such. Respectful treatment then would prevent any worker tearing the bedclothes off a child who is slow to rise in the morning. More specifically, some children may sometimes need more individual attention than others at bedtime: they may want to be tucked up with extra care or to have their own special toy tucked up too, or to have a ritual story or a few minutes' private conversation.

Similarly, everybody's meal times should ideally be conducted in pleasantly relaxed social circumstances and again there is room for individual quirks to receive attention on top of the basic care. Milieu therapy may be a more exacting way of working but it costs nothing extra in terms of time or money. In fact it may save time and wasted energy both in the short and longer runs. For example, it is probably easier to wake children, give them breakfast and see them off to school if they are allowed a few moments' leeway in getting up than if the atmosphere is so tense that it encourages arguments and stubborn resistance. Dockar-Drysdale[3] is quite clear that therapeutic treatment is an economical part of planned provision: 'Ten minutes, properly used, are more valuable than two hours of permissive "floating".' Events in residential life may be planned or unplanned, treated explictly or implicitly, but communication (for better or worse) exists within a real situation as it happens. Words and actions are meaningful as a natural part of the complete pattern of daily care.

To give a brief outline of my research[4] without going into much statistical detail, the material is based on questionnaires completed by forty-four students during their placements in a wide range of residential units (for example, community homes including ex-approved schools, assessment centres, special boarding schools, hospital wards). The forty-four places contained 946 children and adolescents, and 416 caregivers. Respondents described patterns and interactions of twelve aspects of daily life round the clock including methods of discipline and control. It is fair to say that my research methodology is open to criticism, not least because it relied upon forty-four individual impressions. However, certain safeguards were built in; also it can be argued that an impressionistic approach via temporary student-residents may have more research 'significance' than superficially precise scientific measurement by outsiders.[5]

A tentative attempt was made to grade the patterns described, using as mid-point a standard where daily care sounds adequate though not inspired, analogous to D. Winnicott's concept of the ordinary 'good enough' mother. Accordingly, the sample of 946 children in forty-four units fall into three groups comprising 43 per cent living in twenty-one *good enough* residential units, 17 per cent in six *more positive* units (where there seemed to be deliberate efforts to create something akin to milieu therapy) and 40 per cent in seventeen *more negative* places, six quite seriously so. In other words, about 60 per cent of children were receiving at least good enough daily care, while the remaining 40 per cent experienced a hostile environment. It is worth stressing that difficult, disturbed children are spread thickly throughout the sample: no rational question arises of negative units feeling they must be stricter and more regimented because they contain all the most awkward inmates.

There is insufficient space here to illustrate the extraordinary differences in the quality of care. The treatment of absconders is an obvious example. Frequently absconders, once found, are brought back in disgrace from what may have been a frightening escapade; then stripped – punished by being locked up or deprived of 'privileges' and home leave. Now this method is not even logical (let alone humane) – because, if we wish children to want to stay with us, we must give them something positive enough to want to stay *for*. Bettelheim's method[6] of welcoming back absconders, with runaways knowing that whenever they returned they would find food awaiting them and a warm bed, is not only expedient in the short run but a far more effective way of handling actual and potential absconders. However, it is not easy in practice for staff to be welcoming when they naturally feel hurt by the runaway's apparent ingratitude and rejection, worried for his or her safety and fearful of defiance on return. So in practice there is little logic in this whole area of discipline and control. Naturally enough, caregivers react in the heat of the moment, and much heat is generated by fear and irritation.

Once having distinguished three categories of quality of care in the sample (more positive, good enough, more negative) it was possible to link them with other factors such as unit type; settledness in children; their relationships both with staff and with each other; and staff qualifications, length and conditions of service. In short, these are the main points arising from the study as a whole:

First, it was clear that children with similar basic human needs vary greatly in the quality of care they actually receive. (We require no further evidence that negative treatment breeds negative results.)

Secondly, it seems that these variations (particularly in methods of discipline) depend less upon theoretical principles than upon the caregivers' immediate pressures in practice. Almost half the sample of units showed serious conflict between colleagues (let alone between staff and children) about methods of control. There is much greater reliance on the use of punishments in negative units, as well as more emphasis on rewards. If it is surprising that I do not see rewards as positive, let me suggest that they are simply the other side of the same coin of punishment. Lack of reward can imply punishment and vice versa. The sample contains many places where a few workers exert a helpful kind of discipline which is simultaneously friendly and appropriately firm (designed to *protect* children from harming themselves or other people) whereas other colleagues use threatening, bullying tactics, or sometimes are fearful of exercising responsible control when the situation demands it for the sake of safety. Ultimately, I believe the most valuable lesson for children to learn through ongoing experience is that their adults can care for them and control them without becoming exhausted, hurt or hostile in the process but while remaining on friendly terms. Unfortunately this is easier said than done.

Thirdly, looking at the 416 caregivers in my sample, is a slightly surprising finding that staff show a tendency (not marked but noticeable) to stay longer in the more negative units. One of many possible explanations for this might be that workers in 'better' units exhaust themselves more quickly by trying to give positive care against heavy odds. Paradoxically, it may be easier for staff to drift with the tide in negative units, though this is not to say they drift contentedly.

Fourthly, it was more surprising to explore the factor of training. One might have expected there to be more qualified staff working in the 'better' units. In fact there were almost exactly similar proportions of professionally trained staff in negative as in 'better' units – proportions of about 20 per cent in each case, higher than the national average. At first sight, this is a discouraging finding but, on reflection, it is not altogether surprising. We have tended to assume that residential staff, once safely qualified, will continue to put their knowledge, values and skills into practice for the remainder of their career, and live happily ever after. Surely, however, no initial training (even if excellent) can hope to prepare workers for all subsequent pressures they will meet on the actual job. Faced with an awkward situation, we are not immediately inspired by some half-forgotten textbook or lecture from the past. Caregivers react spontaneously to a wide range of planned and unplanned situations in the context of their everyday life. And just because of these spontaneous reactions, it seems staff often welcome background discussion involving their own natural attitudes if they are to respond more positively in meeting difficult situations.

This leads to my *fifth* and most important finding: the clear link between the availability of ongoing support/consultation for caregivers and the quality of care they give in turn. My study shows clearly that most of the 'better' units have good opportunities for staff support, whereas the vast majority of negative units have only poor opportunities. In negative units, staff often feel isolated, neglected, dissatisfied: obviously, if one is already 'feeling out on a limb', one's tolerance for the residents and their problems tends to be low. Training may provide a firm foundation for future work, but certainly cannot prove so effective long term as ongoing support in meeting daily problems as and when these arise.

Lastly, therefore, it is worth trying to consider some of the practical implications of ongoing support and consultation on the job. Perhaps the first step is awareness of the extreme pressures commonly experienced in residential life (whatever the size of the roof) from the caregivers' viewpoint. They are bound to feel isolated, undervalued, unless outsiders empathise by adapting to their frame of reference. Very briefly, typical difficulties fall into three broad categories: those in relation to residents, to immediate colleagues, and to the external environment.

In relation to *residents* (just to take one aspect), the problem of having to handle individuals in groups tends either to lead to unrealistic efforts for 'fair play' by dividing emotional and material resources into deadly equal rations, or to provoke heightened irritation with individual nonconformists whose behaviour might prove infectious. There is often a fear that, if Philip is allowed to slide down the banisters, everybody will start sliding down the banisters and the place will be chaotic. Although it is fairly unlikely that this would actually happen, staff naturally imagine it might.[7] Another common misconception is that it is a luxury to lose one's temper, that it brings relief to lash out when angry or fearful; whereas in reality destructive confrontation is painful for both parties. Certainly it is painful if caregivers perceive their situation as a battleground because this implies their needing 'to win at all costs' and being desperately afraid of defeat. In relation to *immediate colleagues*, there is the highly exposed nature of residential work, where (unlike fieldwork) one's mistakes are obvious in the very act of making them. All residential staff, senior and junior, risk experiencing the worst kind of loneliness: isolation within a claustrophobic crowd. And in relation to *the external environment* there is scope for difficulties on all sides: contacts with parents, neighbours, fieldworkers and external administrators may seem haphazard and neglect-ful on the one hand, or intrusive, critical and unsettling on the other hand.

At this stage, after skating over typical difficulties outlined above, we may agree that the sheer weight of pressure makes it hardly surprising that many residents receive only mediocre or poor care. Small wonder that caregivers commonly describe a sense of being drained of positive feelings and growing full to bursting point with negative feelings. Beedell[8] says residential workers need 'the capacity to withstand threatening cir-cumstances' but, I think, rather than overtax that capacity, it is safer to look for ways of alleviating the stress. (As I have argued elsewhere,[9] similar reasoning can be applied to foster-parents: whether social workers regard themselves partly as colleagues, friends, inspectors, supervisors or educators of foster-parents, we need primarily to act as support figures – and this is not patronising but merely what we ourselves would require in their shoes.)

This introduces the second practical implication of support. Once we are convinced that caregivers' most worrying problems mainly revolve round human relationships, inside and outside the building – once it is clear that these relationships are simultaneously the chief *means of residen-tial treatment* and the greatest *obstacle to providing* positive treatment – it follows logically that the remedy must also be found within a helping relationship specially designed for the purpose.

If so, what kind of help is appropriate, and who might be able to offer it? I believe such support must be offered rather than imposed – it is for the consultant to try to adapt to caregivers' expressed needs, not for them to be forcibly fed against their will, so whatever is offered has to be optional, flexible and confidential.

How far can basic-grade fieldworkers act as support figures? On the whole I think only to a limited extent, and that residential staff are realistic in saying they want 'better liaison rather than support from fieldworkers'. Just because fieldworkers are concerned with individual residents, they tend naturally to focus on that one resident's needs rather than on the caregiver's problem in meeting these needs. [. . .] For this reason I ques-tion how far it is practical or economical for busy fieldworkers to take on a support role *vis-à-vis* residential staff in addition to their main concern for individual residents.

The next possibility is whether opportunities for support and consultation are available *within* units. According to evidence in my study, these opportunities vary enormously in terms of supervision, staff meetings, and formal and informal discussions. But to the extent that colleagues are already in serious conflict with each other (true of nearly half the units in my sample) then it is not easy for them to lift themselves out of this vicious circle by their own bootstraps. It does seem much more possible for the unit head to support his or her junior colleagues internally when receiving external support.

So another possibility is an external consultant (who may be a psychotherapist, senior caseworker, ex-residential worker, social work teacher; full time or part time). This appears to be the most viable proposition, based on evidence in my study and on my current experience of group work with residential staff. An external consultant, just by virtue of coming from outside and having no direct responsibility for inmates, is not bogged down in the unit's daily pressures, and therefore is free to empathise with whatever the staff choose to present as being uppermost in their minds at the time. Through being allowed to define their own immediate problems themselves, caregivers are protected from intrusion into their privacy, and instead are actively engaged in the here-and-now situation of their current work experience. Residential workers, because of the very nature of their work, tend to be anecdotal, so the chance to discuss happenings and events from their own viewpoint can alleviate stress, making these experiences more livable with, more containable. If the consultant creates a climate where uncomfortable feelings and thoughts can be expressed without fear of criticism in return, the caregivers' warmer feelings are less choked with thorns and have more room to breathe naturally of their own accord.

My book (1975, second half of chapter 4) outlines five possible models of consultation drawn from the work of Dockar-Drysdale, Caplan, Bettelheim, Balint and Woodmansey;[10] all five are similar in that they respect the caregivers' competence in the foreground, given appropriate economical background support. Experience suggests that such consultation can be offered either to individuals or in groups, with the proviso that a group is best composed of people who see themselves on a par with each other, rather than a mixture of seniors and juniors having to be wary of mutual vulnerabilities. As the group develops confidence in its leader, members will tend to want to discuss currently troubling situations which have naturally aroused discomfort, such as fear, despair, rivalry, frustration, irritation and hostility.

Not infrequently, people mistakenly assume that my belief (that hostility is anti-therapeutic) means I advocate the employment of superhumans who either 'have no feelings or who hide them dishonestly'. In fact, I believe the reverse: that workers will under great provocation inevitably become hostile (turning it outwards, or inwards against themselves) unless this can be alleviated by a third party. It is important not to collude with the idea that violent exchanges are mutually beneficial in everyday life. Grown-ups who are tempted to be punitive show great dexterity in producing rationalisations in support of their arguments. In any group discussion about controlling children, someone typically recounts an incident in which he (or she) patiently tried to deal with an awkward child for a long time but was not successful until provoked into a temper outburst which suddenly resulted in a much improved relationship. These stories are plausible in attempting to prove that provocative children respond best to spontaneous anger, but possibly the caregiver's original self-discipline contained so much ambivalence that open communication was impossible; warmth was withheld while an over-controlled consistency was maintained. Obviously the child, though not enjoying his adult's brief loss of temper, appreciates the aftermath of compensatory positive feelings and responds accordingly.

This, however, is not an argument in favour of adult temper-tantrums; it simply means that the pieces can be picked up after an unfortunate episode. Also, an occasional angry outburst is very different in its effect from persistent, ingrained adult hostility; and of course there remains a place for firm control as a safety device. Rather than collude with the idea that aggression can usefully be expressed in direct reciprocity (which is impossible with one party in a weaker position) I think it preferable for accumulated negative feelings to be eased by a consultant who is in a strong enough position to respond to the caregiver's viewpoint without evasion, retaliation, or becoming hurt himself.

In contrast with consultation, a purely inspectorial visit tends to defeat its own object, because workers are unlikely to confide in an official who comes looking for trouble, and he has an uphill task in trying to remedy any faults which staff naturally hope he will fail to discover. It is preferable and safer all round for the caregivers to say (under suitable conditions) where their shoe pinches, rather than have an inspector come searching for a wide range of corns and blisters which may not even exist.

The third and last set of practical implications about consultation is linked with selection, education and training of staff. Ideally, training offers an excellent opportunity for students to begin to learn the value of discussing their work; that it is not a sign of weakness but part of their professional equipment to be able to accept and use support in extremely difficult work. Again, they only learn through first-hand experience of receiving effective supervision, not by being told they have a duty to discuss problems. [. . .] One would hope to select students (and caregivers) who in their initial interviews show at least a small measure of trust, some willingness to communicate.

Also, in residential work we need to think of self-awareness and self-knowledge in very practical terms: everyone's interests are served through individual workers having some awareness of the foibles of their own metabolism; whether for instance they tend to have more patience at breakfast or at supper time, whether they are more adversely affected by a delayed meal time than by broken sleep or vice versa. In other words, material aspects of daily life affect caregivers as well as residents, and the status for residential workers is enhanced when their domestic service is truly perceived as milieu therapy. [. . .]

The gist of this paper can perhaps be summed up in terms of hot-water bottles. Dockar-Drysdale is a pioneer enabling a leap forward in residential treatment; amongst other things, she has changed our concept of hot-water bottles from a menial domestic detail into a medium for therapy. However, when actually filling a hot-water bottle, she is a fairly ordinary human being, unlikely to conceptualise at that moment about 'localising symbolic adaptation' – the spirit in which she does it matters far more. So we are all equally capable, once self-confident enough to be willing to recognise and meet an expressed need.

What matters above all is that caregivers should survive the heavy demands of their work – that the hot-water bottle does not burst, leak or perish because that is destructive both to the giver and to the receiver. So I see daily experience in all forms of residential life on more than one level, each level feeding the next below. The actual practice of milieu therapy does not depend on high-flown theoretical knowledge; it happens in small, ordinary ways, conferring dignity on both parties. And the quality of care experienced by children depends upon a parallel experience of appropriate care for the caregivers.

Notes

1   Berry, J. (1972) *Social Work with Children*, London, Routledge and Kegan Paul, chapter 3; (1971) 'Helping children directly', *British Journal of Social Work*, Vol. 1, No. 3, pp. 315–332.
2   Winnicott, C. (1964) *Child Care and Social Work*, Welwyn, Codicote Press, p. 30.
3   Dockar-Drysdale, B. (1973) 'Staff consultation in an evolving care system' in *Residential Establishments: The Evolving of Care Systems*, Conference Report, University of Dundee.
4   Berry, J. (1975) *Daily Experience in Residential Life: A Study of Children and Their Caregivers*, London, Routledge and Kegan Paul.
5   Ibid., p. 157; Patterson, W. J. (1975) *Social Work's Theory of Man: A New Profession's Philosophical Anthropology*, Coleraine, New University of Ulster, p. 28.
6   Bettelheim, B. (1970/71) *Love is not Enough*, London, Collier-Macmillan/Avon.
7   Stevenson, O. (1972) *Strength and Weakness in Residential Care*, Quetta Rabley Memorial Lecture, Bookstall Services, p. 3.
8   Beedell, C. (1970) *Residential Life with Children*, London, Routledge and Kegan Paul, pp. 100–102.
9   Berry, J. (1972) *Social Work with Children*, op. cit., chapters 3 (p. 70) and 5.
10   Dockar-Drysdale, B. (1973) *Consultation in Child Care*, Harlow, Longmans. Caplan, G. (1970) *The Theory and Practice of Mental Health Consultation*, London, Tavistock Publications; Bettelheim, B. (1962) *Dialogues with Mothers*, London, Collier-Macmillan; Balint, M. (1957) *The Doctor, his Patient and the Illness*, London, Pitman; Woodmansey, A. C. (1966) 'The transmission of problems from parents to children' in *Mental Illness in the Family: its Effect on the Child*

(22nd Child Guidance Inter-Clinic Conference Papers), NAMH; Woodmansey, A. C. (1972) 'The unity of casework', *Social Work Today 2*, 19 January, 1972.

20　Senses and sensibility

Leonard F. Davis

Having decided to make use of the title of one of Jane Austen's novels, *Sense and Sensibility*, I thought that I had better read her book again. This I did, thinking that it was only the title I wanted to borrow (and adapt slightly) and that the rest of the work would have little relevance to my theme. In many ways I was wrong. Important strands running through the novel are as valid today as when the first edition appeared in 1811.

Sense and Sensibility is the story of two sisters, Elinor and Marianne, and describes their varied and uneven progress towards eventual marriage with, in society's eyes, two worthy men. Essentially, Elinor is concerned to be socially correct; she strives to maintain her composure; it is natural for her to keep up appearances; and she is tactful, practical and disciplined. Her whole being displays an acceptance that man must curb his enthusiams and impulses, and thereby quietly make his contribution to a well-ordered society. On the other hand, Marianne is of independent mind; responsive to her feelings; some would say undisciplined; certainly sensitive to the finer meanings of language and to what people say; cries without shame or embarrassment; is prone to psychosomatic illness; and communicates freely and directly. Of course, as Jane Austen shows, Elinor is not devoid of feeling, neither is Marianne without common sense, but as Tony Tanner says in his introduction to the Penguin edition of *Sense and Sensibility*,[1] together the two sisters project some basic division or rift in civilisation as the author knew it, and to my mind, as we know it today.

Thinking of our own settings, the differences in outlook and temperament between Elinor and Marianne are not dissimilar from what is still sometimes found among human beings: between adults and young people; between teachers in a school; between groups of care staff; between teachers and care staff in a residential school; between a headteacher and his or her staff; between the school and its external managers; and between the school and the neighbouring community – all of which (in reality, symbolically or by their attitudes and opinions) embody the characteristics displayed by Elinor and Marianne, and provide arenas for conflict, misunderstanding and disagreement.

From my reading of *Sense and Sensibility*, and from Tanner's introduction[2], I am left with a number of thoughts: (i) that nothing comes unmixed, because qualities which exist in pure isolation as abstractions occur in people only in combinations (often in confusion and contradiction, with other qualities) and in configurations which can be highly problematical; (ii) that tensions will always remain between the potential instability of the individual and the required stabilities of society; and (iii) that society forces people to be at the same time very sociable and very private (those who are 'isolated' are looked upon with pity or sympathy). Yet, we have not created the type of society in which a great deal of a person's private self can be shared, because the methods we employ for enabling people, young or old, to share a little more of their inner worlds are, for the most part, one-sided, with power vested in one person, and the pressure to share [placed] on the other.

However, what permits us to be optimistic – and I do remain optimistic – is the potential of the mixture of qualities in the individual to which I referred. This is what we have to cherish, ensuring that such potential develops in ways which are neither self-destructive nor evocative of a repressive response from society; and affording it opportunity to make known its new perceptions of the contemporary scene. The alternative, as we too frequently see about us today, is to lock people into their earlier patterns of behaviour, into their defence systems and into their mistakes.

We often make reference to the problems associated with the 'them and us' syndrome which so easily creeps into our institutions and has its roots in the basic divisions projected by Elinor and Marianne. Sometimes it is a deliberate approach on the part of the power holders so that their positions of authority are maintained, with clear boundaries drawn between those in charge and the residents, inmates or recipients of services. Such structures are found in our toughest prisons and will be experienced in the regimes of the new-style detention centres at Send in Surrey and New Hall in Yorkshire where boys as young as fourteen will be sent. These are extreme examples, but we must not forget that, even in our supposedly child-centred establishments, military-type organisational structures are allowed to develop. I recently identified in a local authority children's home caring for twenty-eight young people in four units the following hierarchy: officer-in-charge, deputy officer-in-charge, assistant officer-in-charge, four unit leaders, four deputy unit leaders, plus basic care staff (full time and part time) and students, all of whom were constantly reminded of their places in the pecking order. Basic-grade staff felt as powerless as the young people at the centre, and, at times, undoubtedly colluded with the residents against the management. I often wonder what the young people think of this setting as an alternative to family living, and to what extent it provides an environment for sustained personal concern, shared decision making and the development of mutually-rewarding relationships, concepts which I see as central to the work in which we are engaged.

While not unmindful of the issues relating to control, authority, experience, accountability, age differences, status, salary differentials, basic human likes and dislikes, competing loyalties, cultural gaps, sexuality and professionalism, and without wishing to labour the point, I would like to suggest that in future the western world is more likely to be peopled by Mariannes than Elinors (both staff and residents) and that, while seeking to retain some of the qualities displayed by Elinor, the crying need is to understand, appreciate, accept and respond to the characteristics shown by Marianne to a degree hitherto unknown. Personally, I have learned

far more from the Mariannes of this world, both about myself and about
other people, than was ever possible from the Elinors.

I place residential social workers in three groups: those content to work
in a very traditional way; those who have freed themselves completely
from the shackles of the past (a rare breed); and those who are making
desperate efforts, in spite of heavy odds, to develop new methods of
working. Most of us, I guess, would place ourselves in the last category.
For some people the transition demands a whole new way of viewing the
residential task, and was recently (dramatically) described by a colleague
of mine as a 'conversion'. Emotionally, I agree with her – and, as we shall
see, the emotions play a vital role – although, intellectually, it may be
better described as an educational process, a process which is never
completed.

A few moments ago I mentioned the 'them and us' syndrome. I see no
conflict between the professional task and narrowing this gap. Indeed,
particularly with young people, the professional task requires us to invest
heavily in narrowing it, while at the same time retaining our adult status.
I am committed to breaking down further the barriers between young
people and adults by providing models of adult behaviour which in no
way replicate for young people the unhappy experiences of the past. To
do so is to confirm all the worst fears of young people about adults and
about the very poor self-images which many of them hold. I do not
underestimate the difficulties in bridging this divide. Some barriers will,
and perhaps must, remain. Young people recognise the need for them
and benefit from the security they afford. In fact, most adults, especially
young adults new to the work (but for most of us for the rest of our lives),
are not able to function without the props which our jobs and our agencies
provide.

The task of working with damaged and damaging children is a difficult
one. We have to deal with the damaged and damaging bits as they present
themselves, both at an individual level and on a group basis; we have to
reverse these traits so that they are replaced by behaviour patterns which
are personally satisfying and socially acceptable; we have to give young
people access to learning; and we have to provide an environment which
ensures the smooth development of those large areas of normality found
in the most abnormal children. The sensitivity of the adult in responding
to these needs is one factor which can make or break an existing pattern
of behaviour within a young person. It is this question of sensitivity that
I wish to explore, sensitivity which is tested in our residential schools and
children's homes in the face of every exchange with a resident. The
rewards for the adult are great because, as his or her awareness continues
to increase, so does his or her own self-image, both personal and professional. The adult finds that the skills required by those working intensively with young people in difficulty are indeed special – special beyond
what traditionally results from the usual training course – as are the
rewards which accompany greater understanding and better communication. I suppose I am now looking for, looking forward to and looking

towards new levels of professional maturity and professional awareness in the residential care and education of children and young people.

All I have said so far is by way of introduction and I come now to the main body of my remarks. Three areas will be put forward for your consideration: (i) the five senses and how we respond to them; (ii) our professional responsibility at every moment of the day to be in tune with the feelings and emotions of the young people with whom we live and work, and over whom we have so much power; and (iii) the young person's right to be different.

The modern philosopher, André Gide, once remarked, 'What will be said has been said before; but no one was listening so everything needs to be said again.' 'No one' is rather strong, but things do have to be said again because there will always be newcomers to the work who need help in determining their own approaches.

First, then, the five senses – *smell, taste, hearing, sight* and *touch* – the mechanisms by which our bodies receive messages from the environment and from the people who interact with us.

Man is a sensual being. He is constantly alert, overtly or covertly, to the signals his body takes in from the environment and from the people who surround him. For me this has been re-emphasised during the last six months as, in connection with a research project, I have recently completed confidential interviews with over 200 fourteen- and fifteen-year-old boys and girls in three comprehensive schools, the young people concerned representing the full gamut of social, educational, emotional and familial satisfaction and dissatisfaction. Above all, their super-sensitivity, where it has been allowed to emerge, has struck me forcibly, pushing me to re-evaluate my own position in respect of the quality of care required in residential schools and children's centres if we are to have a hope of meeting the needs of young people removed from home.

Some homes and residential schools *smell* like institutions: I refer, for example, to the polish we use; to the powerful disinfectants in toilets and bathrooms; to the stench of socks which children continue to wear long after they should have been discarded; and to our failure to eliminate the worst of the cooking smells (and I am not thinking of a roast dinner cooking which can be so inviting to children – and to adults!). If the strong or objectionable nature of these smells is more than we would tolerate in our own homes, what are we doing about them? At a personal level, there is need for thought to be given to ways of making children and young people more attractive to themselves and to others. For instance, the soap provided in many institutions may be functional and efficient, but it does little to encourage its use by the scent it gives off. While showers may have a place in the changing room of a sports field, a bath gives an opportunity for children to gratify their whole being with some of the delightful – and not too expensive – bath cubes, bath salts and bubble baths which, in addition to their soothing properties, help towards building a personally satisfying bodily self-image. There is a natural and instinctive movement – on the part of both adults and other children – towards a sweet-smelling child or young person, perhaps resulting in some form of bodily contact, thus reinforcing his or her appeal as a human being.

Smell and *taste* are, of course, inextricably linked and the latter allows me to focus on the question of food, the ultimate taste of which stems not only from the intrinsic flavour of what is being eaten, but also from a variety of other conditions. A great deal of symbolism surrounds the preparation and presentation of food. For some people, young or old, adapting to new eating patterns is of primary concern on moving away from home:

> We must not forget the significance of food in a dependent living situation. Permanent institutional catering can be nauseating to some palates, the absence of certain ingredients in a dish can make food uninviting to many people and the mere preparation by an unfamiliar person – especially if that person represents the system which has brought about the removal from home – can prevent acceptance and enjoyment of the food which is offered . . . how little we understand the reasons of children and young people for picking at meals or rejecting them; and how little we appreciate the internal conflicts through which they must sometimes match up the processes of rejection with their needs for survival.[3]

We should talk to children more about food, bearing in mind that the thought of food will produce a psychic salivary flow which, followed by a tension-free meal, will provide an opportunity for intimacy and conversation. High levels of anxiety drain away the gastric juices and upset the digestive system. I am surprised that in some residential settings staff still do not sit at table with residents and only supervise them, often eating their own (better-quality) meals later in an adjacent room. Children should sometimes have the chance to eat out in restaurants in very small groups with adults – something in addition to fish and chips hurriedly eaten in semi-darkness in the back of the school minibus – and, in turn, be engaged in the preparation of food for others. Fundamentally, such preparation is a demonstration of what you feel is good enough for another person's body. The attractive presentation of food is to be expected: awareness of individual preferences (lightly cooked or well cooked?) and the opportunity to serve oneself at table (and on other occasions to be served) are essential. To a hungry child, nothing shows parental love more than the individually prepared plate of egg and chips served by a fond mother. We may rarely be able to approach this level of care (although I ask myself what on earth we are doing when we fail to!) but, at least, after eating, children and young people should be left, both literally and figuratively, with the right taste in their mouths.

Hearing, too, calls for our attention as our reactions to sound vary. Pitch and tone, loudness or softness, harmony or cacophony all bring about a range of responses. I know of children who are upset by too much noise and adults who live comfortably amidst a constant din, although we usually associate obliviousness to noise with younger rather than older people. However, we often pay too little regard to the detailed content of a child's daily ration of sound (some would say noise). What is the maximum decibel count to which he or she is exposed? What opportunities are there to escape from noise? What provision is made for the child to be quiet, perhaps in the company of a single adult? Carpets in upstairs corridors, bedrooms and lounge areas do more than provide warmth, comfort and a relaxing environment. They also absorb some of the harsh, hollow institutional noises.

On the positive side, some stereo sounds offer comfort and body relaxation to disturbed, distressed and merely developing young people (adults as well!), reducing anxiety and facilitating communication. We can extend our awareness of this question of sound by, for example, considering the effects of sudden, loud noises. I am thinking especially of adults who find it necessary to shout at young people. Basically, we do this for two main reasons: firstly, to obtain instant reaction (that is, to move them, to stop them doing something or to get them to do something); and secondly, to assert our control and to demonstrate our authority by expressing anger or displeasure. The fear of adults that 'things will get out of hand' is a real one and must be one of the greatest discomforts experienced by people having charge of groups of children. We may need to look more carefully at what sound is received rather than what is emitted. Although a young person may be unable to avoid listening to unacceptable noises whether addressed to him or her directly or forming the background to other activities, he or she may choose rarely to *hear* what is said (I find this distinction between listening and hearing useful both for the young person and the adult) and, indeed, if shouting is perceived as a common behaviour pattern in the adult, will probably block off altogether, thus avoiding as much pain as possible.

Carrying this theme further I would wish to ask for more thought to be attached to the tone, phrasing and points of emphasis we employ in our verbal exchanges with young people together with the frequency and the manner in which we use their names. Using a person's given or Christian name thoughtfully is a wonderful way of communicating, of building identity and enhancing self-worth. Some of the formal modes of address which adults demand from young people – indeed, perhaps, much of our behaviour – will, without doubt, in twenty years' time be chuckled about in the way that those delightful little aluminium men from outer space laugh in the television advertisement about the kitchen implements used today for making mashed potato.

Turning to our fourth sense, *sight*, let us stay for a moment with the impact that person-to-person contact makes on young people. The hurried gesture of dismissal, the quick movement away and, above all, what we say with our eyes convey powerful messages. With our eyes, in fact with the expression on our faces, we accept or reject, show like or dislike, and say 'Come closer' or 'Go away'. In answering the demands of young people it is easy to develop what might be described as a 'shop assistant response' in which the customer is seen as a shadowy figure on the other side of the cash till who receives the standard smile and 'Thank you' (if it is a polite shop assistant!). Again, it is possible to 'hold' a child, to embrace him or her with our whole facial expression in a manner which transmits reassuring signals. Do we pay sufficient attention to the visual cues we give young people, both as isolated responses and cumulatively? It is not difficult, in our own moments of personal anxiety or distress, for our faces – our whole beings – to register boredom, frustration or dissatisfaction and for these signs to be inappropriately absorbed by young people.

A word about the physical environments we create. Just as we say something in the preparation and presentation of food, so the environments we provide speak directly to residents. Frankly, some institutions I have visited in the last couple of years have said quite plainly to them, 'This is good enough for you.' Similarly, we convey a message in the way we show concern for the treasured possessions of a child. Caring for his or her belongings is another way of caring for the child. Society is not willing to spend overgenerously on the comfort of deprived, delinquent and maladjusted children and young people, and those who manage homes and residential schools do have problems in ordering their priorities when it comes to spending money. But let us make no mistake. We will help children much less effectively if we are unable to demonstrate visually by the environments we build – and in the way we maintain them – that this is a setting worthy of them, one in which they are valued and cherished.

I have reserved the question of *touch* until the last of the five senses because of its special place within the context of human interaction, especially adult–child interaction, and would like to refer briefly to the fears and taboos which surround it, notably in work with adolescents. I will not dwell on the feel of the articles we provide in institutions for everyday living (personally, I dislike drinking out of plastic cups and plastic tumblers and prefer cotton to nylon sheets), all of which give scope for cosseting people, allowing them choice and ensuring, literally, that they feel good.

I am particularly referring to physical contact with another human being which provides not only touch, but warmth or heat of a special kind. Eric Berne suggests that of all the forms of sensation the one preferred by most human beings is contact with another human skin.[4] Such contact may ultimately make the difference between physical and mental health or breakdown. I firmly believe this to be so. Young people in our care are often hungry for physical contact. I think that we should indulge them more. 'Touch hunger' is a phrase that has been about for a long time and remains a central concept in our work. Children and young people need compensation for the ordinary bodily contact many will have missed out on during the first twelve or fourteen years of their lives. Without our help their ability to interact physically in later life with their spouses and children may be significantly impaired. Unless young people feel comfortable with their own bodies and with the bodies of others, the pathway to sexual maturity may be guilt-ridden and perplexing. And I do sometimes become concerned about the quality or absence of sex education programmes in residential schools, places where the very intimacy of the living groups makes them even more important than in day schools (where, incidentally, some excellent work is now being developed). Unfortunately:

> The taboo on touch in residential work acts strongly on what is regarded by some as developmental need. As Pease says: 'The story of the loss of this important channel of communication as a child gets older is one of the great untold stories of child psychology.' In much the same way as sex itself, touch has untapped potential as a comforting agent and communication process.[5]

We may not be able to divorce touch from sexuality and, working as I do in this field of adolescent sexuality, and seeing how for some adults everything can go sadly wrong in their attempts at communication, I am very aware of the 'dangers' which may arise in the development of strong relationships. Here again, perhaps, we may recognise one of the fundamental splits between Elinor and Marianne noted earlier. For my part, I am sure that touch is a rewarding and undervalued way of making contact with inarticulate, distressed or emotionally isolated children and adolescents. We must remember that 'touch is also a language' and it has a valuable place in communicating with children and adolescents, demonstrating its healing, soothing quality and thereby counteracting the violent aspects of physical contact experienced by so many.[6]

In one of his most brilliant short stories, 'The Horla', Guy de Maupassant puts a fine point on what I have been trying to convey in respect of the five senses:

> Everything about us, everything we see without looking at it, everything we brush past without knowing it, everything we touch without feeling it, everything we meet without noticing it, has swift, surprising and inexplicable effects on us, on our senses and through them on our ideas, on our very hearts.[7]

The heightened awareness of the senses should enable us to move into closer contact with the emotional beings of the children and young people in our care; to share, really to share, some of the feelings which lie behind their efforts to make sense of the complexities of their lives (both past and present); and to ensure that the responses we make help children forward rather than push them back along the road whence they came.

We cannot determine the future of those who pass through our hands during their formative years (although we can give young people a better chance of understanding it and influencing it); we must accept that some of the formal education they receive will be forgotten or of limited practical use (although the development of a passionate interest may sustain them through crises or periods of despair); and we have to take care not to focus disproportionately on what we read in the thick files which chronicle past difficulties (and I use the word 'past' advisedly) and detail the often unhappy, indeed tragic, social histories they carry with them. To my mind, the best insurance for future mental health – and I would give mental health priority in my list of aims in our work – is a high concentration, firstly, on the quality of our response to the feelings and emotions which surround and invade the 'here and now' of our residents' lives, and secondly, on the worries of young people as they wrestle with growing up, with their bodily development, with their emerging sexuality, with their differences from others, and with the intrigues and disappointments of their relationships. 'Life is nothing but what our feelings make it,' wrote Honoré de Balzac,[8] and so easily feelings hollow out a deep abyss between two people or between a person and his or her environment.

I find it exciting that we are only on the edge of learning to live and work with disturbed and disturbing children and suggest that this has implications for some redefinition of our aims in a number of residential schools and children's homes. Not long ago Spencer Millham wrote a description of the various regimes and the range of treatments he found in his research into some of the residential establishments in England and Wales:

> You could ask headmasters what was their principal objective, and sometimes you got startling replies. The head of a large Catholic school, with a seraphic gaze, said he was preparing his children for death, certainly not a perspective shared by his boys. Another in a rather isolated boarding school, proud of his trade departments and gleaming workshops, felt that his boys were 'practically bent' – he did not know how true he was. There were the great nautical schools, run like battleships; you certainly could have dug a trench round them and towed them out to sea, where they would have floated for several days before anyone noticed. With their bells and bugles, and marching lads, boys were posted not as absconders but as 'having abandoned ship'.
>
> There were other training schools, like preparatory schools where little boys, squeezed into corduroy shirts and marshalled by tiny prefects, rushed from one stimulating activity to another. There were family group homes, there were therapeutic communities where to the sound of four-letter words and breaking glass relationships were discussed and problems ironed out. I can remember waiting with a group of boys for the community meeting. 'What's it for?' asked a new boy. 'To discuss your problems,' volunteered another. 'But I haven't got any problems', and from the back came the worldly rejoinder, 'Well get some, bloody quick, otherwise you'll never get out'.[9]

We may smile – and I could take you to schools where the essential elements of these descriptions live on – but what I wonder about is the extent to which the worries children have, 'the complexities of their lives' as I have described them, could be explored, put into perspective and made less painful in the schools Millham wrote about. Some problems young people come to us with, already weighty by any standards, together with those new ones which result from group living, get out of proportion if they are unable to share them. They can become all-consuming, bring about further irrational behaviour and pervade the whole existence of the young people concerned. Boris Pasternak in *Doctor Zhivago* comments on the harm resulting from the 'constant, systematic duplicity' of our lives:

> Your health is bound to be affected if, day after day, you say the opposite of what you feel, if you grovel before what you dislike . . . Your nervous system isn't a fiction, it's part of your physical body, and your soul exists in space and is inside of you, like the teeth in your head. You can't keep violating it with impunity.[10]

I have identified a number of problems – most not very unusual – that can play havoc with this nervous system, can really screw children up, can upset their bodily mechanisms, can build up their defences and make them a target for the unkind actions and gibes of others. Without sensitivity the adult may unknowingly feed into these personal anxieties. You will each be able to draw up your own list equally well, or add to this one, but these are the worries that I have come across in young people during the last few years: having eczema; having asthma; being unable to read; being enuretic; being encopretic; wearing thick-lensed glasses; having a mentally ill mother; having a father in prison; having a dying parent; being desperately poor; being grossly overweight; being extremely clumsy; having severe acne; wearing a hearing aid; being of mixed-race; having no friends; feeling unloved by any adult, being underdeveloped physically; being underdeveloped sexually; not knowing who fathered them; having a noticeable birth mark; having unpleasant burn scars; having false teeth; having a glass eye; having bald patches; being physically frightened of other children; being fearful of their own death; having an alcoholic father; having frequent and uncontrollable erections; having irregular periods; and having done something really bad.

Working with young people and sharing these problems demands a huge commitment from the adult, a commitment that may cause him or her pain and uncertainty, particularly when the adult is still trying to resolve some of the issues within his or her own being. As Kahlil Gibran says in *The Prophet*:

> You give but little when you give of your possessions.
> It is when you give of yourself that you truly give.[11]

And give of ourselves we must, because the worries I mentioned must be tackled. These are the human problems with which young people often need help, even if the help only enables them to come to terms with their feelings and their bodies. Some things we cannot change, but children and young people respond to assistance in putting into words what they feel. An unhappy child cannot give a name to his misery,[12] and without aid he is likely to hide from us the deepest sorrows of his life.[13] The development of close relationships with a young person serves as a check on all that has been written about him or her. Remember, an autobiographer has many advantages over a biographer because he undoubtedly knows his subject better than anybody else.[14] The following thought, from an entry in André Gide's *Journal* dated 3 January 1892, is of course principally addressed to us as adults, but it may also help in our efforts to build healthy self-images in those with whom we work:

> Our whole life is spent in drawing an ineradicable portrait of ourselves. The terrible thing is that we don't know it; we don't think of making ourselves beautiful. We think about it in speaking of ourselves; we flatter ourselves but later on our terrible portrait will not flatter us. We recount our lives and we lie to ourselves; but our lives will not lie . . . Rather than recount his life as he lived it, man must live it as he will recount it. In other words: his portrait, what his life will be, must be identical with the ideal portrait he desires; and, in simpler terms, he must be as he wants to be.[15]

These are seminal thoughts, awful in their implications, but a first-rate credo for those who aspire to working seriously with maladjusted children.

The context for unravelling these tangled threads in young people is 'love', a word which, for many reasons, is insufficiently used and demonstrated in residential settings for children and young people. And life is so arranged that we cannot do without loving and being loved.[16] The other day I came across a boy leaving care who faced adulthood with four stumbling blocks, which he recognised himself: he could not say 'Goodbye'; he could not use people's names; he could not say 'Sorry'; and he could not use the word 'love'. Young people need the intimate relationships that adults thrive on, or sometimes collapse without. If those in our care are not having such relationships with their families, then we have to provide them all the more. I am thinking most of the hard-to-like child who so swiftly becomes the hard-to-like adult. Urie Bronfenbrenner has said that 'what every child requires is an enduring, irrational involvement and intimate activities with caring adults'. By irrational involvement, he means that 'somebody has to be crazy about that kid'.[17]

Because of their entrenchment over the years, many difficulties facing young people do not always yield easily to adult intervention and concern. Some are too great and too complex for individual workers to tackle alone. They will need their own strong support system. Hopefully in the next decade we can look forward to the establishment of supervision and consultancy in residential settings in the same way that it is built into the best practice of field social workers. In this I would include both teachers and residential care staff. I do not know the extent to which in Scottish schools you have staff consultancy, either in groups or individually, neither do I know the amount of staff–resident problem solving that exists. Certainly in England and Wales it is by no means far enough advanced. I have recently completed two years' consultancy in a community home with education on the premises. In this school I sought to develop a number of vehicles for the exploration of feelings and the further understanding of human behaviour: daily community meetings for adults and young people in each house unit; weekly small group meetings for five boys and two adults; regular meetings for house staff to look at staff–resident exchanges (most suitably programmed after the house unit meetings); occasional staff seminars for formal learning (for example, on such topics as aggression and sexuality); and individual counselling for staff and boys.

Only in a setting where the adults working intimately with young people know that they are surrounded by people who care deeply about them[18] will workers be able to think seriously about my third and final area for consideration, the child's right to be different.[19] We are destined to be different from the moment of conception. The circumstances under which we were conceived, how we were nurtured during the nine months before birth, and thereafter every detailed interaction which took place between us and our environments, determined how we are today. And this latter influence continues until death. We are all delightfully different by virtue of our genetic composition and our environmental upbringing. For this reason we can never move into a child's world completely; he or she can never be like us; we can never make him or her like us. Indeed we should question our right to do so. Kahlil Gibran takes up this point:

> Your children are not your children.
> . . . though they are with you yet they belong not to you.
> You may give them your love but not your thoughts,
> For they have their own thoughts.
> You may house their bodies but not their souls,
> For their souls dwell in the house of tomorrow, which
>   you cannot visit, even in your dreams.
> You may strive to be like them, but seek not to make
>   them like you.
> For life goes not backward nor tarries with yesterday.
> You are the bows from which your children as living arrows
>   are sent forth.[20]

Our society, our institutions, our schools have a tendency to want to make people the same. Sometimes we become fixated on developmental 'milestones', on age-related behaviour and age-appropriate activities. I would defend the individual's right to be different. George Bernard Shaw has an enigmatic thought on the subject:

> The reasonable man adapts himself to the world: the unreasonable man persists in trying to adapt the world to himself. Therefore all progress depends on the unreasonable man.[21]

There is for each child a point between our duties and our responsibilities where he or she has the optimum chance of asserting a right to be different. We are bound to help the child find that point. By virtue of our employment contract with a local authority we have a duty to protect society and its members from the damaging aspects of idiosyncratic behaviour. As professional child care workers (teachers or care staff) we have a responsibility to those in our care to allow them maximum free expression of their personalities and the opportunity to satisfy individual needs and whims. As employees we have a duty to receive, temporarily in the first instance, into our specialised institutions those who have become enmeshed in self-damaging conflicts in their local schools and local communities; as professionals we have a responsibility to ensure that nothing we do in our residential schools and children's homes perpetuates these youthful struggles against often unidentified enemies.

For each admission to a residential setting we are confronted with two children, the child as he or she is and the child society would like him or her to be.[22] In trying to satisfy the demands of society, we must not reject the real child, because it is the real child of today who becomes the adult of tomorrow. I conclude with an extract from John Holt's book, *Escape from Childhood*. Holt has a respect for children; he is responsive to their feelings; and he would uphold their right to be different.

> What we need to realize . . . is that our power over another person's life is at most very limited and that if we try to extend our power beyond that narrow limit we do so only by taking from him his ability to control his own

life. The only way we can fully protect someone against his own mistakes and the uncertainties of the world is to make him a slave. He is then defenceless before *our* whims and weaknesses. Most people would prefer to take their chances with the world. They have the right to that choice.[23]

References

1   Austen, J. (1969) *Sense and Sensibility*, Harmondsworth, Penguin.
2   Ibid.
3   Davis, L. F. (1977) 'Feelings and emotions in residential settings: the individual experience', *British Journal of Social Work*, Vol. 7, No. 1, pp. 25–39.
4   Berne, E. (1973) *Sex in Human Loving*, Harmondsworth, Penguin.
5   Davis, L. F. (1975) 'Touch, sexuality and power in residential settings', *British Journal of Social Work*, Vol. 5, No. 4, pp. 397–411. Pease, K. (1974) *Communication, With and Without Words*, Leamington Spa, Vernon Scott Associates.
6   Davis, L. F. (1979) 'A case of indecent assault', *Social Work Today*, Vol. 10, No. 24.
7   Maupassant, G. de (1971) 'The Horla', in *Selected Short Stories*, Harmondsworth, Penguin.
8   Balzac, H. de (1974) 'The Duchesse de Langeais', in *History of the Thirteen*, Harmondsworth, Penguin.
9   Millham, S. (1977) 'Who becomes delinquent?' in *Working Together for Children and their Families*, London, HMSO.
10   Pasternak, B. (1966) *Doctor Zhivago*, 3rd edn, London, Collins and Harvill.
11   Gibran, K. (1966) *The Prophet*, London, Heinemann.
12   From a film by François Truffaut, *L'Argent de Poche*.
13   Noted in Delay, J. *The Youth of André Gide*, translated and abridged by Guicharnaud, J., Chicago, University of Chicago Press, 1963, and originally published under the title, *La Jeunesse d'André Gide*, Paris, Librairie Gallimard, 1956.
14   Ibid.
15   Ibid.
16   From a film by François Truffaut, *L'Argent de Poche*.
17   Quoted by MacKinnon, F. R. (1977) 'To travel hopefully', an address given to the Conference on Family Policy convened by the Canadian Council on Social Development, Ottawa, and noted in Hepworth, H. P. (1978) 'Where are we going with children: prison house or paradise?' *International Child Welfare Review*, Vol. 38/39, September/December, pp. 76–88.
18   Ibid.
19   A theme developed by Dr Spyros Doxiadis, President, Institute of Child Health, and Minister of Social Services, Greece, at the 31st Annual Lecture of the CIBA Foundation, 1979.
20   Gibran, op. cit.
21   Shaw, G. B. (1966) 'The revolutionist's handbook', in *Man and Superman*, first published 1903, Harmondsworth, Penguin.
22   Developed from a comment by Cravioto, J. (1979) 'The child and the environment', in *The Child in the World of Tomorrow*, Oxford, Pergamon.
23   Holt, J. (1975) *Escape from Childhood*, Harmondsworth, Penguin.

21   Access between children in care and their families

Jo Tunnard

The Family Rights Group is a small national charity that gives advice to families and professional workers about local authority care and child protection procedures, and offers training courses on child care law and good practice. One of the most common problems that we are asked about is the access arrangements between children in care and their relatives. This chapter looks at the law on access and considers some of the problems facing children and their families.

The law on access

Before 1984 child care legislation was silent on the question of access between children in care and their relatives. Case law had established that not only did local authorities have the power to make decisions about access to children in care, but in most cases these decisions could not be reviewed by the courts. New legislation in January 1984 smoothed out some of the existing confusions, complexities and anomalies but left others untouched and created new ones besides. The changes are incorporated into the Child Care Act 1980.

The Act applies to all children in care except those who are in care as a result of orders made in any proceedings in the High Court or as a result of an order made in matrimonial proceedings in the county court. This is because in these circumstances the court already has the power to give directions to the local authority as to the exercise of its powers and thus can entertain applications for and make orders in relation to access. Children who have been received into voluntary care and children under place of safety orders are not covered either.

The Act sets out who can apply for access orders and the circumstances in which such applications can be made. The provisions are limited in that only parents, guardians and custodians can apply for access, and applications for access orders can be made only when a local authority has refused to make any arrangements for access or has terminated existing arrangements.

If a local authority wishes to terminate access or to refuse to make arrangements for access it must *first* serve a notice on the parent or guardian. Once this has happened the parent can apply to the juvenile court for an access order. Children can be made parties to proceedings once they have been commenced but they cannot initiate applications for access. In dealing with an application for access or an application to vary or revoke an access order, the court must regard the welfare of the child as the first and paramount consideration. The court can either make an order or refuse to make one. If the court makes an order it has wide powers to attach conditions as to the frequency, duration and place of access and any other conditions it thinks fit.

If an access order is made, either the parents or the local authority can apply to the juvenile court to vary or revoke the order. Once again, children cannot initiate such applications but can be made a party to them. There is no limit to the number of such applications that can be made. Once an access order has been made the local authority loses its power to make decisions about access. Any further changes to the access arrangements, including termination, must be done through the court and the court can override the local authority's wishes.

In an emergency, when compliance with an access order would put the child's welfare 'seriously at risk', the local authority can apply *ex parte* to a single justice for an emergency order to suspend the operation of the access order for up to seven days.

Any party to access proceedings can appeal and appeals are heard in the High Court.

The final section of the 1984 legislation provides for a statutory Code of Practice on access. The Code provides very useful guidelines for good practice about access arrangements for *all* children in care: the DHSS circular that accompanied the new legislation explained that the scope of the Code was not restricted to the groups of children and parents covered by the legislation described above.

The rest of this chapter describes some of the many and varied access difficulties that crop up for children in care and their relatives, and highlights the way in which practitioners can play their part in helping to avoid or resolve them.

The early days after admission to care

Our society's view of public care, a view shared by social workers, can have a damaging effect on the chances of successful access. The causes of this negative view of care are not difficult to find. For some four decades emphasis has been laid on trying to keep children within their own families and not let them suffer the disadvantages that public care can bring: many changes of placement and people, and poor physical and emotional care. Sadly, the lack of effort to correct the faults of the care system has made it difficult for people to see the value that public care might have for children and their families and has led to a passive acceptance of the way things are.

The first way this negative attitude becomes apparent is in the manner in which children are admitted to care. Many admissions are made in a hasty way, with little preparation of anyone involved. Often such haste, or lack of preparation in planning, is the result of a social worker's reluctance to offer or use care in a helpful way. Care comes to be used as a desperate measure, as an emergency, as a last resort.

Such stalling, followed by hurried admission, can mean that admissions are not planned or discussed fully with the child's family. Work is not done beforehand to reassure the family of their continuing importance for the child and of how that might best be demonstrated. Neither the social worker nor the parents prepare the child for the separation, and so the trauma of the move is considerably, and unnecessarily, heightened. The trauma for all concerned lessens the chances of access starting and of its being successful. Everyone is responding as if there were an emergency (one which has, in reality, been artificially created) and the plan for access cannot be worked out in a calm and thoughtful way. The children concerned not only are impelled to leave home with all the haste of evacuees, they also have seriously reduced chances of seeing in the near future those who are close to them.

Information

When children are admitted to care, the child and family need a clear explanation of the legal implications of care and of their rights and responsibilities. Many are told precious little about departmental policies and practices that might have a dramatic effect on their future as a family, and few seem to get information in writing. When families are given nothing in writing they are prevented from understanding the world that they and their children have entered. They are also prevented from mulling over the information in the comfort of their own home, or with a friend or adviser. Even if a social worker does take time to explain things verbally, it is unreasonable to expect that families will hear and understand information given when they are feeling distressed, confused and perhaps resentful of the social worker. As a result, families can be left with mistaken ideas about what they can and cannot do once their children are in care. This, in turn, can have disastrous effects that are unintended by everyone, including the social worker. In our experience, clients value general information about how the law and child care practice may affect them. They see note taking, if properly explained, as an indication of the seriousness and commitment of the social worker. They are glad to have a written record of what has been discussed and decided.

Contact with the family

When children are admitted to care, the level of contact between the local authority and the family drops off alarmingly. One can speculate about why this happens. After arranging admission the social worker may feel enormous relief – the child is now safe, the heat is off, the anxieties reduced. What also happens is that the social worker has a new client – the child in care – and, as a result, the family may lose its social worker, may no longer be seen as a client as before, and may cease to have access to social services in its own right. The social worker also has to respond to loud demands from her or his agency: to call a case conference, fill in a change report, complete the boarding-out forms, visit the placement and arrange schooling. All of these demands, stemming as they do from the place of work, are louder and more insistent than those of the family who are now out of sight down the road. At the time when the family is likely to be most distraught and most vulnerable, the support and encouragement of the social worker is wrenched from them. Their feelings of guilt about the admission, and their sense of abandonment by their social worker, conspire to make them less able than they might otherwise have been to think what they might do for their separated children. And so the opportunity to start access, to build a place for the family before the jelly is set, so to speak, is lost. Work not done at this time can rarely be done later, but the effect of this lack of contact is likely to be felt and to be reflected in planning for a long time to come.

Initial meetings with children

In the same vein, many families receive little help in preparing for their first meeting with their child in care. There is much to be learnt from the effort and imagination put into initial meetings between children and new families. Social workers spend time with the children explaining what is going on, helping them to understand why the visit is taking place, planning what they might do, and reassuring them about the future. Time is also spent with the new family, helping them to understand what the child might be thinking and feeling, and alerting them to the possibility that the child might appear rejecting or uninterested or might test them out with all sorts of difficult behaviour. They will be told what the child has been doing so that they have something concrete to talk about, and there will also be discussion of what to do during the visit, what to say, what to wear, what to eat, where to go, how long to stay, how to respond to the child's awkward questions, and what to say when the visit comes to an end. The social worker will also ensure that she or he has spent time with those who are currently caring for the child so that they are prepared for the visit, know the sorts of things that might occur, and can think about what they can do to help make the meeting go well.

Anyone who is a parent will remember the anxiety of seeing again their child who has been away for a few days, even where their child has gone to a loving relative who has prepared them for their child's return. Will the child ignore them? They often do. Or go to someone else first? They often do. Or not be keen to go home? Such fears and experiences can shake the confidence of the most competent parents. How much worse it must be for parents with children in care, placed with people they do not know, under the control of a state agency, and perhaps with little influence over what happens or when the child will return home.

Meeting carers

Families find it very difficult to visit their children when they have not had the opportunity to meet the foster- or residential carers and discuss their child with them. It still seems to be unusual for social workers to arrange for foster-carers and families to meet before a placement starts. Yet that is what we expect people to do when the state is not involved: children will most certainly expect their close family to meet up with, and give the seal of approval to, those with whom they are going to stay. The lack of such an introduction can undermine the parent's role and authority in the eyes of their child. Perhaps, more importantly, it can mean that the foster-carers get information about the child and the circumstances of admission to care from a go-between, the social worker. The family do not know what has been said about them and so become apprehensive. The foster-carers have not been able to hear direct from the child's family, what the child likes, dislikes, responds to, eats and so on. They also have no clear image of the child's family, so cannot help the child to retain her or his own image of them in the first crucial days and weeks.

Nor do they have the vitally important opportunity that a meeting offers to realise that they simply are not going to get on together. FRG and the National Foster Care Association have organised several conferences for carers and families and a common recommendation for future social work practice has been that families and foster-carers should meet before a placement is finally agreed so that people can exchange information about themselves and the child and so that, exceptionally, each could veto the other if differences in lifestyle and culture were so great that the adults would not be able to work well together for the benefit of the child.

Participation in other meetings

Families also have difficulties in getting involved in wider discussions about their child's future. It's still rare for families to be invited to attend case conferences, statutory reviews and other meetings. Sometimes social workers claim that parents have been invited to a review when in fact they have been invited to meet a small sub-group of the main meeting to hear the decisions that have just been made. Families consider it an insult to be denied any part in planning and then to be told to come to an office at a certain time to hear what is to happen. That sort of approach can stifle any worthwhile discussion with parents. If parents are not involved in the wider discussion about their children, they are prevented from having a clear picture of their life beyond the relatively narrow confines of their access. Such exclusion can lead to families having tunnel vision about their children, considering them only in relation to access. Families are then in danger of being accused by the social worker of thinking only of their own needs and not their child's. It is difficult to think about what you do not know. Equally, excluding families from the wider discussion can lead social workers to develop a tunnel-vision approach to those families, considering them, in turn, only in relation to access arrangements.

Financial help

Many families find that an easily removable obstacle – lack of money – is put in their way when they try to see their children in care. The majority of families with children in care live on a very low income and have no extra resources to enable them to meet the cost of going to see their children or of having them home for a visit. Few families will know that help is available from the local authority. Those who might think of asking for help are likely to be deterred from doing so in case their inability to pay their way is seen as more evidence of their failure as parents. Sadly, if they do ask for help they may be met with a social worker who does not know what powers are available to her or him.

Section 26 of the Child Care Act 1980 provides for help to anyone – not just parents and other relatives – for any expenses involved in visiting a child in care, provided the local authority considers it reasonable. Apart from direct travel costs, payment can include other essential expenses such as childminding fees for other children, food and entertainment for the child being visited, and the cost of overnight stays. Travel warrants, rather than cash, are not the only way to pay fares; they are often issued as a convenience for the local authority but they can give families unnecessary extra burdens.

When children visit their relatives rather than being visited by them, the cost can be met by Section 1 money, through its provision to assist in reducing the need for the child to remain in care. Its applicability is most easily seen where the intention is to return the child to her or his family. But it can apply also where the plan, in the short or long term, is for the child to leave care through adoption or custodianship proceedings.

Written agreements

It is alarming that so many families who have long had access to their children in care have nothing in writing from the social worker setting down what the access arrangements are and, if relevant, spelling out the difficulties there have been and what solutions have been found for them, explaining the implications of certain actions for the direction of the child's future, and warning of actions that the local authority is considering. Some of the problems that arise over access could be avoided if social workers incorporated the making of written agreements into their daily practice. In relation to access this would ensure that before a placement starts everyone involved should meet. The meeting would include the child's parents, other relatives if they are going to maintain links with the child, the child if old enough, the new carers, and the social worker. Together they should agree the access arrangements, specifying who is to have access, where, with whom and for how long. They should also identify what financial help will be given and what contact the social worker will have with the child, family and carers in order to help make access work well. The agreement should identify clearly when the current arrangements will be reviewed and everyone should sign the agreement and have a copy of it.

In some instances it may not be possible for all the participants to agree the access arrangements and in that case the local authority must make decisions, and should confirm them in writing. It is important to remember that this is not the same as an agreement and so those affected should be informed of the procedures they can invoke if they wish to ask for an independent review of the decisions made. It is vital to make such a distinction: putting pressure on parents to sign an agreement or contract which in reality is a stipulation does nothing to establish that important element – co-operation between the adults involved in a child's life.

The setting for access

Families who already feel like fish out of water when visiting their children in care can be even more disconcerted by the physical arrangements for access. Often parents are not offered private space to talk or play with their children and end up having to cope with other children or curious, if well-meaning, adults in the residential or foster-home.

Sometimes social workers think that a visit will be better if it takes place on what they call 'neutral territory' and then arrange for the visit to take place in the social worker's office. Such a setting is not designed for such intimate meetings: it is not conducive to a relaxed atmosphere, and it is most certainly not neutral. It is the social worker's territory and that is a very powerful influence indeed. If visits cannot take place in the child's parents' home or where the child is currently living, there are other options that can be explored, such as a relative's home, a nursery, or a children's home.

The presence of others

Far from being given privacy for meetings, some families and children find that other people insist on being present. The family will usually be told that their access is being supervised or observed but, unfortunately, sometimes no explanation is given. Observing visits and supervising them require different skills from the social worker. A visit is *observed* in order to make some sort of assessment, so someone with relevant skills should undertake this job. A visit is *supervised* in order to ensure that some behaviour does not occur or that something is not said, and so a much greater variety of people can undertake this role. It does not need a qualified social worker, or even a member of the department, to stop a parent physically punishing a child. Often a friend or relative will be willing to help but may not be invited to do so. A social worker's reluctance to involve outsiders probably reflects the lack of clarity about why someone else is taking part. Is the visit to be observed or supervised? Why? Do the family and child understand the reasons for it? How will anyone know whether the objective has been achieved? How long will it go on for? When will it be reviewed? All these questions need to be answered if the supervision or observation of visits is to be useful and constructive, rather than simply serving to make families anxious about being watched.

Ethnic minority families

All the difficulties mentioned above can apply to any family with children in care. However, families from ethnic minorities are often in double jeopardy because they are likely to be judged from another cultural perspective and dealt with by people who have little or no understanding of their ethnic, racial or cultural background. The whole question of adequate child care is complex and culturally determined. If a society contained only one ethnic group it would be understandable, perhaps, if that culture's way of doing things was seen as the only good way. In a society as multicultural as ours it is quite wrong to hold up one cultural tradition – a western one – as superior to all others. Yet it is by this western yardstick that ethnic minority families seem so often to be judged, and sometimes found wanting. It is wrong for workers to assume, as they have done in our experience, that the information they may have gleaned from a brief training day equips them to make correct interpretations of people's views and wishes. Another tendency we have found is for white social workers, and predominantly white Social Services Departments, to use the little knowledge they have about an ethnic minority group to stereotype families and their problems. Such an approach does not allow an individual approach to difficulties and may result in very important problems being missed.

Relatives other than parents

Links with children in care are not simply an issue about children and their parents, although they are sometimes treated as if they were. Without special attention to relationships with members of their wider family, children can too easily find themselves cut off from everyone except their parents. We at the Family Rights Group are concerned about the lack of encouragement given to links between children in care and other relatives. Grandparents, aunts and uncles have come to us in increasing number in recent years. Mostly they want to see their young relatives in care, sometimes they also want to care for them. Rarely have those who come to us been sought out by the local authority and rarely have their offers been welcomed.

In our experience, although other relatives will sometimes know of the child's admission to care, they often feel hesitant about asking for access in case that is seen as interference or because they do not know the officials involved. Failure to pick up on these possibilities can mean that important opportunities to maintain some continuity for the child are lost, in some cases irretrievably. It is also our experience that children who do have access to other relatives are in danger of losing that if the local authority stops their access to their parents.

If links are not maintained with other relatives then the possibility of children living with them, if unable to live with their parents, is also lost. This is particularly worrying given the finding of Jane Rowe and her colleagues, in their five-year study of children fostered long term (*Long-Term Foster Care*, Batsford/BAAF, 1984), that the children living with relatives were the best adjusted.

Why, then, do relatives find their offers met with no real interest and sometimes even disdain? The department's reluctance may stem from its anxiety to retain power, something it can do less easily if the child goes to a relative. But there is no evidence to show that having total control necessarily serves the child better or that relatives will not welcome the continued involvement of the social worker.

Children making decisions

There is a clear duty on the local authority (S. 18, Child Care Act 1980) to seek the views of children and take them into account when making decisions. It is right that such a duty exists but important that children know that they can rely on adults to make final decisions and also enable them to reconsider their own wishes later. Some parents are told that their access is to be curtailed or terminated because that is what their child wishes, even a young child. It is not fair to leave children with the burden of responsibility for such a major decision when they cannot fully appreciate its long-term effect. Nor is it fair to the families concerned who are then effectively prevented from challenging that decision. This way of responding to children is in sharp contrast to the normal experiences of children living with their families, when they are frequently encouraged, and sometimes cajoled, into seeing people they would rather not see because of the adult belief that in the long term they will value the link they have with those people.

Disagreements and complaints

Before the Code of Practice came into force it was extremely hard for any relative of a child in care to get a review of decisions about access with which they disagreed. The Code provided that each local authority should set up a complaints procedure to deal with disputes over access. Such a procedure should enable senior officers, the director and elected members to decide on disputes and should be open to use by parents and other relatives. Information should be provided for all parents.

More than five years after the Code was issued in January 1984, some authorities still have no appeals procedure while many others fail to involve the director or elected members, or give no information about the procedure, or refuse to let it be used by relatives other than parents. On the other hand, a few authorities allow young people in care to use the procedure if they are unhappy with access arrangements, and ensure that people have ready access to reports that are to be submitted about them and are encouraged to take a representative to help them present their appeal.

Further reading

The following publications, and details of our other work, are available from Family Rights Group, 6 Manor Gardens, London N7 6LA.
About the law on access and on care and related proceedings generally:

RYAN, M. (1985) *A Guide to Care and Related Proceedings*, London, FRG.

About research findings on access, the role of elected members, the views of a practitioner and a foster-carer, and for more detail about the experiences of family members:

FRG (1986) *Promoting Links: Keeping Children and Families in Touch*.

About central and local government cash payments for families of children in care and for young people in care or leaving care:

FRG (1986) *In Care: A Money Guide for Families*.

Postscript: Access between children in care and their relatives

Explanatory note about Children Bill (England and Wales) 1989

At the time of writing this chapter the Children Bill is being debated in Parliament. It is expected to gain Royal Assent in the summer of 1989, and to be implemented in 1991.

The bill uses the word 'contact' to describe what is referred to here as 'access'. It makes some welcome changes to current provisions: it places local authorities under a general duty to keep a child in care in reasonable contact with parents, and gives parents the right to apply to court for a contact order. The definition of parent now includes non-married fathers. The bill also provides for other people to seek the permission of the court to apply for a contact order, thus giving new rights to brothers and sisters, grandparents, other relatives, and family friends. The Code of Practice will not be retained as part of the new legislation, but may be reissued as guidance to accompany the Act.

The final position should be clear later in the summer of 1989, although regulations and rules of court will still remain to be written once the bill has received Royal Assent.

Index

absconders, 242–3
access, 76
access to child in care, 114, 136, 263–73;
complaints 272; contact with family, 265–6;
disagreements, 272; early days after admission,
264–5; ethnic minority factors, 270–1; financial
help, 268; information, 265; initial meeting with
child, 266–7; law, 136, 263–4; meeting with
carers, 267; order, 263–4; presence of others,
270; relatives other than parents, 271; setting,
269–70; written agreement, 269
Achievement in Primary Schools (1986), 143
Acts of Parliament: Child Care Act (1980), 8, 18,
access, 263, 268, 272, children's views, 272, day
care, 43, 144; financial help, 268; Children Act
(1948), 18, 26; Children Act (1975), 24, 25, 26,
30–1, 106, 133; Children and Young Persons
Act (1969), 169, 172, 185; Children Bill (1989),
273; Education Act (1944), 183; Education Act
(1980), 142; Education Act (1981), 142, 150;
National Health Service Act (1977), 143, 150;
Nurseries and Childminders Regulation Act
(1948), 143
Adcock, Margaret, 132
admission to care, 20, 21, 105–7
adolescents: containment, 176; delinquent, 134,
168, 176, 181; homeless, 7; in penal
establishments, 168; severely disturbed, 168,
181, 184; short-stay residential care, 180;
special placement schemes, 134; suicidal, 184;
Swedish model of community care, 134;
units/hostels for, 169
adopters, transracial, 54–5
adoption, 25, 28, 34–5; black families, 52, 66; class
nature, 34–5; fostering compared, 26, 28, 133;
long-term effects, 35; open, 46; permanent
family finding, 48; relation to fostering, 133;
security, 48; without consent, 45
Adoption Agency Regulations, 46
adoption allowance, 133
adoption hearing, 133
Adoption Resource Exchange, 45
adoptive parents, 23
Afro-Caribbean children, 215, 216, 218, *see also*
black children
Almeda project, California, 121
anal dilatation, 4
angry, hostile child, 198–9
antenatal support group, 152
approved school (*latterly* community home with
education), 169, 172
Area Child Protection Committee (*formerly* Area
Review Committee), 84 (table), 85–6
Asian children, 216–16, 217–18, *see also* black
children
assessment of children's needs, 203–13; child in
residential care, 175–6; compilation of
assessment, 212; emotional development,
209–10; goal formulation, 212–13; history
taking, 205–8; illustrative children: Angela, 205,
Clifford, 204, 205–8, 211–13; outcome, 213;
preparation, 204–5
assessment centre, 106, 169, *see also* child
development centre
assessment report, 219
Association of British Adoption and Fostering
Agencies, *see* British Agencies for Adoption
and Fostering
asylums, 69–70
attachment, 209–10
Austen, Jane, 250–1

BAAF, *see* British Agencies for Adoption and
Fostering
baby-battering, 3
Balzac, Honoré de, quoted, 258
Barnardo's, 187; Cambridge Cottage, 138;
schemes, 135
Baron's Close Young Family Centre, 156–7, 161–2
BASW, *see* British Association of Social Workers
Beckford, Jasmine, 19, 82, 208
bedtime, child's attitude to, 241–2
behavioural pedagogies, 73
behavioural problem, 177, 185, 241
behavioural psychology, 178
behaviour rating scale, 231–2
Berkshire Social Services Department, 134
Berry, Juliet, quoted, 119
'best interests', 31–2, 93
bicultural experience, 61
Birmingham, children in care, 121–2
Birmingham University, UNESCO study, 217
black children, 50–65, 215–19; acknowledgement
of differences, 57–8; adaptation of family/child
to existing/future conditions, 64; adoption, 58;
black homes for, 51–2; colour and identity,
56–7; coping strategies, 217; development of
positive identity, 10–11; fostering, 58, 137;
identification with white adopters/black
community, 64; in care, 8; in white families,
60; interests promotion, 61–5; life-style of
adoption family, 63; overcompensation, 217;
school environment, 65; selection/preparation
guidelines, 62–3; self-image, 216; socialisation
outside family, 64; transracial placements, *see*
transracial placements
black people, 50–61; assimilationist tendencies,
218; culture conflict, 218; political position in
white society, 218; resistance to adoption, 61;
teachers' attitudes, 65; traditions/family life, 56
'blood tie', 26, 28, 30, 33, 123
boarders, 185–6
boarding-out allowance, 134
Boarding-Out Regulations (1988), 47, 133, 138
boarding schools for children with special needs,
168
borstal (*latterly* youth custody establishment) 172
Bowlby's work, 13, 143
Bradley, M., 149–50
British Association for Adoption and Fostering
(BAAF; *formerly* Association of British
Adoption and Fostering Agencies), 30, 132,
133; training pack, 136
British Association of Social Workers (BASW),
26; *Guidelines*, 133
British Deaf Association, 187
'broken family', 14
Bronfenbrenner, Urie, quoted, 260

Cambridge Cottage, Barnardo's, 138
Camden girls' centre, 226
Campaign for One-Parent Families, 15
care: adoptive, *see* adoption; foster, *see* fostering;
long term–short term compared, 117, 132;
shared, 3, 124; substitute, 18, 24;
supplementary, 18, 21
caregivers: care for, 239; conflict between
colleagues, 243, 246; self-awareness/self-
knowledge, 247–8; support/consultation for,
244–5; tendency to stay in negative units,
243–4; training, 247
care order, 20
Carlile, Kimberley, 82
case conferences, 86–7, 90

275